To Tony – with all my love – Min – 8-9-2019

D0707380

SPLASHDOWN:

The Rescue of a Navy Frogman

John Wolfram

Splashdown: Rescue of a Navy Frogman
Copyright © 2008 by John Michael Wolfram
ISBN: 978-1-61005-233-7

All rights reserved. No part of this publication may be reproduced, stored in a retrieval system, or transmitted in any form or by any means—electronic, mechanical, photocopy, recording, or any other—except for brief quotations in printed reviews, without the prior permission of the author.
www.Johnwolfram.com

Events described in this book including BUD/S (Basic Underwater Demolition/SEAL) training and Hell Week are presented to the best of the author's recollection, and to best allow the reader to experience these events in an autobiographical format. The author apologizes for any unintentional misrepresentation of the order of events. Should the reader wish to learn more about BUD/S training, detailed books and videos are available both in print and online.

The maverick behavior of early UDT/SEALs which the author describes in this book is no longer tolerated by the United States Navy. In present day, an arrest by law enforcement for drunk driving, fights and drug use can be grounds for termination. It is the author's hope that the mindset of the period as presented has been phased out and that what he relates here will in no way diminish people's respect for the SEALs or for anyone in the military's Special Warfare Community.

The author strongly cautions the reader to not attempt any of the inherently unsafe events described in this book without proper professional training. The author will not be responsible for any accidents, injuries or losses incurred.

Special and sincere thanks to Mr. Michael Esslinger who graciously shared a number of facts from his personal research of the Apollo 11 spacecraft and mission.

All Scripture quotations, unless otherwise indicated, are taken from the Holy Bible, New International Version®. NIV®. Copyright © 1973, 1978, 1984 by International Bible Society. Used by permission of Zondervan. All rights reserved.

The Apollo 8 astronauts' reading of Genesis 1:1-10 is from the King James Version of the Bible.

I believe that this nation should commit itself to achieving the goal, before this decade is out, of landing a man on the Moon and returning him safely to the Earth.

~ John F. Kennedy, 1961

Dedication

I affectionately dedicate this book to three wonderful women: Deborah, my loving wife who exemplifies Proverbs thirty-one in every way possible; Laurissa, our only child, who oftentimes (oh my!) reminds me of myself; and the precious lady who brought me into the world, my caring and selfless mother, Marion.

Acknowledgments

I have numerous people to thank for this manuscript. Tammy Barley, my talented editor, worked hard organizing and making my manuscript "sing." Her tenacity and perseverance reminded me of my BUD/S training. Hooyah, Tammy!

My daughter, Laurissa, earned every bit of the camera that I promised to share with her for typing out the initial manuscript. Thank you, Riss, for allowing me to interrupt your school work, phone calls, text messaging, iPod listening, net surfing, summer vacation, and time with friends when I needed to ask your opinion or solicit advice.

My devoted wife so graciously allowed me to *hide* from family, friends, shopping, sightseeing and a hundred other tasks in order to immerse myself in this project. Thanks, Deborah, you have always been there for me.

Wow, the cover. Rebecca Stevens from Australia was especially helpful. She created the logo. Josh Murtha and Samantha Shorr of Pixelution Studios, Inc. designed this cover. I got dozens of opinions from Deborah, Laurissa, Tammy, Jim, Brenda, Dave, Kathy, Lisa, Gordon, Afton, Linda, VicToria, Carlos, Jho-ir, Jen, the paper boy, the guys who mow our lawn, neighbors, the mail carrier, passers-by, and just about anyone else I could corner.

Jho-ir Alcaraz and Jerrober Ramos from the Philippines helped with the initial pictorial layout. Laurissa did the typesetting, touch-up and rework for printing. A great big *salamat*.

Thank you, Brenda Ghiloni, Michael Esslinger and Steve Fortosis, for your contributions to this book. My former UDT-11 teammate, Mike Mallory, provided many of his cherished photographs.

The final phases and publishing of the book and working with the printers—we finally made it! Several people at Entry Way Publishing helped greatly to see that this book is a success. Thanks go out to R.D. Foster, Linda Phillips and VicToria Freudiger for their efforts and talents.

Heartfelt appreciation goes to Rev. Allen Picklesimer, his gracious wife Elaine, and their four wonderful children, John, Julie, Jolene and Jeff for adopting me into their Christian family when I was at a critical point in my life. I will never forget their hospitality and friendship.

I have deep respect and appreciation to all of our United States military personnel. America is truly indebted to you and the sacrifices you have made. Any comparisons between the different branches are merely an indication of the playful rivalry that was prevalent during the time period expressed in this book.

Last, but not least, I want to thank my Lord and Savior, Jesus Christ for Calvary.

Contents

Introduction

The landing of a man on the moon is unquestionably one of the greatest technological achievements in the history of mankind. Nuclear power, computers, and the Internet have changed the way we live, but still nothing compares to the day Neil Armstrong took that famous "one small step" off the lunar module *Eagle* and into the books of history. His copilot "Buzz" Aldrin then joined him on the moon, and two human beings spent two and a half hours walking on the lunar surface, collecting moon rocks and other samples.

After their historic walk on the moon, they successfully docked again with the command module *Columbia*, piloted by Michael Collins. On July 24, 1969, these brave men reentered Earth's atmosphere. The capsule screamed back at 24,800 miles an hour, landing in the choppy waves of the Pacific Ocean. I was the first person on planet Earth to greet them.

The dream of space flight is as old as mankind. The folklore of many cultures is filled with myths and legends of heroes who tried to reach the heavens with the help of birds or by magic. The first known story was told as early as AD 160.

The idea of flying into space and perhaps walking on the surface of the moon has for millennia driven the dreams of poets, storytellers, philosophers, visionaries and engineers. A thousand years ago a Chinese emperor thought he could fly to the moon by strapping gunpowder rockets to his throne. He blew himself to pieces.

In my generation the space race raged between the Soviet Union and the United States. As a young man I listened to John F. Kennedy's now-famous speech, challenging America to land a man on the moon before the end of the decade of the 1960s. I watched countless newscasts and read numerous books, editorials and magazine articles leading up to this monumental event. The public seemingly couldn't get enough, and the media fed us until we were stuffed.

While growing up and nearly drowning in the moon hysteria, I never in my wildest dreams imagined that one day I would be so close to the action. But as providence would have it, I would witness firsthand history in the making.

The story I'm about to share, however, entails more than my involvement in the Apollo 11 recovery. It's also a fast-paced journey of a young man coming of age in a world bombarded with the rapid cultural changes of the turbulent '60s.

Discover what it was like to go through the rigors of BUD/S (Basic Underwater Demolition/SEAL) training, and the controversial Vietnam War.

Even more fascinating than experiencing the complexity of our vast universe with its billions of stars, numerous galaxies, planets and their moons vicariously through the astronauts, is the journey we each take in discovering ourselves.

Herein lies an adventure, a call to redefine "impossible," and a dare to reach for more.

SPLASHDOWN:

The Rescue of a Navy Frogman

—Chapter One—

Splashdown

At last! After staring at the bunk above me most of the night, my alarm clock sounded. I fumbled around in the dark, found the 'off' button, and reached for the light—2:00 a.m. I'd hardly slept. I doubt my teammates who were sharing this once-in-a-lifetime event with me did either. The moment had finally arrived. This was no drill. It was the real thing. It was July 24, 1969, and the astronauts were just minutes away from splashdown.

Hours earlier I had been surrounded by dignitaries who attended our final briefing—the ship's captain, senior officers, NASA officials, helicopter pilots and crews, fellow UDT/SEAL swimmers, and news reporters and photographers. As a twenty-year-old seaman, I was awed to be included in this gathering of seasoned military personnel and scientists. When I had graduated high school two years earlier, it had never crossed my mind that I would be a player in something as monumental as the Apollo 11 rescue. I was *ecstatic*!

Even so, challenges lay ahead. I pushed myself up on my elbow and mentally ran through them.

In a quick decision the night before, Houston's Mission Control changed the splashdown site. Now splashdown would be two hundred fifty miles from where the USS *Hornet* was positioned Wednesday afternoon. Turbulence and thunderstorms at the original landing site could have caused structural damage to the spacecraft. However, the weather forecast for the new splashdown site wasn't much brighter for us frogmen. Winds were sixteen- to twenty-four knots (eighteen- to twenty-eight mph) with potential swells nearly as high as a man, making the seas notably rougher.

The two hundred fifty miles wasn't a problem for the aircraft carrier USS *Hornet* which could travel at a speed of thirty-three knots (thirty-eight mph), and everything could still be coordinated with the other communications ship. The President of the United States would still be flown in.

Bottom line, everyone could tolerate the last-minute shift, but up to this point we had never rehearsed in seas as high as the one forecast.

Though we'd practiced rescuing the command module and astronauts until we could do it blindfolded, we didn't want any mistakes. High swells would complicate everyone's job. We would be thrown around in our rafts—a greater challenge in getting the astronauts out of the module and into a helicopter. The boisterous seas would hamper the entire water sequence.

"Well, Joe?" I swung my legs over the side of the bunk. "We've trained hard for this. We're in the best shape of our lives. We can handle this." I felt invincible.

Joe Via shot a cocky grin at me. "We've been through *Hell Week*. Nothing can be as hard as that. Unless the landing site is in the middle of a typhoon, we'll be up for the challenge."

I agreed and jumped down from the middle rack I occupied in our stuffy, barely cooled compartment in the *Hornet*. Our barracks had housed troops during World War II, but today they were claimed by a handful of elite members of the United States Navy's Underwater Demolition Teams (UDT) 11 and 12.

Around us others hurriedly shaved, showered and prepared for the day.

"This is it, John. This is what we've been waiting for," said a smiling Mike Mallory, the second team member of our designated trio, Swim 2.

I grimaced. "I just hope I don't jump into a bunch of sharks."

When we drilled two days earlier, sharks swarmed around us, and one rubbed against my wetsuit. I yelled to the others, "Sharks! Get into the rafts, quick!" Everyone scurried for safety, as sharks are unpredictable. The media picked up on our dilemma and printed a story that went out over the AP: "NASA officials and swimmers say they've never encountered as many sharks in the area of any previous space shot recoveries."

I was quoted as saying, "The sharks watch us. We watch them. They've been nibbling away at our gear all week." It's comical how journalists could make us look like idiots. Helicopter crews saw the sharks too. Night ops were the worst. Chopper lights shining down on us attracted the pests. But lately they were drawn to our daylight practices as well. One shark had bitten off a chunk of the Styrofoam surrounding the base of the Billy-Pugh net, and another had taken a piece of the sea anchor.

I had to jump into the water first—and alone. I didn't want to be shark bait, but my job was to secure the capsule. That came first. Once showered, I pulled on my wetsuit bottom and top, my life vest, and coral booties to protect my feet. I slipped a lanyard over my head and secured my web belt around my waist, which held a Navy-issue K-Bar knife with a flare attached to it by black electrical tape. I grabbed my face mask and tan fins. In the chow hall I had a quick predawn breakfast with the other frogs. We then headed up to the flight deck. I don't remember what I ate. I was totally focused on the splashdown.

The ship was surprisingly busy. From the boiler room deep down in the belly of the ship to the quarterdeck topside, all phases of recovery crews readied themselves. The air was damp from the mist and spray coming off the choppy waves as the *Hornet* raced toward the revised landing site.

"It's showtime, guys. Let's get moving!" Michael Bennett, the backup BIG (biological isolation garments) swimmer, slapped us on the shoulder. He didn't have to remind us. Nothing could have slowed us down.

I took in the sensations—the smell of salt water and diesel fuel, sailors hurrying to complete their tasks, the whining shrill of helo blades revving up and beating. Over the PA, an announcement blared to clear the flight deck.

Mike Mallory and I hurried over to the Sea King SH-4, our designated chopper. Lieutenant (jg) Wes Chesser, the third team member of Swim 2, was there to greet Mike and me. "Got your act together, guys? This is the real deal, you know?"

We nodded and checked to be sure everything was in place—the package holding the collar, the sea anchor and mandatory scuba gear we loaded a few hours before—then climbed aboard and strapped ourselves into our webbed seats.

Swim 1 and 3 likewise prepared while the helicopter pilots and crews went through their checklists. Then we anxiously waited for the signal to be airborne.

When the signal came, we lifted off the *Hornet's* flight deck and began our mission.

The door in front of us remained open. Beyond it, the ocean called to me.

It was a familiar call, as the water had beckoned to me since my childhood. I could still hear the voice of Bill, my swim instructor, as he challenged me.

"Johnny, why don't you join the swim team?"

I was nine and couldn't swim well. Mom enrolled me in swim classes and I had just successfully dived down to get the wrench. I had become a *pollywog*.

"Really?" You want *me* to swim on the team this summer?

Wow! "What would I have to do?"

"Just come to the practices each morning," he said.

"That's all?"

"Yep."

"I'll ask my mother," I said excitedly.

I couldn't wait to get home.

Fort Atkinson, Wisconsin is a small town named after General Atkinson who built and maintained a fort for his troops. The first settlers of Fort Atkinson arrived in 1836 and built log cabin homesteads. I was born there on October 21, 1948. Fort (as the locals fondly called it) was in Jefferson County, a region in southern Wisconsin with dairy farms and fields of corn, mint and hops.

The land around my hometown was beautiful—lush vegetation and deep-green forest over rolling hills separated by winding, slow-moving streams and lakes that sparkled in the morning sunshine.

My father, Orville (Ollie) Wolfram, was a World War II veteran. The government offered modest tin houses in Jones Park for the returning GIs until they could get their feet on the ground. My father wisely took advantage of this. The park was thick with elm, oak and maple trees, which provided profuse shade. It had its own baseball diamond and grandstand, plus playgrounds with swings, slides, and sandboxes.

Some might say my childhood was charmed, because frankly, I survived more than my share of brushes with death. When I was two I fell from the top of a set of outdoor bleachers to the hard asphalt below. Those who saw it told me I was lucky I didn't break my neck. When I was five, a semitruck hit me in front of our house. That same year, I buried myself in a pile of leaves while playing hide-and-seek with some friends, and someone lit the leaves on fire, not knowing

I was hiding underneath. I escaped unharmed as the pile went up in flames, though the fur on my hat was singed.

Although my family wasn't impoverished, I had my share of struggles. My father and mother, Marion (Larsen) Wolfram, didn't get along, so my dad was usually gone. My mother raised the six of us (Gary, John, Jeff, Pam, Paul and Tom) essentially alone, but she was equal to the task.

I was always curious and had the heart of an adventurer. This would be an asset in my chosen career, but as a child it always landed me in trouble. Mom had to dig BB pellets out of my arm after the neighborhood bully used me for target practice; I got a stone stuck up my left nostril—the doctor lectured me on why I shouldn't do that again; and my five-year-old girlfriend's mother scolded us when she discovered Diane and me playing in the buff in her playhouse.

I was curious but always felt a painful emptiness, like the core of me was missing, so I tried to fill this emptiness with excitement.

When things went sour between my parents, and my father's heavy drinking deprived us of a more comfortable life, Mom decided it was better to live around a personal support group—her mother, sister, and childhood friends. Grandma Larsen owned a couple of rental houses in Fort, and when things got really tight she gave us a roof over our heads. Her loving generosity carried us through the lean times.

The house I remember best was a duplex. One side had two bedrooms, a living room, a kitchen and side porch, all on ground level. Mom, Pam, Paul, and Tom slept on that side. The other side was two stories that we shared with a lady named Delores. She lived on the lower level, and had sole use of the bathroom upstairs. Gary, Jeff and I shared the two upstairs bedrooms. I always got paired with Gary, my older brother, because Jeff would never have survived his shenanigans and bullying.

Each unit had its own front door, though the stairs were shared.

The upstairs rooms on our side didn't have any heat except what came up through the floorboards from Delores' apartment below, so we suffered in the winter. The other side of the house wasn't much better. A wood stove between the living room and kitchen was all that kept the chill back. On sub-zero days and nights, we fought for space around the stove to get warm. I wrapped myself in quilts and wore wool-footed pajamas to bed. Gary always got the warmth of the dog or cat, because he insisted they sleep with him.

Memories: Ed, who lived across the street to the right of us, dashed out onto his lawn, grabbed a blue jay with his bare hands, and broke its neck. The jay had been picking on a robin. Mrs. Will, the lady next door, died and wasn't discovered for several days. My grandma slipped on ice up the street and broke her hip one winter, and mom held Mrs. Guess' hand while she quietly passed away. I also have memories of my uncle Gene lining us boys up on the side porch to cut our hair. We knew what kind of haircut we were going to get. One just like his—a butch.

I needed a real family and self worth. I wanted more than what I had.

The chance to be on the swim team was like an answer to a prayer. When I arrived home and asked Mom if I could, she said yes.

With that invitation from my instructor, I found my first love. Swimming was more fun than I had ever imagined. I could hardly keep my head above water, let alone swim to the end of the pool, but my instructor believed in me, and I started on a journey that would eventually fill my summers and school days with new adventures and friends. It wasn't long until I conquered floating, the dogpaddle, and discovered I could actually swim—and fast.

At 0539 hours air support made visual contact of the Apollo 11 command module, *Columbia*, and at 0540 radar contact by the *Hornet* was confirmed. The spacecraft decelerated through the atmosphere.

For more than three minutes, the astronauts were separated by a blackout of radio communications due to the generated heat of 5,000° Fahrenheit. The heat shield of the command module was built to withstand this scorching heat. The radio was not.

I searched the sky through the helo door. Everyone waited in tense silence.

By now our three frogmen crews had been circling over the Pacific Ocean in our respective helicopters close to an hour. The roar of the engines made our eardrums throb even with the headgear on. For months we had gone through endless rehearsals, and now it seemed surreal.

The Navy had made certain we could do our jobs backward and forward. Houston Space Center provided us a boilerplate (a mockup that resembled the actual space module) to rehearse with. We honed our skills by repeating the recovery process dozens of times, step by step, which included jumping out of a low-flying helicopter, attaching the sea anchor and collar, and maintaining the equipment before securing for the day. This also provided the helicopter pilots and their crews a time to train.

While we trained, various military, civilian, and NASA personnel likewise drilled. Since the success of all space missions depends on cohesive teamwork between all participating affiliates, numerous conferences took place in many locations with the goal of successfully recovering the space module and astronauts. Representatives from NASA, NELC, GE, Western Union, Affiliated Press, ABC, the *Hornet* and capsule recovery teams had to blend their individual skills and contributions into a very complex operation in which they were highly dependent upon each other.

While aboard the *Hornet*, everyone continued to rehearse their jobs. We frogs assumed the role of the astronauts to allow helicopter crews to practice hoisting us up in the one-man Billy-Pugh nets. Boatswains honed their skills retrieving the bobbing capsule from the ocean. Radiomen fine-tuned their communication equipment, and quartermasters practiced their navigation skills until we all felt we could do all our jobs expertly.

The radio crackled, and the USS *Hornet* confirmed that the command module's chutes had opened. It was too far away for the ship's filming crew to cover the actual opening, but the photo helicopter was fortunate to be closer to the action. Gathered around the landing point to greet these space travelers were 9,000 men in nine ships and fifty-four aircraft, all led by the *Hornet*.

At 0546 hours, VHF voice radio and recovery-beacon contact was made. Four minutes later at 0550, the command module splashed down into the choppy Pacific Ocean.

The command module was dragged across the waves by the chutes and was turned upside down. Our helicopter raced toward the drop zone at full throttle, the bulkheads shaking and vibrating like they were going to split in two.

—Chapter Two—

Into the Deep

Though not all my childhood was a battle, I was no stranger to adversity. The early 1950s were a time when we never locked our doors at night. We watched *Jack Benny*, *The Twilight Zone*, *I Love Lucy*, *Ozzie and Harriet* and *The Lone Ranger* on our plain black-and-white TV. We played tag, kick the can and hide-and-seek under the street lamps at night. Marbles, baseball cards, *Boys' Life* magazines, *Archie* and *Superman* comic books, hula hoops, yoyos, Slinkies, Monopoly, Lionel trains and Lincoln Logs competed for our attention. Another pastime was watching Linda from across the street neck with her boyfriend in his parked car.

Dick Clark's *American Bandstand* and *The Ed Sullivan Show* were also family favorites. Ed Sullivan was awkward looking, had horrible posture, spoke with an odd accent, and couldn't sing, dance or act, but was on television for twenty-three years. Sunday nights we all gathered around the TV and watched jugglers, opera, ballet, lions, tigers and bears (oh my), singers, comedians, puppeteers and ventriloquists. But nothing prepared us for the night Sullivan hosted Elvis and his "pelvis." I got my first whiff of "girls gone wild" when our neighbors Judy and Cheryl came screaming from across the street to tell us Elvis was on next.

Barrie Park was just down the street, catty-cornered from Trinity Lutheran. We wiled away hours at the park, challenging each other to see who could leap the farthest off the swings, climb the tall slide without using the steps, and to see who could stay on the small merry-go-round the longest without vomiting—all escapades that would have rattled our mother if she'd known.

Each summer the city sponsored an ice-cream social there, and a band played inside the bandstand. Booths and tables were set up where pies, cakes, cookies, candy and soda pop were sold until long after dark. Early the morning after, we combed the park for dropped coins, a scavenger hunt we always looked forward to. The bandstand was boarded up during the winter and made an excellent obstacle course. It took a lot of skill to inch our way around the structure on what was left of the outside ledge. Maneuvering past the concrete pillars between the sheets of plywood was especially tricky. Only a few of us were able to successfully make the full circle.

The four seasons were a big part of life in Wisconsin. We had hot, humid summers and winters colder than a penguin's bottom. Blizzards were common, but winter wasn't all bad. Shoveling snow was a great way for us kids to make money, and there were plenty of widows around who we could help. They were more than happy to give me a dollar to shovel snow that came up to my chest. Come summer, I earned those dollars by muscling a push mower across their yards.

During the summer an ice truck dropped off blocks of ice for neighbors who had iceboxes. Milkmen delivered glass bottles of milk and cream twice a week and placed them in insulated milk boxes on our front porches. On cold days the cream on top froze and expanded, lifting the milk caps from their bottles. Mosquitoes were a big problem. City trucks drove through each neighborhood spraying insecticide, leaving gigantic white clouds of poison in their wakes. Dutch elm disease hit with a vengeance and the city sprayed to save the trees. Some were spared, but the chemicals killed thousands of birds. We cuddled the quivering creatures in our hands until they died.

Grandma knew all the nursery rhymes by heart and could say, "I picked a peck of pickled peppers" faster than anyone I knew. She set aside a day each year for us kids to celebrate a private Christmas in her upstairs apartment. Granny had all the props—the fake red fireplace with the cellophane flames, a small Christmas tree on a table and all sorts of other Grandma-type things around the place. The best part was opening up dozens of little inexpensive gifts that must have taken her ages to wrap, like candy bars, a wooden whistle, a pack of chewing gum, a bar of soap and other practical things. She was my mentor when it came to Economics 101.

The whole Wolfram clan went to Barrie Elementary School. It was a good mile walk to Barrie Elementary, but we learned how to take shortcuts through people's backyards. During winter storms we took the sidewalks. For a while I stuck to the longer route so I could walk with Sue. It usually took us half the walk home to get up enough courage to hold hands. We were nine at the time.

Grade school was interesting. We celebrated everything back then—kids' birthdays, Halloween, Thanksgiving, Christmas, Valentine's Day, May Day and even the chicken-pox, measles and mumps. When someone broke out with a communicable virus it wasn't long until everyone was infected. The kids loved to share. We took turns staying at home until the welts, rashes, and scabs weren't considered communicable then returned to school to show everyone our scars.

On occasion we were bussed down to the municipal building for vaccinations for smallpox, flu and polio. As we stood in a long line waiting to get to the "spot", some of the cowardly boys cried, and I remember a girl fainting once. The smallpox shots were administered by pricking the skin on the upper part of the arm with a needle a dozen times. After the scab fell off we were marked for life.

A few students who were unfortunate enough to have contracted polio attended school in leg braces. I will never forget: the tall boy who had wooden legs; the Dutch boy whose parents put a bowl around his head and then gave him a haircut; the retarded boy who could draw; me, drinking my daily pint of chocolate milk in the school's basement, joining the square dance team, being chosen for traffic patrol and hall monitor, playing the drums in the school band, singing "Go, Tell It on the Mountain" during the Christmas program; Fran, who was developed way beyond her years; the chiropractor's son who could sing all the TV commercials; my cousin's birthday party where we played spin the bottle; my Cub Scout den mother taking our troop to the Janesville YMCA where we boys all swam in the nude.

Mom did her best to provide us with the things that really mattered like love, self-acceptance, and character. She tried to make us feel special and was careful to give us plenty of hugs every day.

I can still hear her say, "John, I wish things were better. I never wanted things to turn out like this. This is not what I had in mind when I married your father. But we'll make it through this, believe me. I love each of you very much and we will pull through this." Then she would break down and cry.

She tried to be optimistic, but unfortunately her emotions were tied to her rocky relationship with Dad and to her apprehension of raising six children under harsh circumstances. Mom did her best to keep things as normal as possible, but came close to a nervous breakdown in the process.

At first my father's absence during the week didn't bother me, but eventually it became a source of irritation and hurt. Whenever I visited my friends' homes, I was reminded of what it might be like to have a functional family and a father living at home every day of the week, a male figure to talk to about adolescent problems, or to help with homework.

In the beginning he tried to make it home on weekends from Chicago where he worked and had a small apartment. But as we got older and most needed a father in our lives, his weekend appearances became more and more sporadic. We never knew for sure whether he would show up at all.

Some people called my father a romantic. Others said he never grew up. However one described him, he knew how to bring adventure and excitement into our otherwise dull lives. When we were very young, there had been outings, fishing trips and campouts in Kettle Moraine State Forest. One time, he scattered real arrowheads in a creek and then took us swimming. When we found them, he acted as though we'd discovered them all by ourselves.

My father also loved to tell us homespun stories when he put us to bed at night. Growing up, he had us believing that a little bear came and knocked on the window to talk to him each evening. Of course, the conversation was always one-sided. By the time we rushed to look out the window, the little bear had always conveniently disappeared. It never occurred to us then that a bear would have a hard time looking into our second story window.

Also, thanks to our father, we had dogs, cats, horses, motorbikes, and silly contraptions that claimed our attention. Mom, of course, would have preferred that the money be used for food, clothing, and furniture, but that didn't register with Dad. Because he had an inventive imagination, we never knew what to expect next.

It didn't take us long, however, to realize these fun times were only occasional, since we only got to see him for two days every other weekend, if we were lucky. His absence left a huge hole in my life. I spent most of my weekdays eagerly awaiting Dad's return, so his broken promises and failures to show up crushed me. Since I took his word as his bond I often stayed glued to the window for hours waiting.

Mom tried to comfort me. "John, why don't you go and play with Tom from across the street? It's so nice out. Your father probably had something come up, and he just couldn't make it this weekend."

I had a hard time figuring out why Mom and Dad couldn't get along. "How come Dad doesn't live at home? Why does he have to live so far away?" I frequently asked.

Mom always downplayed it. "That's where your father was able to find a good job. He's tried other places, but he can make more money working at Continental Can."

I often wished our home life was different, but each time I did, I came to the same conclusion—there was nothing I could do to change it. Because we didn't have enough money to live on, Mom was forced to work to make ends meet. This made life even more chaotic because the six of us had the run of the house with little supervision. The sitters Mom was able to hire were old, odd or eccentric, and they never stayed on the job long.

One thing was for certain—when I grew up, I would not live like this again.

I did have great admiration for my mother. Not everyone could have persevered under the terrible pressure she did. Wisconsin is known for its heavy alcohol consumption, but Mom never tried to escape her problems through either drinking or smoking cigarettes. Instead she took advantage of the wisdom of a Lutheran pastor's son who was studying psychology. Their sessions seemed to help.

Mom was an excellent example, modeling for her children how

to withstand pressure from others, how not to become someone you didn't want to be. She encouraged us to form our own convictions, choose our own friends, and not follow the crowd. "Be careful who you run with. Find someone to play with who knows how to stay out of trouble."

During lean times we lived on American staples like macaroni and cheese and peanut-butter-and-jelly sandwiches. We rarely wore new clothes, so we were always glad for the hand-me-downs and offerings we received from concerned friends and the church. But accepting charity was extremely embarrassing for Dad, who had a warped sense of pride. When he learned the church brought us groceries, he was furious. "What are you trying to do to this family? We're not beggars! We don't need some da—church to feed the kids!" The next time he visited, he came bearing gifts, and Mom received her usual monthly allotment, but that only lasted until Dad's next binge.

I don't blame my parents for splitting up, but I know Dad's drinking either caused his problems or his problems drove him to drink. Even at my age, I saw that alcohol did nothing to make life easier. It only made things worse.

At the time, it didn't seem odd to walk everywhere because Mom couldn't drive, but when the temperature dropped below freezing I would have loved a ride to school. I envied my friends who had both parents living at home, nice clothes to wear, and a car to lug their groceries home from the store. We managed without too much complaining.

My older brother, Gary, took his frustrations out on me. One of his favorite outlets seemed to be making my life more miserable. God must have stuck him in my life to prepare me for boot camp, because at the time there didn't seem to be any other good reason.

Our house was always full of people—loud and stressful. There was no place to call my own unless I hid in a closet to get away from it all.

Boys will be boys. In fact we made the newspaper a few times. When Jeff crawled out of his upstairs window onto the back porch roof, he fell and broke his elbow in two places. The article's headline was "Local Boy Tries to Fly." We almost lost Tom once when he climbed through the garage window and fell through several double-paned glass storm windows leaning against the wall. The jagged glass tore into his abdomen, just missing his spleen. Another time he tried to pet a friend's dog, and it bit a huge chunk out of his face, leaving a nasty scar. Mom had her hands full.

One day I found Mom locked in the bathroom screaming hysterically. Dad was on the outside trying to force his way in. I was too young to understand what was really going on, but I ran all the way up the back alley and across Madison Avenue to get help. "Uncle Gene, please come to our house! Mommy's in the bathroom and she's crying really loud. She needs help. Hurry!" My parents divorced shortly after.

Our strained home life not only affected Mom, it also affected me. I broke out with hives, battled migraines, and had a hard time focusing in school. The school nurse often sent me home because my head ached too much to continue my studies. Nausea accompanied the migraines that were only relieved after I vomited, which usually happened as I walked home from school.

After various allergy tests, the doctor told Mom that my hives were caused by stress. "Marion, the tests are inconclusive. I don't think Johnny is allergic to anything. Perhaps it's tied to his nerves. How is he doing in school? Is he worried about something?" My mother's highly emotional state and the fact that she sometimes cried on my shoulder only added to the trauma.

In some ways my mother was like an insecure child, but who could blame her? She never expected to draw the hand she was dealt. Mom was in way over her head, but she was a fighter. I was more than willing to be her confidant if she needed one, though I was too young to offer much more than a hug and a listening ear. "It will be okay, Momma. I just know it will. It's gonna be just fine," I'd tell her.

The swim team became my savior. There I found a family away from home. I made new friends like Jim Simdon, a guy my age who was attending a private Lutheran school, and sisters, Dianne and Joni Dean who came up from Illinois to work as lifeguards and help coach the swim team. They were related to our city manager. Joni and Dianne called me their adopted little brother, and gave me the attention I craved. For three blissful months every summer, swimming and hanging out with my new family was my escape to a much more normal life. Receiving encouraging letters from them lifted my spirit during the long winters.

Because of my swimming connections, I got to go on my first airplane ride with the pool administrator, spend time at the Simdon's family cottage up north, go on picnics and waterskiing with Joni and Dianne, and enjoy lots of out of town swim meets with some great kids. The connections from the swim team helped me to make friends who spanned several age groups. I loved the praise I got from my coaches and friends when I won races, and I worked extra hard to get a pat on the back.

We were challenged every year to see how many miles we could swim by doing laps. We kept tally by marking a chart on the bulletin board. Swimming laps provided me with a door to my inner self. The water became my secret place. I could lose myself in a make-believe world and dream big dreams. My thoughts and I became one. It was my inner sanctum, a welcome escape from the noise at home.

I attended Sunday school at Trinity Lutheran Church, a half block from home, and enjoyed the Bible stories. It was comforting to hear about God's love and learn that Jesus died to forgive all my wrongdoings so that I could join Him in heaven one day. Discovering Him brought a new dimension to my life and gave me hope.

My teacher said, "Jesus loves all the little children, and never turned one of them away. He enjoyed holding each one close." She later explained He was like a shepherd. "Once He counted his hundred sheep and noticed that one had strayed. So He left the ninety-nine safe in the fold and went looking for that one lost sheep. And He is still looking for anyone who is lost today."

I related all too well. That lonely, lost sheep was me. If only Jesus would come and find me, so I'd know that someone besides my mother cared. I wanted that approval, that acceptance. I wanted to matter.

One sweltering hot summer day, I was feeling particularly down. My father was on one of his drinking binges and behind in his alimony payments, which once more left us with little money. Like most children I craved sweets, so I earned candy money by canvassing the neighborhood with my wagon, going door to door collecting empty pop bottles, then returning them to the store for refunds. It was during one of these pop bottle runs that something remarkable happened. I can still remember the exact spot on the quiet, shrub-lined street where it occurred.

While deep in my thoughts, something flickered in my mind, the same way a scraped match takes on flame. At first I thought it was me, but then I realized it wasn't. The sensation was more vivid, more alive—more sentient.

My somber mood vanished and was replaced by wonderful calm. I felt all alone with God, just Him and me. I felt a physical embrace of love, of affirmation. I glanced around. No one was there. A voice whispered, "John, I love you and am watching over you. You are in this world for a purpose." That was it.

The experience didn't last more than a few seconds, but *whew*, I felt like I was flying. It was God talking to me. *Me!* I realized then that God was more than just some Bible story. He was real and He knew my name. More importantly, He loved and valued me.

Did God just say, 'I have a purpose for your life'? I thought. *What does that mean? What is my purpose for being here?* It was puzzling, yet reassuring. *There must be more to my life than all the depressing stuff I'm going through. There has to be.* I craved my Dad's attention and wanted his approval, but he seemed oblivious to my needs. We were poles apart. I tried to enter his world, but I don't remember him ever trying to enter into mine. Though my earthly father was absent, apparently my heavenly father wasn't.

Like many of my school friends, I attended church but eventually stopped going. The God-awareness took a back seat.

I exuded energy—lots of it—so I kept myself busy. As if the swim team wasn't enough, Little League and later Pony League baseball in the summer, basketball and wrestling during the winter, plus Cub Scouts and Boy Scouts helped to keep me busy. I made all the practices and pushed myself to be a strong athlete. I loved the discipline it brought into my life, and soon discovered I enjoyed competing with myself. Some of my friends were now smoking regularly, but I couldn't figure out why they would want to.

When I turned twelve, I added a job as a morning paperboy and delivered the *Milwaukee Sentinel* through rain, sleet, snow, and the freezing cold of winter. Like everything else I did, I thrived on the challenges.

I wasn't satisfied with being an ordinary paperboy, so instead of getting up at six in the morning, I crawled out of bed at four. I loved the early mornings. It was quiet and peaceful as the townsfolk slept. The morning mist and dew that formed on the grass during the summer months provided a fresh smelling fragrance that mysteriously disappeared after sunrise. Only a few melodious birds chattered high up in the trees as they slowly woke, along with the occasional tapping sound of a lone woodpecker. It was mine alone to enjoy. I didn't mind that there was no one else to share it with; I liked having it all to myself. It gave me plenty of time to reflect. I cherished being alone with my thoughts. There was this little game I played. I called it "elimination." What if there were no trees? What if there were no bushes? Birds? Animals? Flowers? Grass? Houses? People? Stars? Moon? Sun? One by one, I would make everything disappear until there was nothing, just total darkness. Then I would ask myself, "Is that all there is?" Then there would be an explosion of sorts inside me. Something exciting. Something unique. Something that led me to believe there was more.

Often I arrived at the *Sentinel's* office, which was on the opposite side of town from where I lived, before the papers arrived from Milwaukee. I had no choice but to wait. That wasn't so bad in the summer, but during the winter it was miserable. Occasionally, I backtracked in the freezing weather to locate the delivery truck. I usually found the driver at the 24-hour eatery at the edge of town. I never could figure out why he didn't drop off the papers first and then enjoy his breakfast, but he must have assumed that nobody in their right mind would keep getting up at that hour to deliver papers. But because I derived great pleasure in knowing my customers received their papers before most other paperboys even got out of their warm beds, I continued the madness.

Early in life I learned that if I wanted to accomplish something I had to motivate myself. I had no cheerleaders. I simply decided to do something, then went about doing it.

I went through a brief stealing stage. Several of us converged on Main Street during our school lunch hour like a pack of marauding wolves, and helped ourselves to anything we could sneak from the local stores. Group stealing was easier because you had the cover of many, but doing it solo was terrifying. The rush it provided was addicting, but the real challenge was defying the establishment by not getting caught.

Heading down the aisle, I slipped a box of candy into my *Milwaukee Sentinel* news bag. Then I heard the voice.

"Hey, young man, where do you think you're going with that? Let me have a look inside your bag."

It was the store clerk. I was busted. My face undoubtedly turned several shades of red and I felt a knot tighten in my stomach. Everyone in the store must have witnessed my embarrassment. But that wasn't the worst of it.

"Young man, you're going to call home and tell your parents what you have just done. Come along now and follow me to my back office. You can use my phone."

I started to sweat and felt clammy all over. Dealing with the police would have been easier than making that phone call. I didn't want to cause Mom any more grief than she already had. She'd had enough. Mom thought she was doing a pretty good job of raising us, and now I had let her down. The man stood there as I dialed, which made it even more humiliating.

"Hi, Mom. Say, ah...um...I'm down here at the Five and Ten and ...well...I got caught taking a box of candy without paying."

It was very quiet on the other end. Then I heard her voice break and she began to sob. It tore my insides out. I'd heard too much of that through the years. I hated to see her unhappy and now I was the one who caused her pain. Mom would blame herself, of course. She always did.

When I got home she didn't even scream at me. All she said was, "Hon, I'm so sorry we don't have the money to buy those kinds of things. Really, things will get better soon—I just know it. Next time you want something, check with me first and let's talk about it."

She was too nice. Too loving. Too understanding. That made my shame even more unbearable. I wanted her to punish me, ground me or take away some privileges. But all I got was her tenderness. Perhaps she used a mother's wisdom? Maybe she knew that by her doing nothing, my conscience would kick in.

I didn't steal because I couldn't afford it—my paper route was earning me money. I stole because I liked the thrill of getting away with something dangerous. It was another challenge. Besides, I hated to spend my money.

One of the biggest hurdles I struggled with was acceptance. I think everyone wants to fit in somewhere. Young people can be very cruel by poking fun and playing gags on the kids who don't seem to fit a certain mold. School was fertile ground for emotional pain, especially when couples broke up or when someone didn't make the team or the honor roll.

Competing for friends or striving to be accepted into some type of clique or club wasn't my thing. I resolved not to get caught up in peer pressure. Learning to be my own best friend gave me the option of choosing who and when I wanted to be with someone. I was friendly to everyone, and careful not to put myself in a place of rejection.

I was sensitive toward the underdog—those who were not popular or had few friends. When I was in the seventh grade a girl in my class played a cruel prank on me. She passed out a fake announcement for a sleepover I was supposedly having. She only invited the shy and backward guys that no one hung around with or liked.

Fortunately, one of the fellas asked me about the party before the last school bell on that Friday, and I was able to defuse what would have been a very embarrassing experience for both them and me. Not that I was ashamed to have had these guys over for a night; I was horrified that someone might see the condition of our house. Our sofa was old and torn with springs sticking out in all directions, and most everything else we had was in similar shape due to our roughhousing. I about died when I realized how close I had come to being humiliated.

My self-discipline and love for solitude continued when I started high school. After I quit my paper route, I still got up at an unreasonable time, walked two miles to school, and tried to time my arrival with the milkman. Because his arrival wasn't always predictable, a few sub zero winter mornings I stood outside the door freezing, until I discovered a hot air exhaust vent under some steps on the far end of the building. When the milkman was on time, however, I could go inside and had more than an hour to myself before the bus kids arrived, and they arrived a good half-hour before the city kids.

During my teenage years, lack of money demanded I become creative. The cheapest way to attend the movies was to go to the second showing—stand by the rear exit doors and walk in while everyone from the first show was leaving. Outdoor theaters were easier—it's surprising how many people we could pack into the trunk of a car. Local dances were more challenging, but we learned how to admit five for the price of one. One of us paid and got stamped, then ran into the bathroom while the ink was still wet, and stamped the others. It was an act of faith, because with the invisible ink we never knew if the transfer was valid until we put our hand under the black light. Lake Ripley Park was a piece of cake. We could get in for free by avoiding the main entrance and instead walking through people's yards and climbing over a fence or two. Plus there was always the option of being dropped offshore by a boat.

Dating was expensive, so that was never an option. Why pay for two when you could pick-'em-up for free? I never went to one homecoming dance, prom or any other function at school that required tickets, corsages, or rented tuxedos. I didn't waste my money on a class ring. Those things didn't seem practical.

Rock River ran straight through Fort, encased by rock and

concrete walls. A few hundred feet from the Main Street Bridge downriver was the railroad bridge. The bridge had wooden walkways on both sides that were great to fish from. High electric wires on both sides displayed fishing lures, flies, bobbers and hooks—a testament to the skill of the local fisherman. When the white bass ran during spring, the guys and I could each catch a stringer full in no time. We had other favorite spots where we caught bluegills, crappies, bullheads, catfish and carp. We spent the evening before gathering night crawlers, a flashlight in one hand and a *Campbell Soup* can in the other.

The railroad bridge was a favorite place to play. Huge concrete pilings held it up. Underneath the wooden walkways and train tracks, steel girders webbed together formed the superstructure for the bridge. It was dangerous, but we could hold on to the top pieces and walk on the bottom pieces all the way across the river undetected. After we got to a concrete post we had a private chamber all to ourselves. It was especially fun when the train passed overhead.

Cruising was big. Anyone who had a car to drive, whether borrowed or owned, wasted gallons of gas going up and down Main Street for hours on end. Drivers were always on the lookout for passengers willing to chip in for gas. At twenty-three cents a gallon, who could complain? No car had seatbelts, and in a fast car you could bury the needle. Drag racing, burning rubber and doing donuts in parking lots were favorite pastimes of local hotshots.

Driving blindfolded was an adventure. Tom Belzer became my eyes while I drove his 1958 Cadillac the entire ten miles from Cambridge to Fort while sightless. We traversed winding, hilly roads without a scratch by his calm directions. "Move the steering wheel a little more to the right, now to the left...hold it steady...okay, step on the gas...now let up a little, we're approaching a curve that bends to the left. Easy now...turn the wheel just a little more... That's it. Now we have a straight road, we can go a little faster. How would you like to pass a car? There's one just ahead of us poking along...okay, we have to get into the left lane so turn the wheel to the left, that's it, now step on the gas."

I needed a role model. The local church helped, but it was short lived. My father could have played a major role in my life, but when I needed him most, he disappeared. My mother did her best, but was loaded down with the responsibility of raising six children and, with all her duties at home and on the job, she could only point me in the right direction. The public school had a few exceptional teachers, but there were hundreds of students and I got lost in the crowd. I had no one. I was left to form my own opinions, and I did. I rebelled against most authorities in protest of not having my innermost needs met. I was a perfect candidate for the myriad of voices of the world that were vying for my attention. I couldn't wait to graduate and get away.

John F. Kennedy's murder shocked everyone. November 22, 1963 was a dreary Friday for us all. Anyone old enough to remember can tell you what he or she was doing when they heard about the Dallas shooting. It was that kind of moment. I was a fifteen-year-old in freshman geography class. Someone stuck his head in the door and said, "Have you heard the awful news? The president has been shot!" I can still remember the stunned faces of my fellow students and teacher. We were terrified that someone wanted our president dead. The rest of the school day was a big blur.

Just prior to this, we feared World War III because of the Cuban Missile Crisis. We lived in fear that we might be bombed without any notice at all. Kennedy's assassination brought back memories of having to dive under our desks in grade school during mock nuclear attack drills. I was too cocky then to have a real concern about dying.

I earned a varsity letter in swimming my freshman year, and then gradually began to lose interest in sports. Sports might have been more enjoyable if it had been a family affair. The spectators at most sporting events were the other kids' parents. Mom was able to attend a few times, but Dad never even attempted. I'm not condemning my parents, because if I were to walk a few miles in their shoes, I'm sure I would better understand why some of the things were the way they were. Besides, by that time in my mind, there were better things to do than to compete on sports teams. I was interested in getting a job, drinking, and just plain fooling around.

One event pushed me over the edge my junior year. During a

preliminary track meet, my coach called me into his office and said, "John, your hair is getting too long. I'm going to cut it." Before I could blink he opened up a locker and pulled out a pair of bush trimmers with twelve-inch blades. I stood there in shock thinking this was some kind of joke when he and his assistant grabbed my hair and snipped off the bangs to the scalp. I pulled away in horror. *Did he just do what I think he did?*

Not only was I taken aback, but also furious when I gazed into the mirror. I looked like a moron—a disgusting resemblance to Moe, one of the *Three Stooges*. I don't know if he intended to cut off that much hair or not, but he offered no apologies. That angered me the most. I stormed out of his office, grabbed my school-issued wool beanie, and pulled it over my head to hide my embarrassment. Then I went straight to the track field, directed my fury on competition, and won first place in the broad jump and high jump.

After talking it over with a couple of friends on the track team, they agreed I had grounds to quit, even though they wanted me to stay because of our close friendship and my contribution to the team. I really was looking forward to my junior year of track, but found it hard to serve under a coach who had no remorse for what he'd done. So I turned in my uniform and track shoes and found a good paying job.

In times like these it would have been nice to have had a father who busted down the coach's door and knocked him through the wall. But since that wasn't an option, I sucked it up and handled it my own way. It fueled my rebellious streak.

Due to all my walking, running, swimming, bicycling and horsing around, I had powerful spring in my legs. At five-foot-ten I could stuff a volleyball into a regulation basketball rim with six inches to spare. I also performed some good jumps during spring practice. To rub it in, during a gym class, I set the high jump bar two inches above the school record and hollered, "Hey, coach! Watch this!" He turned just in time to see me sail over the bar with ease.

When the *Beatles* invaded the United States, the atmosphere drifted from the depressing state of American affairs to lightheartedness. Their music was uplifting and fun. Almost everything they recorded was a hit. *The Fab Four* changed the image of rock bands forever. Overnight, singing groups formed and their one-hit wonders took the world by storm. It seemed like everybody who could pick a guitar, play a drum or keyboard, got together to perform.

We went from Barry Mann's "Who Put the Bomp (In the Bomp, Bomp, Bomp")" to the Kingsman's "Louie Louie" in a flash. Other favorites in succession were "Hang On Sloopy" by the McCoys, "Mrs. Brown, You've Got a Lovely Daughter" by the Herman's Hermits, "96 Tears" by ? and The Mysterians, "Wild Thing" by the Troggs, and "Light My Fire" by The Doors, to name just a few.

It was a brand-new day. Clothing styles changed dramatically; the young could be expressive and experiment with their identities. The older generation thought we were weird, but we felt we were cool. The music charmed us with a hypnotic pull, and we followed it as the children who followed the *Pied Piper*. Songs were cunning, subtly seductive, and had an uncanny way of leading us to wherever they wanted us to go. The older we grew the more consuming the music and fads became because they were no longer just words to listen to or fun jingles to sing, but a lifestyle to emulate.

During my sophomore year, Mom remarried. William Krebs was a truck driver who reminded us of Hoss Cartwright, the burly guy from the TV show *Bonanza*. His appearance in our life was quite an adjustment. He braved the fact that he was marrying a woman who already had six children, all living at home, not to mention his own three. We quickly realized the benefits to having a man around the house seven days a week. Our quality of living rapidly improved, and we noticed it especially at the dinner table. All of us were happy for the security it brought our mother. Bill, as we called him, turned out to be a great guy.

Dad tried to get some roots back home. He bought land out on the edge of town on the Rock River. At first it was going to be a Mexican restaurant—*The Eldorado*. It eventually turned into a house—that is, a half-finished house. He never did finish it, but it was his home until he went to the veterans' home up north.

One thing Dad could do well was make awesome chili. We

called it "Ollie's Fire Brand Chili."[1] Everyone loved it. Dad's place became a hangout of sorts. He hosted all kinds of beer parties for us kids and provided the chili. Those were some very rough years for Dad as he hit the bottle pretty hard. He knew he was an alcoholic, but it would be a few more years before he sought help.

During Easter break while I was a senior in high school, I went to Florida and the Bahamas with two carloads of young men and one gal. While we were in Fort Lauderdale, thousands of college age kids rioted. They got drunk and pulled down palm trees, vandalized cars and trashed the beaches. We happened to be in the wrong place at the wrong time. Hordes of police drove thousands of us off the beaches and out of the city with shotguns, clubs and trained dogs. I discovered that even normally good people can get caught up in mass hysteria and do wrong things.

On the airplane to the Bahamas, a man in the seat next to me spoke to someone across the aisle. From what he said I gathered he was from San Francisco. Then the man turned to me.

"Hey, young man, what's your name?"

"John."

"Hey, have you ever tried some of this?" He was holding a small heart-shaped pill.

"What is it?"

"LSD. This stuff is totally radical. It'll change the way you see the world forever. It is mind expanding. Here you can have this. Take it with you."

I was tempted but I refrained.

The vacation itself whetted my appetite to discover more of the world, and I determined right then and there to see more of it.

Wisconsin and drinking are synonymous. People love their beer and bratwursts. I was drinking in bars before I turned eighteen (I had a false ID), but after becoming legal the teen bars were even more inviting. I thought it was *cool* playing adult. There wasn't a weekend

---

[1] *Recipe is at the back of the book.*

that went by that I didn't get drunk. One evening I drank a whole case of beer. It was stupid and dangerous. My drinking was getting out of control. Guess I was trying to follow in my Dad's footsteps.

When Vietnam first became front-page news, my friends and I couldn't even find it on the map. Things happening 8,000 miles away didn't seem relevant. We were too busy being teenagers. By 1966, the media was feeding us a steady diet of daily updates on the growing involvement. We watched the evening news in our comfortable living rooms as Walter Cronkite led us step by step through the escalation.

The year of my graduation was full of news. In January 1967, astronauts Air Force Lieutenant Colonels Edward H. White, Virgil "Gus" Grissom, and Navy Lieutenant Commander Roger B. Chaffee met a violent death as a fire spread through their space capsule during a full-scale simulation of a launching. Jack Ruby (the man who shot and killed Lee Harvey Oswald, President Kennedy's alleged assassin), then fifty-five, died of cancer in Dallas, Texas. For the first time in the Vietnam War, U.S. planes bombed targets in the North Vietnam port city of Haiphong. In a startling Space *first*, the Soviet Union landed an instrument capsule on Venus, and it immediately started sending back information about the planet's surface and atmosphere.

The '60s belonged to the young. Seventy million children from the post-war baby boom became teenagers and young adults. The movement away from the conservative '50s culminated and eventually resulted in radical ways of thinking in the cultural fabric of American life. We were no longer content to be mere images of the generation ahead of us. We baby boomers wanted change. Those changes had an effect on education, values, lifestyles, laws, and entertainment. It was a revolution.

The '60s generation made its mark in music, arts and dress, led by spokespeople such as the *Beatles*, *Andy Warhol*, *Twiggy* and the hippies. Those of us under thirty were the innovators, and the people over thirty either strove to keep up or became our best critics. We dressed, acted and lived to suit ourselves, and were not overly concerned with what others thought. Much of our clothing was salvaged from secondhand shops, old storage trunks and Army-Navy surplus stores. Wall designs were done with fluorescent paint so they lighted up in the ultraviolet (black) lights of discotheques. Psychedelic posters, flowers, buttons and body painting were vogue.

This wasn't a healthy time for anyone without strong moral roots. The winds of change swept many unsuspecting young people into debauchery, and the country became full of teenage runaways. Youth rebellion was at an all-time high, and the floodgates of hell were wide open. Jingles like *If it feels good, do it* and *Do your own thing* were bywords of the day. The charm of sin had recruiters on every corner, and the enlistment rate was extremely high.

Those days were an ideal time for the misdirected to become rebellious, and I was right in the middle of the first wave of change. When I grew my hair long, it was a style a few years premature for Wisconsin. The older people in my hometown didn't know what to think of it, and spent plenty of time gawking whenever I was in sight. The high school teachers acted dumbfounded. Even if they didn't mind the long hair, they were still attached to the "respectable" part of society and felt it was their duty to keep this fad from spreading, as if it were some newfound disease. Because my senior class picture was taken with hair over my ears, the yearbook staff felt it was their moral responsibility to have it banned. When my picture was returned to me with the explanation that my hair was too long to fit their standards, I decided to boycott all picture sessions that year, and carefully avoided any school photographers. As expected, there were no pictures of me in the 1967 yearbook.

Long hair proved to be a battle throughout my final year, just as miniskirts were for some of the girls.

I was trying to get a head start on letting my hair grow for the summer. With only four months left before I left for Navy boot camp, and knowing my hair would be shorn upon entrance, I wanted my hair to be as long as possible. So I pushed the limits of our school's hair policy. A couple of other guys did too, but I felt that the principal, Mr. Lepley, had a personal vendetta against me.

He gave me a backhanded compliment once. "John, you're a leader. People look up to you. Others follow your example. But what kind of influence are you having on them?"

When I stopped wearing socks with my shoes, others followed me. So the school adopted a policy that we had to wear socks with our shoes. I wore flesh-colored socks to school one day and was sent to the office. "John, you know you're violating school policy. I'm going to have to send you home."

When I asked why, the principal said, "You're not wearing any socks."

"Really? What do you call these?" I contemptuously pulled up my pants to show him my socks.

I wasn't afraid to be different. To do what everyone else was doing seemed boring. Earlier in high school, I took perfectly good jeans and poured bleach over them to make them spotted. (Back then this was absurd. Today people pay big bucks for this stuff.) My grandma frayed the bottoms for me. She also sewed permanent creases down the front. Soon others followed my lead. I cut the sleeves off my sweatshirts and frayed the armholes. The sweatshirts complimented the long-sleeved shirt I wore underneath. Again, others followed suit. I took a knife to my penny loafers and cut away the leather to make splotches. Once more, my schoolmates copied me. I replaced my leather belt with a piece of woven cloth. Yet again, others adopted my fashion. But it was probably my long hair that bothered school officials most.

At dress rehearsal the day before our graduation ceremony, Mr. Lepley inspected the class. I was one of the few given the mandate: Get a haircut or don't graduate with the rest of the class.

Thinking this through, I decided to play his bluff. I talked it over with Laura, a cheerleader I was asked to walk with, and she told me it was okay by her if I didn't comply. So on graduation night, with greased-down hair, I walked with Laura to the front of the gymnasium for my diploma. All I got was a dirty look from the principal, because it was too late for him to do anything without creating a scene. He handed me my coveted diploma. I graduated.

After all the fuss everyone made over my hair, the popularity of long hair a year or two later made it the fashion. It was even deemed acceptable by the local school board and teachers. I thought it was a hoot that after I joined the Navy and came home with short hair, I found several of my high school teachers sporting long hair and beards.

Greasing down my hair didn't leave a good impression on Mr. Lepley the evening I graduated. It probably looked shorter than those who had blow-dried theirs, but he knew I hadn't complied. I couldn't help but wonder what he might be thinking of me now—the first man scheduled to welcome home the Apollo 11 crew.

~

At 0546 hours, VHF voice radio and recovery-beacon contact was made. Four minutes later at 0550, the command module splashed down into the choppy Pacific Ocean.

The command module was dragged across the waves by the chutes and was turned upside down. Our helicopter raced toward the drop zone at full throttle, the bulkheads shaking and vibrating like they were going to split in two.

Air Boss One with Squadron Commander Colonel Robert Hoffman reported, "It's still in Stable 2 (upside down). The bags are inflating."

Armstrong added, "Air Boss, Apollo 11. Everyone is okay inside. Our checklist is complete. Awaiting swimmers."

The module uprighted into Stable 1 just as we arrived. We were cleared for recovery.

Lt. Richard J. Barrett piloted our helicopter close to the bobbing space module. I unstrapped from my seat and stood in the open door, hoping I wouldn't make any mistakes.

I reminded myself the United States' military had given its all to prepare me. I was a Navy UDT frogman.

Aware of the world's eyes on me, I leaped into the choppy ocean alone.

Early Days

Marion and Orville Wolfram - John's Parents

317 Lincoln Street - John's boyhood home

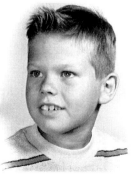

John, 8 years old

Fort Swim Team - John, third row sixth from left

Fort Swim Team - John 12 years old

John 1967

—Chapter Three—

Anchors Aweigh!

U.S. boys were drafted at age eighteen. Before graduation day arrived I realized I had some important decisions to make. The big question was; what should I do with my life now that high school was almost over? Because of the draft, hanging around town working a part-time job was dangerous. If you didn't have any concrete plans, Uncle Sam had some for you.

Many of my friends rushed off to college to avoid the draft. Others enlisted so they could pick the branch of service of their choice. Those who took their chances were usually drafted into the Army and hurried off to fight in the jungles of Vietnam. Many never made the return trip home alive.

Deciding wasn't all that difficult. College was expensive and, for me, would have meant mostly parties and fun—time and money wasted. Being drafted into the Army wasn't an option, so after a little research, I chose the United States Navy. When I was younger, I saw a television special on Navy frogmen and was mesmerized. That focused my interest.

A California boot camp seemed like a dream come true— goodbye Fort Atkinson, hello beaches! The Navy's campaign slogan was "Join the Navy and see the world." That was exactly the kind of education I wanted! No more of the tedious book learning, tests, and term papers I had to endure throughout high school. Nope. There was a big world out there and I was going to see it firsthand.

Just before I entered boot camp, a group of us went to the "Poplar Point," a teenage bar just outside town. We met up with Terry Beck, a friend on his way to Vietnam. Terry quit school after his junior year to join the Marines. His father, a local banker, had sent him to a military academy in an attempt to discipline him. Big waste of time. Terry was someone you couldn't easily tame. He was mature for his age and big. He was extremely well liked, especially by the girls. We had one thing in common—we both loved to play drums.

A few of us were sitting at a table drinking, talking, and minding our own business when someone from behind me started to pour his drink over my head. (I assume he didn't approve of my long hair.) In reflex I jumped to my feet and, with one solid punch to his nose, knocked him to the floor. Before you could blink, the group at my table jumped up and a free-for-all erupted. When it was over, several chairs and tables lay busted, and we sent the young college kid who'd poured his drink on my head, along with his friends, headfirst out the tavern door onto the pavement. Thankfully, the owner was a friend of ours and didn't call the police.

After our altercation at the bar, we were in for yet another surprise. Terry somehow managed to smuggle off his base several live grenades, parachute flares and a few mortars. I had no idea until we were out in the country on a joy ride, when Terry suddenly stopped his car and opened the trunk.

"Hey, guys, watch this." For the next few minutes we had a prophetic view of Vietnam. The dark evening sky suddenly lit up as the mortars and grenades exploded underneath the canopy of bright flares, which left clouds of smoke like ghosts suspended in the sky. Cows in a nearby field bellowed, bucked and scattered in every direction. *Terry, the grenade-launching cowboy*, I thought. Surrounding farmhouse lights blinked on. I hollered, "Hey, let's get out of here before the county police arrive!" We sped off toward town.

My happy-go-lucky days were over. It was time for me to put away my childish ways and become a man. Because I didn't want some government employee to ravage my head in twenty seconds, I planned to show up in San Diego bald. I chose Nancy, the girl I was dating at the time, to cut it. It was a sad moment when she put the scissors to my long locks, which by then had reached my shoulders, because it symbolically marked the end of my carefree days. We documented it all on Polaroid film as if it were a life-shattering event.

At boot camp I met some interesting guys from all over the United States. One had come straight from Haight-Ashbury in San Francisco and told stories about flower children, communal living, rock and roll concerts, weird people and LSD. Others came from as far away as Alaska, Hawaii, Maine and Puerto Rico to become sailors in the United States Navy.

Even so, I had always hated sharing a room with anyone, especially my brother Gary. He was bossy and controlling. Now I had a barracks full of Garys and a company commander—the Navy's version of an Army drill sergeant—even more domineering. Since guys will be guys, fights broke out, and people got picked on and made fun of. When someone messed up they got a "blanket party." That was when, in the middle of the night, a bunch of guys threw a blanket over someone's head while they were sleeping and beat them with their fists. Gradually rebellious attitudes gave way to camaraderie and we pushed through boot camp as a team.

The biggest battle for many was being away from home. Leaving friends, family, familiar surroundings, teen bars and partying for a disciplined environment under the iron glare of our company commander didn't seem a fair trade. There was a distinct lonely, left out feeling. We were locked behind huge fences for twelve weeks of military training while the whole world was passing us by. Most of us had hometown friends whose weekly letters kept us up-to-date on new goings-on at the local hangouts. Their lives were blissful in comparison.

That winter, in sunny southern California, it snowed for the first time in twenty years. I'd avoided boot camp at the Great Lakes Training Center to get out of the cold. Yet there I was; one of the unfortunate to witness this spectacle. Outside I shivered as frozen white flakes covered the *grinder* where we marched, exercised and stood inspection.

For some reason, after weeks of being yelled at, doing countless push-ups, sit-ups and marching until blisters tore from our feet, we felt we had graduated to manhood. We couldn't wait to go home after boot camp to show the old gang how much we had matured in such a short time.

During boot camp I asked about the Underwater Demolition Teams since that was the main reason I joined the Navy.

Frogmen were used as long ago as the Revolutionary War.

The sailors of our infant Navy attacked British men-of-war anchored in our harbors with the use of underwater torpedoes. When other nations saw the advantage of this kind of fighting man, they also developed this combat technique.

On May 6, 1943, Seabees from the NCB Training Center at Camp Peary, Virginia, chosen for their knowledge of blasting with high explosives, answered the call to form the United States' first Underwater Demolition Team (UDT).

These frogmen were used during World War II to clear the proposed invasion beach areas and their offshore waters of both natural and manmade obstructions, mines, and entanglements. The UDT also performed river recon, pre-landing intelligence, harbor penetration to attack sheltered ships, the destruction of seaport facilities, plus recovery of guerrillas and agents on enemy-occupied beaches.

An Underwater Demolition Team was made up of thirteen officers and one hundred men. It was organized into four operating platoons and one headquarters platoon. The complete Team could operate as one unit or be divided to operate in a platoon size or in smaller elements if required.

All UDT members—present day SEALs (sea, air, land)—were highly trained in advanced underwater swimming, deployment and retrieval techniques, the utilization of high-speed boats, submarines, low-flying helicopters, and parachuting from both helicopters and aircraft. Although the UDT didn't normally operate inland, they were trained to, and were occasionally called upon for reconnaissance and demolition missions.

The UDT saw action again at the outbreak of the Korean War in 1950. A new war and challenges brought about the development of new skills and techniques. Besides doing their traditional jobs of beach reconnaissance and clearance, the *Teams* (referring to all UDT/ SEAL teams today) were called upon to assist in night demolition of enemy factories, bridges, railway tunnels and other targets.

Their job also required them to clear heavily mined rivers and harbor entrances that were too restrictive for conventional mine-sweeping operations. The UDT methods were sometimes atypical and extremely dangerous, but very effective. A line of swimmers would move into the harbor mouth or river and, as they came across a mine, attach an explosive charge with a time-delay fuse. Once a charge was placed, UDT members had to swim rapidly away because the shock would slam into their bodies at an alarming force. An unfortunate swimmer who was knocked out by a shock wave would almost certainly die.

The UDTs hadn't changed all that much when I applied for training, and were already being used extensively in the Vietnam campaign. Soon I heard numerous firsthand accounts of hair-raising missions conducted by those fortunate enough to have made it back alive.

The UDTs were a brotherhood of the daring—Mavericks. I had to be one of them.

The day finally came when our company commander announced there would be testing at the end of the week for those of us interested in becoming frogmen.

Only two from our barracks joined the few other adventurous souls early that morning—Mike Anderson and myself. We crossed the base through thick fog to the swimming pool for preliminary screening.

"So, you want to be frogmen, do you?" said the grinning recruiter. "Hurry up! Move your bodies to the shallow end of the pool. We'll soon find out."

We had to swim 500 meters doing the breast or sidestroke in less than 12 minutes 30 seconds; then all of us were herded to the track. We had to do at least 42 push-ups in 2 minutes (followed by a 2-minute rest), 50 sit-ups in 2 minutes (with a 2-minute rest), 8 pull-ups with no time limit but as fast as possible (followed by a 10-minute rest), and then run a mile and a half in full dress and boots within 11 minutes 30 seconds. We had to complete the entire screening in less than 60 minutes.

For those of us who competed in several sports in high school and kept in shape, the screen test was a breeze, but for others it was a challenge. The most interesting part was the interview with the psychiatrist.

"Okay, young man, tell me why you want to belong to a group of people like the SEALs. If you were put in a place where you would have to kill or be killed, how willing would you be to take a life?"

After initial screening, we had to wait for the results.

Despite my hopes to be accepted into Underwater Demolition Training (UDTRA) in Coronado, California, my orders were cut for the USS *Chicago*. I was one disappointed sailor as I returned home to Fort Atkinson for Christmas.

While on leave, I received a telegram notifying me to disregard my previous orders—they were cut before I took the screen test for UDT—and report back to Coronado for Underwater Demolition Training. I was *in*! I was headed for the biggest physical challenge of my life.

Sadly, before Christmas leave was over, Terry Beck, the young Marine I partied with just two months earlier, was laid to rest. Terry, the grenade-launching cowboy was killed in Vietnam while out on patrol with his dog just seventy-five days in-country.

I attended his funeral in my uniform and watched dozens of his high school friends break down in tears while the minister did his best to comfort the grieving family.

Death drove me to think. Think really hard—the kind of thoughts that knocked me out of my normal routine. *Is this all there is? Is there life after death?*

Country Joe and the Fish's popular "I-Feel-Like-I'm-Fixin'-to-Die Rag" wasn't much comfort for Terry's family or me.

Well, come on mothers throughout the land,
Pack your boys off to Vietnam.
Come on fathers, don't hesitate,
Send 'em off before it's too late.
Be the first one on your block

To have your boy come home in a box.

And it's one, two, three
What are we fighting for?
Don't ask me, I don't give a da—,
Next stop is Vietnam.
And it's five, six, seven,
Open up the pearly gates,
Well there ain't no time to wonder why,
Whoopee! we're all gonna die.

~

In 1968, UDTRA—now called BUD/S (Basic Underwater Demotion/SEAL) training—was divided into three phases, each six weeks long. Phase One was physical training. Phase Two, swim training. Phase Three, survival training. A class ahead of us had already gone through the First Phase, including Hell Week. We tried to extract as much information from them as possible before our training began, but rarely got an honest answer. I ran into a guy named Greg Moore on his way to take a shower.

"Hey, mind if I ask you a question?"

"Shoot."

"How tough were the instructors on you during your first week?"

He looked at me, dead sober. "If you've ever had a bad case of Montezuma's revenge and had no means to stop the cramping, just magnify that a thousand times. That's what you're up against." Then he busted out laughing.

Right, I thought. My initiation to BUD/S training had begun.

Many of us were right out of boot camp and in our late teens or early twenties. There were a few seasoned sailors, airman and submariners, but for the most part we were all *new guys*. No one wanted to admit it, but all of us were feeling a little tense and uneasy. We did a good job of keeping it hidden.

I had grown up surrounded by patriotism. I had occasional

problems with authority, but I was proud to be here now among these men.

Chapter Four

So You Want to Be a Frogman?

"**H**it the deck! Start pushing California away!" *Welcome to UDT/SEAL training*, I thought. I had no idea what the ogre of a man was talking about. I soon found out. We kicked both feet out behind us and threw our arms out in front of our chests. If we landed right, we "hit the deck."

Now we were in the position "lean and rest." Our bodies were parallel to the ground—no sag—our extended arms and toes held us up. *Hit the deck* put us in push-up position. *Lean and rest* held us in that position until every muscle in our body screamed.

"Hit the deck! On your feet! Hit the deck!" the man barked until we could do it as a group. Apparently this would be part of our lives for the next four and a half months. We began to drip sweat.

"Lean and rest!" We did. The man swaggered through the ranks—six feet tall, bronze skin, zero body fat. His eyes were hidden beneath a navy-blue cap with instructor logo, and behind mirrored sunglasses atop a hooked, broken nose. That was good for me. I didn't care to see his eyes. His khaki military shorts were meticulously tailored to him, and his white socks were rolled precisely three times so they rested just atop carefully spit-shined combat boots. Between his shorts and socks, his skinny legs knotted up at the calves, which gave the impression he was in pain. His teeth dug into a wad of tobacco. "You puke faces are nothing but bananas!" Translation: soft inside and out. "I've seen better looking specimens of the male gender on an old ladies' bowling team! Keep your backs straight, get your head up and use your arms, girls!

"My name," he announced, "is G-O-D. I'm going to make your lives as miserable as I can." Either he was brash or he halfway believed it. On the left breast of his blue windbreaker, huge white letters spelled *God*. Groups of other instructors stood nearby. Their jackets simply bore their names.

His real name was Vince Olivera, Boatswain's Mate First Class. Olivera claimed to be an Apache Indian, but he appeared part Mexican. He definitely was s-p-o-o-k-y. Even if the myth behind his villainous reputation was larger than life, there was enough mystery about him that I wondered if he was a little more than human.

Once we stood, he made a point of pulling off his sunglasses. The man had demon eyes. His face floated toward me like a cobra being charmed by music. His eyes drilled into mine. They dared me to move my eyes one fraction of an inch. I could tell he loved this game. I wasn't so sure I did.

He was good at his ruse. Without words he communicated he was the mountain that stood between us and graduating.

Olivera introduced Lieutenant Commander James Wilson, the CO of our class, Class 44. Wilson stepped forward. He was short and built like a tank—an inspiration to guys under five-foot-five to keep pumping in the weight room.

Wilson said, "Listen up, tadpoles. We didn't invite you here. You invited yourselves. If you don't like what you're about to go through, you can return to the ordinary Navy fleet any time you want." He eyed us. "There is a war going on, and our job is to find out who has the right stuff to join other SEALs or UDT frogmen to fight alongside us in battle. Understand?"

"Hooyah, sir!"

"In six weeks sixty percent of you won't be standing here. It's our job to make sure you're not. All your instructors are seasoned men. We can spot a loser long before he DORs—drops on request. If you're a loser, we'll find you and get rid of you ASAP so we don't waste our time. You may want to be a UDT frogman or a SEAL, but time will tell. Know that we also have a good eye for those who have no quit in them. We are looking for only the best. Understand?"

"Hooyah, Mr. Wilson!"

I learned that *hooyah* was the universal word for *yes*, *I understand*, *right away* and a bunch of other things. *Hooyah* (emphasis on the first syllable: **hoo**-*yah*) is unique to UDT/ SEALs, especially to

BUD/S training. Other branches of the armed forces use the word *hooahh*.

Our first muster was packed with instructor introductions and speeches. I stood among seventy-nine men who wanted to be UDT/SEALs. Roughly 1,900 had already been eliminated at the screen test. UDT/SEALs, I learned, were unique in how they trained. All other services trained their officers and enlisted personnel separately during their basic warfare instruction. At BUD/S, officers and enlisted men trained and suffered together, side-by-side.

BUD/S was billed as the toughest training the military had to offer. We were among the last classes housed on the Naval Amphibious Base. Shortly after we graduated, the Navy built a new training complex across the Silver Strand Highway on the beach next to the former UDT and SEAL compounds. Today it is called the Naval Special Warfare Center. Class 44 was "old school" all the way.[2]

After our initial muster, we ran to the athletic field. Chief Richard Allen, our First Phase PT (physical training) and judo instructor, ran alongside us. A former Navy heavyweight boxer, he was a duplicate of "Smokin' Joe" Frazer—huge, tough and amiable.

"SEALs don't ditty-bop and they don't walk," he said. "SEALs run. They run to the chow hall. They run to the barber, to the post office, the exchange, the head and even sick bay. Or for great distances SEALs hump, one foot after the other, one step at a time, for as long as necessary. SEALs work hard. Only girls try to avoid work. Only girls try to skate. SEALs are clean, not skuzzy. You are the Navy's best. Act like it at all times."

"Hooyah, Chief."

On the athletic field, PT began. Push-ups, jumping jacks and sit-ups were exercises the other guys and I had done for years. *Flutter kicks*, however, were something new.

---

[2] *Special note: Class 44 was full of great guys and instructors. However, in telling my story I will only focus on a few of these fine men. Those I have chosen to mention are a composite of all who made up class 44 and who instructed us. The men of Class 44 are listed at the end of the book.*

We lay flat on our backs and held our legs straight, boots six inches above the ground. First one leg and then the other was lifted three feet then lowered. At no time could a boot touch the ground. The strain on the leg and stomach muscles soon transmuted into horrific pain. We growled our way through dozens of sets of flutter kicks.

"Helen Kellers" were sheer torture. It looked like someone throwing a tantrum on the ground. Someone with a sense of humor must have come up with the name after watching Patty Duke play Helen Keller in the movie *The Miracle Worker*.

We started with a half sit-up, our hands cupped lightly around our ears, legs parallel to the ground three inches above. Then twisting, we drew one knee to the opposite elbow, then threw out the leg, then rapidly switched knees and continued. Helen Kellers required coordination, balance and resolve to do them right, and strong abdominal muscles to do them for any length of time.

Chief Allen worked our abdomens until we thought we would scream. A hard, strong gut was essential. It was the foundation for crawling, running, climbing, swinging, jumping, swimming or anything else we might have to do.

A Chief Allen favorite was having us run in place. Then he would say, "On your stomach." As soon as we were, "On your back." Then, "On your feet." Things got really difficult, and humorous, as the pace grew faster and faster, and he randomly changed the order of commands until we all looked like pigs on skates.

It was hard not to admire Chief Allen. You could tell he loved leading PT—nearly all UDT/SEALs get addicted to exercise. If we had to do two hundred push-ups, he did them along with us. The same with sit-ups, flutter kicks, leg squats and everything else he threw at us. He was a big man with tremendous strength in his arms. He could do one-armed push-ups all day long.

Like all good instructors he was there for a purpose. The Teams were no place for wimps. Allen's job was not only to forge our bodies into fighting machines, but also to help us decide if we really wanted to be a Navy UDT/SEAL. He drove us toward perfection. He was going to make us into elite warriors or we would die trying.

On our first day's PT, we did more than a thousand push-ups and stood at the leaning-rest for hours. At least that's how my arms felt.

I was getting to know a few of the guys. Frank Sparks was hard to miss. He wasn't an inch over five feet tall and was a powerful gymnast who loved to show off. A show-off myself, we hit it off. His name fit him well. Sparks was a firecracker. While most of the guys struggled to do chin-ups, Sparks flew through twice the number required. Of course he had an advantage—he only had half the weight to lug up that bar. The bigger the guy, the harder it was to drag his weight off the ground.

That was another surprising factor about BUD/S. There was no guarantee that someone more muscled than Atlas would make it through training. UDT/SEALs did (and do) place a premium on brute strength, but there's an even bigger premium on determination and resolve. Another quality they look for was perception. Some people are gifted with the ability to anticipate and discern. Making the right decision at the right time can be the difference between life and death. The average-sized guys seemed to have an advantage over others when it came to agility, but the bottom line was still heart. If a person didn't have the "want to," there was no way he would survive UDT/SEAL culture.

Not surprisingly, few could do chin-ups like Sparks. But I was surprised that quite a number had to struggle to meet the chin-up entry level requirement. Chief Allen and other instructors screamed in their faces. "How did you pass your screen test to get here? Did you bribe somebody? Because either you're not trying or you're a weakling! Which is it?"

After PT we did a four-mile timed run on the beach in T-shirt, pants and boots. I figured we must have run an additional eight to ten miles just getting from one venue to the next. It was a two-mile run to get to the beach from our barracks. Two miles there and two miles back—four miles just to go on a run.

We must have gotten "wet and sandy" a dozen times. That meant taking a plunge in the ocean then roll around in the sand.

Getting wet was bad enough (it was winter, the ocean felt like ice) but the sandy part was worse. After rolling in the sand until every inch was covered, we looked like creatures that crawled out of a sewer.

For IBS training, we were split up into seven-man teams. Each team trained with a clumsy thirteen-foot rubber IBS (inflatable boat small; unofficially, itty bitty ship), useless except for teaching BUD/S trainees to work together, IBS training's primary goal. Complete with paddles, repair kit, first-aid box and spare ropes, the raft weighed more than two hundred pounds. It was to accompany us wherever we went—on our runs through soft sand and surf, over rock jetties, and over or under barbed wire obstacles—a portable torture chamber. We would carry the raft, swim with it, sleep on it, and occasionally even get the luxury of using it.

Balancing a 200-pound boat on top of our heads was not easy. Until we learned how to walk in rhythm as a unit, and not as individuals, the boat bounced up and down, making it impossible to handle.

The instructors intentionally assigned mismatched boat crews. Teams ranged from guys five-foot-nothing to six-foot-five, making it even more awkward for everyone to carry his share of the boat. In IBS training, learning how to work as a team was critical. Mismatched crews brought out the best and worst in all of us. If we didn't bear our share of the boat, the rest of the crew would make sure we were gone. (Later on we were grouped with teammates our size.)

Handling the IBS forced us to be team players. There was no way we could handle a boat by ourselves, and absolutely no way to transport it from place to place on land without a team effort. Teamwork was everything. Making it through BUD/S without the help of teammates was just as impossible as surviving combat without the aid of others.

"Surf passage" was elementary but necessary to solidify teamwork. Each crew learned to correctly rig their IBS and align it on the beach for inspection. When the boats were rigged and ready, we stood at attention in life jackets by our boats. Our paddles were wedged between the main tube and the two cross tubes. Bow and stern lines were neatly coiled on the rubber floor.

This time and always, we would race against the other boat crews.

Since every part of training was intended to help create competent operators for the Teams, everything we did in terms of exercises or training was referred to as an "evolution." Each exercise was another step in "evolving" from a tadpole to a frogman.

A typical IBS evolution was to paddle out past the surf line, dump boat, and then paddle north or south to a given marker. Dumping boat was pulling the rubber boat up-side down while in the water to empty it of its human cargo, paddles and salt water. After reaching the marker we would dump boat again then come straight in to the beach. On the beach we would lift the boats to a head carry, run around a given obstacle—a sand dune or vehicle—then sprint down the beach to the starting point.

There would only be one winner. Everyone else was a loser. Winners would get a break. Losers would do push-ups, get wet and sandy or drag their boats over a dune and back, or worse. The races were spirited, but also designed to give a taste of leadership to each crewmember and to force us to think and work together.

One of the instructors ordered, "Hit the surf!"

All boats charged the ocean. At the beachhead we dropped our boat to low carry, just off the sand, one hand grasping the lifting strap, the other clutching a paddle.

"Ones in!" the boat captain ordered. The first two swimmers jumped into the bow and started to paddle.

"Twos in!" The next two boarded amidships and picked up the stroke.

When the water surged to the boat captain's chest, he ordered the last two men in. After we boarded, we reached back to drag the boat captain in over the stern.

"Let's go for it! Stroke!" the captain ordered.

"Stroke!" we shouted. The IBS surged forward.

While we paddled, the boat captain fought to keep the bow pointed straight into the breakers, using his paddle as a rudder. Hopefully we would punch through one dangerously high wave after another until we were safely through the surf zone out to calmer seas.

"Dig!"

"Dig!"

If we hit the wave too weak, without digging in, the wave would knock us over onto our backs. Sometimes the waves were just too big to manage and there was nothing we could do but dump boat and try again.

Getting past the surf zone was an art. We observed the breakers as they rolled in, and learned to anticipate. When there was a strong set, we lay back and let them spill over before taking them on. If it was impossible to wait for a slack set, we waited until we could take the wave directly bow on. If our boat turned sideways, the seaward rowers had to back-paddle hard to straighten it out. If not, the wave would knock the boat over, spilling us and the paddles out.

The return to beach was just as challenging. We knew if we did it right we could get a free ride for fifty yards or more. If we did it wrong, the boat would tumble over into the freezing water once again, and we would have to dump boat before continuing toward shore.

We positioned our boat straight on, bow toward the beach; then waited for the right wave. When it came the boat captain yelled, "Stroke!"

"Stroke!"

"Dig hard!"

We dug.

The captain glanced back at the swell. "Starboard side back! Starboard side back!" he yelled.

The three of us on the right side of the boat back-paddled

furiously to keep the boat straight. The IBS was stubborn, but we managed to straighten out just in time to ride the next wave into the shallow foam of the shore.

"Ones out!"

"Twos out!"

"Threes out!"

Once ashore, we dumped the water from our IBS. Then we slung the boat between us at a low carry and ran to the instructors at the starting point. We positioned ourselves for reporting, inspection and critiquing.

When we were all in, each coxswain (the person in charge of a boat and crew) lined up in front of his boat with paddle at the order-arms position, as if it were a long-barreled musket. When the instructor approached, the coxswain saluted and gave his report. Meanwhile other instructors roamed the boat crews looking for discrepancies. They always found something. When they did, the whole boat crew dropped for push-ups, which we had to do with our boots atop the main tube of our boat and our hands down on the sand. To make it more fun, an instructor used a paddle to scoop heavy sand onto our backs.

The last team to shore paid dearly by hoisting the raft over their heads with arms extended upward for minutes on end. This was achievable until the instructors filled the raft with sand, or even worse, crawled up into it, which quickly fatigued our already weak and exhausted muscles. Winners were always rewarded. Losers paid.

We repeated surf passage over and over until our bodies ached and we were shaking uncontrollably from the wet and cold.

The raft had to be kept in perfect working order throughout the entire training. It was never to be seen in a deflated condition and could never be left unattended or an instructor would let out the air. Inflating the rafts by manual pumps was a chore nobody wanted to do.

Afterward came log PT, designed to strengthen individual

bodies and teams. Each boat team would be required to lift a 150-pound log—a telephone pole ten feet long, one foot in diameter—and hold it over our heads for an extended period of time. We would also do sit-ups with the log lying across our chests, do squats or jumping jacks with it, or toss it.

"Now pay attention," an instructor named Jones said. "The safest way to do this is to work as a team. If you work as a team, nobody will get hurt."

We quickly learned that if everyone carried his own weight, the workout was doable, but if just one person on the team held back, everyone suffered. Most of these exercises were four counts and we would grunt, "One...two...three...four," as we struggled to coordinate our efforts.

Next we were ordered to take our logs into the surf and get them wet and sandy. We lifted the log onto our shoulders, climbed a sand dune and walked twenty-five yards to the beach. After we got our log wet we had to walk back to the sand dune and roll the log down the other side. The log was now wet and sandy.

Boat Crew Three tripped as they were hoisting their log, and it fell to the ground. Olivera pounced. "Don't pick it up. Go get wet and sandy!"

Meanwhile Chief Allen instructed another crew doing push-ups. They too were having problems. "If you can't pick up a log as a group, you'll never make it in combat. Work as a team. Understand?"

"Hooyah!"

Eventually all boat crews stood under their logs. While we held them overhead, arms straining up, instructors roamed among us with paddles, tossing sand onto the logs. They constantly looked for anyone not carrying his load. When one instructor spotted a "skater" among us, he was dropped for more push-ups. The rest of our boat crew also paid because now we had one less man holding up the weight of the log. As we trembled and twisted under the weight, more individuals were dropped for push-ups.

Olivera walked along us. "This puke-head wasn't carrying his share. Do you want him back?"

"Hooyah, Olivera!"

"Get back under your log, banana, and hold up your end of the load, or you'll really pay next time."

"Hooyah!"

As with all other exercises, our class endured log PT over and over again. The instructors had an ace in the hole to help teach lousy boat crews to pay attention and work together as a team—*Old Misery*.

Old Misery was a log three times bigger than the one we were holding up. This monster weighed in at 450 pounds. It was strictly used for punishment. Once you've had to lift her, you'd never want to again. Old Misery had this painted on her side: "Misery loves company, but nobody loves misery."

The obstacle course, *O-course*, as we called it, was a series of obstacles that we had to climb, run, crawl, slither through, or handle. It was designed to force us to use every muscle in our bodies at one point or another. Added pressure—we had to get through the course under a limited time, which had to be improved every time we did it.

From a distance the O-course looked like a huge playground. Up close it proved to be a nightmare.

"Form," an instructor told us, "is important. You can't simply attack the obstacles and expect to get through them, though an aggressive attitude will help. Many of the obstacles are dangerous if you don't do them right. You need to develop technique to get a good time, and that will only come about by trial and error."

We began. Some of the obstacles were familiar, like the Tire Sequence, especially if we'd competed in high school football. The Monkey Bars—a long horizontal ladder like those on playgrounds— were high enough that no one could hang from his hands and touch the ground with his feet. We all had our favorite obstacles as well as those we despised.

One of the worst we called the "Dirty Name." (You don't need an imagination to know why it was called that.) It was a series of three spaced horizontal logs that had to be climbed over. From the first log, only a foot high, we had to leap to the second log, six feet away and six feet higher. From there we leaped to the third log, another six feet away and six feet higher—on posts twelve feet above the ground. They all had to be climbed over before we could drop to the sand and continue the course.

Another dreaded obstacle was the "Weaver." Shaped like a monstrous ladder, the weaver looked like giant Monkey Bars with both ends in the ground and the middle ramped up. We negotiated this by weaving over and under the widely spaced bars, up to the top then down the other side. The Weaver took a lot of coordination and muscle to get through, and slowed us down more than any other obstacle. Slim and wiry trainees were best at this challenge.

Some struggled mentally while climbing the suspended "Cargo Net." It wasn't the physical difficulty that stopped them, but the fear of falling from the top of the log frame forty feet up. The net swayed and moved as we climbed, and when we got to the top we had to figure a way to swing our legs over and climb down the opposite side. Movements of the others climbing made it all the more challenging. Some froze up at the top of the net. They had to be encouraged not to look down, to conquer their fear and finish the evolution or they could be dropped from training.

The "Tower" was one of the last obstacles in the course. Like a three-story log house with no walls—corner supports only—the Tower consisted of three platforms we had to climb, one by one, to the top platform and then back down again to complete the obstacle. There were no stairs. We had to pull ourselves from the outer edge of one platform to the next.

Many just grabbed hold of the next platform edge and pulled themselves up to where they could swing a leg over. Then they would lever themselves up and do it again. Other students, especially the smaller ones, went with the backflip method. Facing out from the tower, they would jump up and grab the edge of the next platform above them. Then they would swing their legs out, up, and over to get onto the next platform. It was the fastest technique for the obstacle, as well as the hardest and, may I add, the most dangerous.

On some of the obstacles, taller, bigger trainees had an easier time. On others, shorter students found other obstacles easier to negotiate, because they didn't have as much mass and bulk to drag through, over, or up the obstacle. The variety on the O-course made everyone work at about the same level. It took more than twenty-five minutes for us to go through the course the first time. In order to graduate we had to eventually do the course in less than ten minutes.

Each instructor had his favorite ways of disciplining us for some minor infraction, for not obeying an order correctly or for botching an activity. The favorite was dropping for twenty push-ups. If the instructor felt like it, he could have us repeat that order several times to get his point across.

Another favorite, if you were near the beach, was the "sugar cookie," dipping in the surf and rolling in the sand while still wet. Having sand in your boots, down your pants and shirt, and in your eyes was akin to torture.

Some preferred making us do the "dying cockroach." That was when we'd lie on our backs with both arms and legs wagging in the air, all at the same time, until our abdominal muscles felt tight enough to snap.

Trainees began quitting on day one. They took a good look at where all this harassment was leading and decided to cut their losses and bail out. A person who wanted to DOR—drop on request—was required to bang his helmet on the doorjamb of the instructor's hut and yell, "I quit!" I kept telling myself over and over, *That's one thing I'm not going to do, I'm never going to quit. Never.*

Today, at the new compound, recruits are required to ring an old tugboat bell that is attached to a stanchion outside the First Phase office three times.

I was making a few friends in the barracks. Jim Gore, John Durlin, Richard Solano, Tommy Bracken and Forrest Harness all bunked around me. In those days we didn't share a room, we shared a metal Quonset hut, a relic from World War II. There were two long rows of bunk beds. I chose the top bunk about halfway back on the left. Durlin had the bunk below me. I found out he was from Iowa. Gore was from Montana, Solano and Bracken were from California, and Harness was from Oregon. We nursed our sores, bandaged each other's feet and talked about the challenges ahead of us.

Gore and Bracken could have been brothers. They both were thin and wiry and had similar features. Solano was over six feet tall, had dark hair and spoke with an accent. He was much huskier than the rest of us. Durlin was the quiet one. He had a gentle side to him that was refreshing among so many macho types that filled the barracks.

I asked Bracken how he heard about UDT/SEALs.

"When I was in boot camp, three men from the Navy Special Warfare Group gave us a thirty-minute presentation. I was in awe of them. After watching that film I was hooked. I signed up for the screen test that very day. The rest is history."

We often talked while we spit-shined our boots and polished our brass belt buckles.

Gore and Durlin were also recruited in boot camp, but Solano and Harness were like me—we went to boot camp already knowing that we wanted to be a part of Naval Special Warfare.

Forrest Harness was one of a kind. He was less than six feet tall, skinny with sandy brown hair and light freckles. He was a wild card and loved being audacious. The weekend before we started training he had ticked off an instructor and was restricted to the base. That didn't bother Harness. He simply climbed into the trunk of a friend's car and headed off to town. If he was caught he faced being dropped from training, but he thrived on taking risks.

Morning came fast. When we awoke, it was torture to move.

I was not going to quit.

Obstacle Course / PT

Cargo Net   *The "Dirty Name"*

Arrgh...

Ughhm...   *Grrrr...*

BUD/S Training

Lean and Rest

UDTRA - Teamwork

BUD/S Training

IBS Carry

Cold Water Torture

IBS Preparation

Drop and Pick Up

IBS OPS

—Chapter Five—

The Only Easy Day Was Yesterday

In order to allow time to shave, shower, dress and eat, our training started with 5:00 a.m. reveille. A ten- to twelve-hour workday awaited us.

The laundry truck arrived. We handed over yesterday's greens and picked up freshly washed, starched and pressed ones for the morning inspection.

When it was muster time we ran to our posts and did our best to line up four deep, but we were all over the place. An instructor stepped in. "Come on, girls, you can do better than that. Line up nineteen wide and four deep. Can't you count?"

Olivera arrived, this time with a fat cigar between his teeth. "Drop!"

All seventy-five of us hit the pavemet. We waited, holding our bodies in a rigid leaning-rest position.

"Well, bananas, a few of your classmates decided UDT/SEALs wasn't for them. Anyone else want to quit?" He strolled about. *Puff. Puff.* "You can save yourself a lot of misery right now." We still held the leaning-rest position. My chest muscles burned.

"Push 'em out. Down!"

Push-ups were a welcome change.

"One!" we counted.

"Down!"

"Two!"

After twenty, we returned to the leaning-rest. By this time some of the guys struggled to hold themselves up. Butts were sagging then rising again.

"Straighten those backs! Arms straight!" Olivera screamed.

Olivera's mirrored glasses scanned the trainees. His grin was that of a wolf hunched over its prey. "This is going to be another long day. If you aren't sure you want to finish the day, now's the time to say so. Before you get dirty."

No one stepped forward.

"Whether you're at graduation or not is entirely up to you. Some of you will take whatever pain we dish out because you think it's worth it to get into the Teams. But statistics show that two thirds of you won't make it. It's my job to find out who that will be." *Puff*.

We were still in the leaning-rest position, all of us having a hard time keeping our bodies off the pavement.

"Push 'em out," he ordered. "Down!"

"One!"

"Down!"

"Two!"

By the time we'd completed four more rounds of twenty push-ups each, all of us had been squirming on arms and toes for more than twenty minutes. I heard grunts and groans coming from every direction. Our buttocks twisted and thrashed around, trying to relieve the fire in our leg muscles and lower backs.

Finally we heard that beautiful word. "Recover!"

"Feet!" We jumped up in unison.

"Give me a report, Mister Lomas."

Lieutenant (jg) Lomas stepped forward. "Instructor, Class 44 is formed. Seventy-five assigned, seventy-five present."

"Seventy-five men present, Lieutenant?"

"Hooyah, Instructor Olivera."

Lomas had done his homework. He was aware of the four who had quit the night before and counted seventy-five people at muster.

No one else had quit before morning roll call.

Next came our dreaded daily inspection. Olivera stepped toward Lomas, the first man on his right in the front row. His eyes went up and down, checking to see if Lomas had taken the time to shave, and that he was wearing a starched shirt, starched pants, had polished his belt buckle and shined his boots. Lomas had no discrepancies. Olivera moved down the line.

Olivera found fault with fifteen recruits. They all ended up in San Diego Bay. Winners were rewarded. Losers paid.

Afterward during PT, Chief Allen said, "Listen up. If you want to make it through to graduation, you better take care of your body like you take care of your gear. Keep it well fed and watered. You need to stay hydrated, so get in the habit of drinking two gallons of water a day. Eat balanced meals and stay off the junk food. If you take care of your body it will perform well. If you don't you'll be lagging by midday."

"Hooyah, Chief!"

Chief Allen was a good mentor, one who wanted everyone to be the best they could be. He was tough when he needed to be, but he was also human. Olivera was a different story. I was starting to believe he thrilled being the bad guy and didn't care whether anyone liked him or not.

Our daily morning PT usually lasted a good hour, depending upon the order of the day. Sometimes it would be shortened if we were to go on a long run or swim afterward, and it seemed to go on forever when instructors wanted to work on our stamina and endurance.

Our first full inspection was the worst. I think the instructors wanted to make a point. They found fault with our waxed floors, urinals, dusty windows, and just about everything. I don't think it mattered how hard we swept, mopped, wiped and polished, they were going to find something to harp about one way or another. They went through our lockers like burglars tossing shirts, pants, socks and skivvies everywhere. It was a good thing we had our names stenciled on each article or we would have been on a treasure hunt. Even our personal things like shaving gear, toothbrushes and family pictures, were thrown about. It left us feeling violated.

~

UDT/SEALs had to master the water. If a trainee didn't perform well in the water, there was no place for him on the Teams.

We headed to the pool for swim training, every one of us glad to be free of clinging, chafing sand for the first time all day.

First, instructors had us swim several lengths without the aid of swim fins. Legs are what propel us through the water, they explained. Legs are the engines. Arms are basically for balance. (For people who swim without fins the opposite is true—legs are more for balance and the arms provide the power.)

Their point made, next came fins. Swimming UDT style with fins is different than swimming without them. UDT/SEALs use a form of sidestroke and flutter kick with their fins. Instructors showed us that just by rotating our legs a few degrees, we could rest tired muscles while using other muscles to save us from leg cramps.

To get maximum speed, we were taught buoyancy control and how to position our bodies in the water. Kick, stroke, and glide are the Navy way. The goal was to swim more like fish than humans.

After learning surface strokes, we moved on to underwater swimming. The secret to underwater swimming, one instructor explained, was to go deep. Swimming along the bottom in deeper water would increase the partial pressure in our lungs, allowing us to hold our breath longer and swim farther. We were also taught how to hyperventilate to rid our lungs of carbon dioxide and fill them with oxygen—a skill necessary in order for us to qualify for the fifty meter underwater swim without fins. This was the most critical evolution of pool basics—if we didn't complete it, we'd be dropped from training. The instructor explained that we were required to swim a full fifty meters without a diving start. We had to jump into the water, do a front somersault below the surface—then begin our swim across the twenty-five meter pool. After touching the wall we had to swim back. Four trainees would be in the pool at a time. Instructors prepared to swim as well, to make sure we didn't drown.

I had never done this before. When it was my turn, I stood at the edge of the pool and hyperventilated until I felt dizzy. When I felt like I was going to pass out, I jumped into the pool and did my underwater flip. I went deep then headed to the far end of the pool by using a version of the breaststroke. When I hit the wall my lungs screamed for air, but I knew that was just my brain telling me that my gas tank was on empty. It was similar to the little red warning light that comes on in your car when it's low on gas—you know it's just a warning—you still have a few miles to go. I ignored my body's warning system and stroked on. Halfway back my legs and arms became weak and I felt light-headed. The instructor at my side watched me closely for any signs of distress. I knew he would rescue me if I passed out. I kicked and glided all the way to the finish. When I hit the wall, I burst to the surface gasping for air. I had passed.

Some of my teammates weren't so fortunate. This was their Achilles' heel. They couldn't hold their breath that long. They came up short with each attempt, and one guy passed out while trying. His body had turned a dark blue color from lack of oxygen and he looked like he had died. But after a few slaps from the instructor he revived.

While at the pool, instructors taught us basic knot tying skills, first on land then underwater. Later in training we would have to use these knots to rig underwater explosives in simulated combat conditions. We stood shoulder-to-shoulder working a piece of line in our hands. Instructors walked among us making sure our knots were tied right. When we made a mistake, push-ups helped us to remember.

Drownproofing was our security blanket. If we could conquer the water, make our bed in it and sleep, we'd always have a home. The water couldn't be our enemy. It had to be our friend.

This was how drownproofing worked. I'd sink a few feet under, but when I relaxed and bent my head forward, I formed an air pocket in my neck. That air pocket helped me float to the surface. I'd gulp a mouthful of fresh air before sinking once again. Then I would repeat. The key was to stay calm.

This technique (I was told) would come in very handy if I were ever captured by the Viet Cong and transported downriver in a sampan (a small flat-bottomed boat). Even while tied up and blindfolded, I would have a fair chance of escaping without drowning. Right...

Eventually we had to jump into the deep end of the swimming pool with our hands and feet tied behind our backs. We were required to float for fifteen minutes. Afterward, we had to swim (bobble) forward fifty meters. The fun challenge was jumping into the deep end, doing a somersault then wiggling down to retrieve our face masks with our teeth. All of this was done with our hands and feet tied. Sometimes we were blindfolded.

During new challenging requirements like this one, I kept myself calm by talking to myself: *John, you've always been a good swimmer. This stuff may be new to you, but it has been done before. Others have done it, and you will too. Just stay calm. This is a piece of cake. Attaboy."*

Actually, drownproofing proved to be quite easy. That is, unless you were a sinker. Some people just don't float well because they have heavy muscle mass. Those who couldn't master drownproofing were dropped.

Timed swims were next. We had to swim 300 meters in less than 8 minutes, then 1200 meters with fins in less than 45 minutes, but that was just the beginning. After the swimming pool phase, we were required to swim a mile in the frigid San Diego Bay to earn our much-coveted wetsuit top. Wetsuit bottoms were never issued during training.

Steve Wolf, a former Michigan high school swimmer, and I jumped from the boat into 54° Fahrenheit water. San Diego Bay in January felt like ice water.

"Burr!" I mumbled to Steve, my swim buddy for the day. My breath came in puffs of vapor as I panted. My skin tightened. "I thought ...snow was cold. This is murder."

Staying with our swim buddy was paramount. We would always work in pairs, and the pairs could be changed at the whim of an instructor. But once assigned a swim buddy, we were to know where that man was at all times, especially in the water. In the water we were to observe the six-foot rule.

In the operational environment of the Teams, an instructor explained, our swim buddy could be the very means of our survival if we had an accident or malfunction while underwater or in combat. The punishment for violating this cardinal rule varied. One erring pair were harnessed together by a six-foot hawser (a thick rope used to moor boats) and forced to do all their evolutions as a twosome for the day.

Steve and I kicked our legs wildly trying to generate some body heat. I had never worn a wetsuit top before, but I imagined it had to be much warmer than this. Nothing was going to keep me from earning mine that day. I didn't enjoy torture.

One instructor shared the tidbit that bay swims could be very slow going, especially when half of it was against the outgoing or incoming tide. By daydreaming I kept my mind off the pain. This was something I was good at. I had plenty of practice while I was growing up during those early morning paper deliveries and on my lone walks to school. I enjoyed retreating into deep thought where I could listen to my conscience and think. This self-taught skill helped me swim the mile. If I focused on how cold and miserable I was, it would only make matters worse. So I let my mind wander to something else.

"Hey! Over here!"

It was Kearsh. He waggled his arm over his head to signal an emergency. Again he shouted, "Help! Over here!" His swim buddy, Tommy Bracken, was in trouble.

Tom's skinny body had run out of fuel and froze. He was unconscious and sinking to the bottom. Kearsh dove under and pulled the pin that inflated Tom's life vest. The vest shot Tom to the surface and buoyed him until the safety boat arrived. Kearsh's quick action saved Tom's life, proving the merits of the buddy system.

Two instructors grabbed Tom's collar and yanked him aboard the boat. Instructor Doc Heatherton threw a blanket around Tom, slapped his face and then asked him a few questions. "Hey, recruit, how many fingers am I holding up? Can you count to ten? What's my name? Do you know where you are?" They rushed Tom to the hot showers to raise his body temperature.

This was early training and the instructors were looking for weaknesses. It was weeding out time so Olivera pounced on Tom. "Why don't you just quit and go back to Mommy?" he screamed. "You don't have enough meat on you to keep you warm."

Tom was skinny, but he wasn't a quitter. The berating just made him more determined. After thawing, he joined the rest of us on our next evolution. A few others who were pulled out called it quits.

Tom had to redo the swim in the morning in order to stay in training. He probably fought a huge battle overnight, wondering if he would be able to master the cold water come sunrise. After all, his body had frozen up once; would it cooperate the next time? (So as not to leave you hanging—in the morning, Tom got back into the cold water, and this time he succeeded.)

Hypothermia would prove to be our biggest enemy in UDT/ SEAL training. It lurked silently behind every evolution almost undetected. But it was there, ready to freeze the life from its victim.

It wouldn't be the physical challenges of the swims, long runs, calisthenics and obstacle course that would bring our demise. It would be the treacherous cold—that miserable biting chill that slowly robbed us of our sanity—that subtle, insidious, unbearable cold. When the body temperature falls to dangerously low levels, it can be deadly.

Harassment was always the plan for each day. Many cold mornings, after the instructors took time to look us over at inspection, we were treated to an additional surprise. With a loud command of "about face!" it became obvious what would happen next, since the San Diego Bay was staring at us. Our "spit and shine" and finely starched clothes were ruined by the slimy waters of the bay. PT was next, in wet clothes. Soggy pants caused our legs and crotches to chafe, which made walking and running painful.

As the days passed, we volunteers were treated infinitely worse. We were goaded, harassed and intimidated with deliberate maliciousness. The instructors were ever on the watch for even the slightest trace of retaliation, resentment or anger from us. These negative traits could not be tolerated, particularly when we were under pressure in combat situations.

UDT/SEAL training was based on one core principle: The human body can take much more than what is normally considered humanly possible. Some have said ten times as much. That main principle extracted more from us than even the fittest volunteer knew he was capable of achieving.

The extremely difficult and carefully enforced physical training we had to bear tested much more than our physical ability. It also tested our minds and will to continue, especially when we felt our bodies couldn't tolerate any more.

Of all the battles a BUD/S trainee had to fight, none was more important than the battle of his mind over body. One's inner voice played an enormous part in the outcome of his success or failure— quitting or pressing on through the freezing ocean, with the nonstop harassment and the pain of muscles driven far beyond exhaustion. That small, self-doubting inner voice spoke whenever the going became intolerable. "This is crazy! Why are you making yourself go through all this? Why don't you just quit? Imagine standing under a hot shower and lying in a warm, comfortable bed."

If we'd listen to that wimpy voice too long we'd eventually surrender to its reasoning and give up and quit.

The body often lies to the mind. Being vulnerable to excruciating pain and exhaustion, it begins to believe in its frailty and waves the white flag. This was the brutal fight that many candidates lost. But for those of us who wanted to go on and become Navy UDT/SEALs, we had to learn to push the boundaries of our physical and mental limitations. Learning to squelch the voice would be critical to surviving all subsequent training and operations.

The concept of mind over matter was reflected in an oft-chanted phrase during early training and the aptly named and dreaded Hell Week: *If you don't mind, it don't matter*. One of our instructors loved to say, "It's just mind over matter. We don't mind, and you don't matter."

There was another popular saying among them which said it all: *The only easy day was yesterday.*

Beach runs were gradually increased from an easy-going two-mile jog to an excruciating fourteen-mile endurance test, often in the soft sand while wearing combat boots and long pants. We formed four columns with about twenty men in each. The safest place to be was near the front because runners toward the back had the tendency to lag further and further behind, and the consequences for lagging were severe.

Once again I retreated into my escape mode. It was my way of blocking out pain. If I thought about how much longer I had to run, I'm not sure I could have endured. Cross-country running was never my strength. The most I had ever run in high school was a mile and a half—six laps around the track during football season. Blocking out pain was much easier when I retreated to my secret place, that serene place I learned to love when I needed some solace while growing up. To keep in step and distract our minds from the pain, everyone chanted *hooyah* each alternating time our left feet landed on the ground.

We also sang songs. Usually one man sang out a line then the rest of us sang it back.

> Saw an old lady walkin' down the street,
> She had tanks on her back and fins on her feet.
> I said, "Hey, old lady, now you're too old,
> You ought'a leave that stuff for the brave and the bold."
> She said, "Sonny, sonny, listen here,
> I checked the Navy out in this gear!"
> Hooyah, Hooyah, Hooyah-aaae
> This is another easy day.

The unfortunate souls who lagged were rounded up to form what the instructors called the "Goon Squad." This sorry group quickly discovered it doesn't pay to fall behind. The Goon Squad received concentrated, nonstop harassment. Instructors screamed in their ears, made them run in and out of the surf, roll over and over in the hot sand, carry heavy logs, do push-ups, sit-ups, the dying cockroach and compete in nuisance races until they collapsed from exhaustion.

Everything had an objective. The Goon Squad was to drive the point home that winners were always rewarded, losers paid. It was also useful for the instructors to turn up the heat on someone they wanted to get rid of. I made up my mind I was never going to end up in that pitiful group. Fortunately, I never did.

Days passed. We were still being indoctrinated and learning about UDT and SEAL culture. There was a certain ethos to this warrior group. Most of us didn't have a clear idea what that culture was yet, but we were learning a little more each day. One thing we were picking up was that we were to work as a team and be accountable to each other.

An association of encouragers developed among us. Even before we knew each other well, the encouragers found other encouragers and we formed an unspoken alliance. This is how it worked. If I fell or got knocked down on a run, and Gore was close, he would help me up. I might give Bracken a little push over the top of a dune if he was bogged down in the sand. Solano and Sparks might each take an arm and give Harness a little support if he was lagging on a difficult run. By the end of the second week, the guys who didn't give didn't get. A safety net was forged. We were evolving into a team.

We were closing in on Hell Week. The first five weeks were mostly physical, preparing us for what was to come if we made it that far, and our instructors gradually increased the pace and intensity of our ordeal, causing more men to drop out daily. Apart from staggering amounts of exercises, long runs, IBS training, log PT, the O-course and miles of swimming, there were commando-style assault courses and brief respites for classroom courses such as marine life, fear of sharks, first aid and lifesaving techniques.

Additionally, we were required to maintain our personal hygiene and keep our clothes and personal items in order. Our living quarters had to be spotless due to surprise inspections, and we took turns at regular night watches.

As time crept by, the instructors seemed less patient, and life became one continuous hurdle, both physically and mentally. The biggest battle, however, continued to be within. We were constantly told, "It is mind over body, nothing more. Just mind over body."

At the end of each week, reviews were carried out. Our original group of seventy-nine was shrinking fast. To make sure everyone was assessed fairly, instructors rotated. A single instructor alone couldn't make a final decision on the removal of a volunteer without all his fellow instructors' agreements. Trainees dropped because of injuries were held for a future training class. Those who quit or were disqualified because they couldn't meet the qualifications were sent back to their old units and were never allowed to reapply for the BUD/S training.

By now most of us had some injuries or ailments. Some complained of respiratory problems or had fluid in their lungs. Others had cuts or abrasions from the IBSs or the O-course. Most all were experiencing some tendonitis or joint pain, and a good many had blisters on their hands and feet. Everyone was required to have a good physical review from the corpsman before heading into the biggest challenge of our lives—Hell Week.

"Motivation Week," more commonly known as "Hell Week," is six days of unbearable physical endeavors, feats of endurance, and tests, surrounded by nonstop harassment and pain...and virtually zero sleep.

It is designed to take you to the edge of exhaustion, and past it. The instructors recreate a combat environment then throw you into the middle of it. As the week progresses, it's more about mental harassment than physical strength as your body gets very tired. However, the push-ups, lean and rest, boat carry, jogging, swimming, obstacle course and other events keep you exhausted. Instructors had to know if we were the kind of men who could stay wet and cold and still bounce back without complaining or quitting.

Hell Week starts with "Break Out" on Sunday night, a simulated combat experience where absolute chaos reigns. Instructors use loud noises, flashing lights and putrid smells to disorient trainees. After the shock of break out, boat crews begin a series of well-choreographed training events that pit boat crew against boat crew, student against student, and the individual against himself.

The weekend before Hell Week, we were encouraged to take things easy and not party too hard. No one needed to remind us that getting plenty of rest was vital. A week without sleep is a long time. A group of us were lying around when our BUD/S commanding officer, Mr. Wilson, paid us a surprise visit.

Someone yelled, "Captain on deck!"

Before we could stand to our feet the captain said, "At ease." We gathered in a semicircle for an impromptu pep talk.

"This is it, guys. Are you guys mentally prepared for the upcoming week?" He didn't wait for us to answer. "I certainly hope so. Because if you're not, you'll never make it past the first day. Believe me, I know what I'm talking about. The instructor staff and I are going to challenge you like you've never been challenged before. It's not going to be easy. You'll be cold all the time. I mean really cold. You've heard that 'if you can't stand the heat, get out of the kitchen'. Well, boys, this is going to be hell backwards."

A few groans sounded behind me.

"I hope you've been eating well and taking care of your bodies because this week is going to be a test of your endurance. Your energy level is going to be constantly drained so you will have to resort to your own willpower to keep yourselves motivated. And you can do it, believe me. When you go for chow make sure you eat a balanced meal, but don't go too heavy on the meats. You don't want to spend all your energy digesting a big fat steak. Eat foods that are easy to digest and will give you lots of energy. Drink plenty of water, often. Take care of your body and your body will take care of you." As he spoke, his eyes took each of us in, one by one.

"You've been around long enough now to know that Hell Week is more mental than it is physical. Your bodies are going to get tired and they're going to hurt and believe me they will be cold, but your bodies can handle it. God made your bodies to withstand the likes of Hell Week. You can make it through this week. Do you know why I believe that? Because I was once where you guys are. I faced the same questions you are facing. I wondered if I could make it through Hell Week myself. I wondered if I could stay awake that long, stay cold that long, but you know what? I went into it with my mind made up, and that's all you have to do. And if I could make it, then so can you."

"Let me give you a little tip. When you become physically drained, your mind will try and trick you. It's going to tell you that you need a break, that you need a rest. It's going to tell you that a hot shower is a lot better than the icy water you're swimming in. That's when you need to trust your training. That's when being a team player pays off. You're going to need to encourage and motivate each other. You'll need to help each other get back up when you fall down. Remember your teammates are your best friends. You'll have to gut it out as an individual, but never forget that Hell Week is a team effort. You can't make it through this week by yourself. Understand?"

"Hooyah, sir!"

"Stress will increase as the week goes on, and your head isn't going to want to be there. Let me tell you when you need to be careful. You need to be ready to fight off the comfort of the chow hall. There will be nights when you are so cold that you'll think you're an icicle. The chow hall will seem like an oasis—warm comfy room, hot food, hot drinks and soft music. Don't let that cushy atmosphere seduce you. That little voice, that demon, will be working overtime to get you to throw in the towel. Trust me."

"He's going to say, 'Hey, pal, this is stupid! I'm tired. I'm beat. I'm exhausted. Who needs this?' And you know what? If you listen to him long enough, you're going to start believing him."

"But before he talks you into quitting, I want you to listen to the voice that told you to come to BUD/S in the first place—that inner voice that encouraged you to take the screen test. Listen to that fellow, not the little demon who is telling you to quit. Don't think about your pain. Don't think about how cold you are. Don't think about tomorrow, because tomorrow isn't even here yet. Just take it one step at a time. One minute at a time."

Captain Wilson was telling us how to survive. I absorbed every word.

    "Remember, it pays to be a winner. Work as a team. If you do, it will pay off. If you come in first on these evolutions you'll be rewarded. You may earn a little rest, a little less harassment for a while, a short reprieve while your classmates continue to be dealt with for not being winners. And a little rest here and there during Hell Week goes a long way. Believe me."

    "Now, gentlemen, get some rest—you'll appreciate it later. Then get together with your boat crews and talk about how you're going to make it through this. Encourage each other. Motivate each other. Teamwork—that's what it's going to take. I can't stress that enough. You'll have to work together as a team in order to get through the next week. So get together and make a commitment to each other that you're going to be winners and not losers. Good day, gentlemen, and good luck."

    The captain's pep talk did its job, but I knew I had issues to settle if I was going to make it through Hell Week. I would have to take a deep look within my soul and find the strength, inner resolve and self-determination to be a winner. Hell Week had to be won inside my head before break out. Nobody but me could make myself want to complete this week of torture.

    Our class, which started with seventy-nine, had been whittled down by injuries, failed tests, and those who dropped on request. We would start Hell Week with forty-nine.

    Mike Anderson, my boot camp friend who took the screen test with me, was rolled back due to injuries.

—Chapter Six—

Hell Week

Sunday 10:00 p.m. Machine guns blasted. *RAT-TAT-TAT-TAT-TAT.* Barracks lights flashed on and off and air horns screamed. Gunpowder stung my nostrils.

"Get out of those racks, you maggots!" Olivera shouted. "I want you dressed and outside for muster in three minutes!" *TAT-TAT-TAT.*

Other instructors yelled like demons and ran among us hammering garbage can lids, banging pots, blowing whistles. They were loud, harsh, scary. Smoke grenades hit the floor and the room filled with smoke, burning my eyes. I choked on the putrid odor.

I knew Hell Week was coming. I thought I'd be prepared but I was completely disoriented in the chaos. Banging and machine gun fire stunned my ears.

Someone ran into me. A student yelled, "Who took my socks?" An instructor blared, "Hurry, slugs! Outside now! Do you know what *now* means?"

Between flashes of light I grabbed my pants, green fatigue shirt. Yanked them on. Socks, boots and hat came next. No time for anything else.

Lights flashed. My eyes burned. Trainees shoved to get out into the fresh air.

Once out the door I was thrown to the side by a throng of rabid students. Every instructor was screaming yet I heard my name.

"Wolfram, what do you think you're doing? On your stomach!"

I fell to the ground. Saw a hose. A blast of freezing water struck my face and hair. For a moment I was unable to breathe.

"Give me twenty!" Olivera screamed.

I started pumping them out. He didn't seem satisfied. The water hose shot streams of icy water all over my body. San Diego's wintry wind was a knife to my skull. My body shivered. The voice in my head told me I needed to get warm. I had no choice but to ignore it. No turning back now. I only had six nights and five more days to go.

After extended harassment and our initial muster in dripping, freezing clothes, we separated into our designated boat crews. Our boats lay over to the side, deflated.

"Someone must have let the air out of your boats," an instructor taunted. "Let's see which boat crew can be the first to fill their boat with air."

Using a manual pump to fill a boat this size was torture. IBSs were a good thirteen feet long and five feet wide. We took turns pumping one section after another until it had a tight skin all around. Boat Crew Five finished first. When we finished, we grabbed our red-orange kapok life jackets and strapped them on. All losers were ordered to put our toes up on the tubes. Everyone did push-ups until our arms ached, but Boat Crew Five was afforded the pleasure of not having cold water sprayed on them during the ordeal. Winners were rewarded. Losers paid.

"Up boat!"

"Hooyah, Instructor Allen!"

We lifted the 200-pound boat and balanced it on our heads while holding on to the side straps.

"Extended arm carry!"

Holding a 200-pound boat high above our heads wasn't easy, especially for long periods of time. Five minutes went by. Then ten. Everyone struggled.

"What's the matter, Durlin? No more strength?" an instructor ranted. "Would you like to be in combat with someone just like you? Answer me!"

"No, sir," said a bewildered Durlin.

"You'd want somebody to carry his own weight, wouldn't you?"

"Yes, sir."

"Then get those arms back up in the air."

"Hooyah!"

The instructors worked on our arms for another half hour before we were ordered to *elephant run* to the beach.

The ocean was a mile and a half from our barracks. A heavy boat balanced on top of six heads looked like an elephant moving—not a graceful sight. For all of us underneath this mammoth creature, it was worse.

Fifty pounds of heavy boat ground down on my head as we ran. Each bounce crunched my neck, shot pain down my spine. My raised arm steadying the boat cramped. More than a mile to go, but I couldn't afford to think about that. Hell Week would be won by taking one step at a time.

We sang a cadence to keep our minds off our pain:

Everywhere we go
People want to know
Who we are.
So we tell them,
We ain't the Air Force
Playin' on the golf course.
We ain't the Army,
The backpackin' Army.
We ain't the Marines—
They don't even look mean.
We are the Navy,
The world's finest Navy.
The mighty, mighty Navy!

Monday 1:00 a.m.

We arrived at the beach. The wind picked up, cut through us. The distant lights of Hotel del Coronado flickered coldly on the waves.

"Down boats!"

We were happy to lose our load.

"Before we head over to Hotel Del for rock portage, we thought you might enjoy a little surf torture," joked Chief Allen. "Line up facing the beach, lock arms with the men beside you, and head to Hawaii!"

"Hooyah, Chief!"

When we walked into the water, raw pain like a thousand needles filled my boots then stung my calves. Being submerged in fifty-four-degree water wasn't something I ever looked forward to. We walked out twenty feet.

"Stop! You know what to do. Lie on your backs with your feet facing the sea."

"Hooyah!"

We submerged up to our necks. Wave after wave of freezing water crashed over us. Salt water shot into my mouth and up my nose. I spit out the foul tasting liquid. The frosty night air added to my misery. The ocean was merciless. But under the constant gaze of the instructors, there was no place to hide.

I lay there for what seemed like hours. My lips quivered and my body shook uncontrollably.

Mr. Freezing was faithful, constant and relentless. He was good at whispering discouragement in my ear. He knew how to rip off my winter parka, earmuffs and long johns, and send me out into a blizzard naked as a jailbird.

I had to be able to endure the cold without question. I had to put this pain out of my mind.

I came into the Navy looking for direction. My trainers were using strange ways to mentor me, using the cold as a means to an end.

I realized there was a method behind their madness. They knew that being cold was a good way to measure a man's tolerance, something all UDT/SEALs would need if they ever ended up on a battlefield mission. While that was certainly true for a combat warrior, it was also true for everyday life. I convinced myself I was learning important principles that would help shape my thinking for the rest of my life. I didn't want to go through all of this for nothing.

Monday 2:30 a.m.

"Rock portage" was carried out on the south end of the beach in front of the famous Hotel del Coronado. Hotel Del, as the locals refer to it.

To protect the resort's beach from being destroyed by the heavy surf, piles of massive rocks had been placed to act as a breakwater. This rock pile jetted outward into the ocean roughly forty yards. Low tides exposed its enormity. During high tides, the waves crashed over their rugged, sharp edges.

We had to land on these rocks, then, while strong waves threw us into them, carry our 200-pound IBS over them to the beach. The point: to learn teamwork and to overcome fear. Getting hurt would be easy. Not breaking an arm or leg was the challenge. Even a small cut could be hazardous—an infection could swell a leg or arm beyond usefulness, then the injured would be dropped from class.

As we approached, the night's darkness played over the rocks. They looked massive as we paddled closer, and oddly foreboding. They exuded a kingly presence, one that said they'd stood there long before we arrived, and they weren't about to be conquered by mere humans. We were about to prove them wrong.

I was a part of Boat Crew Seven. We weren't the tallest men, but no one had more heart. Paul Plumb was our officer and coxswain. Jim Gore, Tom Bracken, Jim Berta, Frank Willis, (plus another fellow who eventually dropped) and I completed the team. Later instructors gave us "Rocky" in an attempt to slow us down.

We quickly learned to grip the sides of the boat with our legs, and keep our knees on the inside during impact. Our effort was wasted. The boat tipped and we were thrown between the waves and the rocks. Holding to the boat, our feet in front, we used the soles of our boots to absorb the force of the impact. Painstakingly, we helped each other climb into the boat. Then we paddled the rest of the way.

"Bow-line man out," called Mr. Plumb over the crash of a wave.

The nose of our boat slammed into the rocks. Jim Berta, with one line in hand, jumped out onto the boulders amid churning foam and scrambled for higher ground. Jim wedged himself between two rocks and wrapped the line around his waist.

"Bow-line man secure!"

"Bow-line man secure!" we hollered back.

"Water!" yelled Plumb as a breaker smashed into the stern of the boat, nearly capsizing us again. The back-surge tried to suck us back out to sea, but we hung on.

"Paddles forward!" Plumb called.

"Paddles forward!"

I grabbed all seven paddles into my arms, stepped over the bow and ran, stumbling and climbing over the slippery rocks. I stacked the paddles on the beach then hurried back to Mr. Plumb and the rest of my crewmates, now out of the boat steadying themselves against the oncoming waves. The only thing more miserable than being cold and wet, I decided, was being cold and wet in the dark.

"Bow-line man moving!" Plumb yelled.

"Bow-line man moving!"

Together we horsed the IBS onto the rocks, then moved it, one boulder at a time, up and over to a new position on the rocks. This was a crucial time. We'd been taught never to get between the boat and the rocks, but incoming waves kept trying to drive us there. We steadied ourselves and moved the boat.

"Bow-line man secure!"

"Bow-line man secure!"

"Ready!"

"Ready!"

"Heave!"

We continued forward, the waves shoving us, our eyes on the beach. Finally, we reached sand, safe but exhausted.

"High and dry! Bow line over!"

A rare compliment from Olivera followed. "That's not bad for beginners. Now go do it again!"

"Hooyah, Instructor Olivera!"

Several hours of conducting surf passage and rock portage again and again left us bone tired. Instructors harassed us in between with push-ups, the leaning-rest, and holding the boats over our heads until our arms nearly buckled.

With rock portage complete, we wobbled our way down the beach for log PT, minus two trainees who'd had enough. No one needed to remind us that this was just the first few hours of a nonstop week of hell.

That frigid damning cold was what made people quit. The cold was the culprit. Always. But it also challenged the determined men to seek strength through teamwork and through helping their fellow students. Hell Week was and still is the defining moment in the life of every UDT/SEAL because it made us confident that we could endure and accomplish many times what we had previously believed possible.

To the casual observer watching from the sidelines, Hell Week probably looked like an overly zealous college hazing, except this was much more intense and lasted forever. The Special Warfare Center had meticulously planned out each segment to the hour in a well-scripted blueprint. Each evolution was designed to equip UDT/SEALs for emergencies that might develop during a real combat mission.

Monday 5:00 a.m.

Log PT could rapidly sap our strength. There was no way to carry a telephone pole without everyone giving 100 percent. The guys at the two ends of the pole carried the brunt of the weight. The guys on the inside could fake their efforts if they wanted to, and some took advantage of the situation to conserve energy. The instructors knew this ploy well, and were on the lookout for slackers. There was no place in the Teams for guys who wouldn't give 100 percent.

Chief Allen jumped on Edwards. "What are you doing under there? Sleeping? You're not carrying your own weight. Drop. Give me twenty push-ups!"

Edwards fell to the sand to push 'em out. This left five guys holding up the log.

"You see what your lack of cooperation is doing to your teammates? You're nothing but a burden, Edwards! Get wet and sandy."

Edwards dunked in the ocean then rolled in sand. It covered him from head to toe. His face was unrecognizable. Now he was more miserable than he had been underneath the pole. Winners were rewarded. Losers paid.

The instructors continued to watch Edwards closely. With so many teammates eliminated, he stood out as someone who may not have what it took to be a UDT/SEAL. His times were slow, and he hindered his boat crew from doing well as a team.

Monday 6:30 a.m.

Running wasn't my strongest trait, but I was determined to learn. According to Chief Allen, next was a four-mile timed run on soft sand. I'd have to do it under the thirty-two-minute time limit, or die trying.

"Hey, Walsh, how do you run so fast?" I was curious. He was hardly five-feet-three, but was as fleet footed as a deer.

"I don't know. How do you swim so fast?" He laughed.

Walsh was right. I could swim and he could run. Not everyone had the same skills, but real teamwork meant being able to pull from each other's strengths.

Chief Allen interrupted our chatter. "All right, tadpoles. You got thirty-two minutes to hike down to the North Island fence and get back here. If you want to be standing with those who graduate, you'd better shake a leg.

"Ready, set, go!"

The long-legged gazelles took the lead. Walsh was among them, taking two steps to their one. It was perplexing seeing those who could make running look so simple. For the rest of us, it was hard work.

Silver Strand Beach was a great place to run—miles and miles of empty beaches, the only sounds being the crashing waves and occasional high shrill of a passing gull. Salty sea wind and rotting seaweed filled my nostrils. The top edge of the sun glimmered at the horizon, but Hotel Del's amber lights still glowed as we ran past her. The beach belonged to us, except for a few early morning walkers.

I focused on the positives. I had another three miles to go.

By dawn Class 44 had lost ten students. Only thirty-nine students remained.

Monday 7:15 a.m.

The early morning run gave me half an hour of uninterrupted solace. Afterward, screaming instructors badgered those who didn't make their times, and sent them into the ocean to get wet and sandy.

The rest of us were ordered to stand and strip down to our shorts for a medical checkup. I had been up all night. My legs were tired. My body ached. It would only get worse.

Monday 7:30 a.m.

We were given thirty minutes to eat. Steaming, hot pancakes—pastry of the gods. Greasy sausage went down like prime rib. I shoveled my food in. It disappeared into a bottomless pit. I needed the fuel to keep me going.

If I didn't eat enough, I would peter out before the next meal. Wrong food choices could also be detrimental—the sluggishness of a heavy meal would work against us.

We would consume four meals a day, about 7000 calories during breakfast, lunch, supper, and "midrats" (midnight rations). We burned those calories with a vengeance. Our personal furnaces burned fuel as fast as we took it in, to keep our bodies warm.

By the end of breakfast, our joints had stiffened and muscles tightened so severely we could hardly move. It was brutal just to stand up.

As soon as we got outside we heard the command, "Up boat!" We lifted the heavy boat once again. It ground down into my head.

We'd be lugging it around all week. I figured we might as well be friends.

Monday 8:00 a.m.

Boat crews were selected by height for Hell Week. The shortest group was nicknamed the *Smurfs*. Frank Sparks and Mike Walsh belonged to that boat crew. It was hard for the instructors to put the Smurf crew together because Sparks and Walsh were under five-foot-three. The taller ones in the boat crew complained. Cold and lack of sleep ratcheted up the tension.

Olivera pulled Lang away from the boat. "Good operators can't afford to lose their cool, Lang. If you lose it on the battlefield others will get hurt. Understand?"

"Hooyah, sir."

To drive his point home, Olivera ordered the Smurf team to do leg squats with their 200-pound boat.

"Down! Up! Down! Up!"

Monday 9:00 a.m.

"Take off your greens, boots and hat and put on your wetsuit tops," Chief Rose instructed. "You're going on a four-mile swim!"

I raced to the pickup truck and grabbed my sack. Inside were my wetsuit top, life vest, web belt, knife and fins. I stacked my wet clothes and placed my boots and socks on top. Hopefully they would dry out during the long swim.

Rose instructed us to find our swim buddies and do an equipment check. We complied.

"Hit the waves!" he yelled.

Two by two we jogged out into the higher than normal winter waves. At least the long swim would take us away from the taunting instructors.

In some ways the required swims were peaceful. That is, when I could block out the feeling of swimming in ice water.

I spit into my mask and washed it out with the salt water. My swim buddy, Steve, and I dove under the first wave and kicked hard. Between strokes, the cold Pacific streamed between my skin and the rubber, and it froze my bare legs. It would take awhile for my body to generate heat. I pumped my legs to keep from being dragged back to shore by the pull of the breaking wave. Just three more waves to conquer. Diving under each one, I kicked to propel myself out to sea. Once we were past the surf zone, the sea was calm.

Steve and I got our bearings then we headed north toward our target. I liked to lean on my left side, Steve on his right. It worked well for us. We both could see each other. Safety came first on long swims. We applied the six-foot rule, knowing any number of unpredictable circumstances could appear at a moment's notice. We watched out for each other.

Thousands of flutter-kick exercises had made my legs powerful, and years of swimming paid off for both Steve and me. We were in the lead.

My body heat soon warmed the water inside my wetsuit, a

welcome relief from the cold. This would also help deter hypothermia. Wetsuits don't keep you warm unless you sweat, and you have to work hard to sweat. Every jerking movement I made allowed a fresh stream of cold water to flush out the warm. The contrast was shocking—a reminder to keep kicking hard. Only three and three-quarters miles to go. *Oh, the pain!*

I got out of my wetsuit and into mercifully drier clothes. Steve and I were the first to finish. For our reward we stood by the instructors' fire.

As soon as everyone was dressed, Olivera yelled, "Hit the surf!"

Reluctantly we obeyed and submerged in the ocean again. This was Hell Week. It wouldn't be hell without being cold, wet and miserable.

Monday 12:00 p.m.

The elephant walk to chow hall helped generate heat.

Inside it was warm, a welcome relief from the wind outside. I grabbed my tray and slid it down the long counter. Pretty faces smiled at me as I chose my meal. Everyone had his favorite server. The young ladies provided invaluable doses of sanity.

Log PT followed. The first hour was nothing but nonsense races. The long log became our barbell, our weight machine and our personal gym. It was six men against a telephone pole. We carried the log fifty yards through soft sand, each man cupping the log to his chest. My arms went numb. My back ached. My legs felt like they were bending in on themselves. But it wasn't over yet.

"Up Log! Down log! Up log! Down log! Extended arm carry. Up! Down! Up! Down!" over and over again until we thought our bodies couldn't take anymore. But we were wrong. We endured this torture another hour.

Chief Rose had a smile on his face. "Go wash your log off in the ocean, men. I don't want to see one grain of sand on that log when you get back."

"Hooyah!"

Afterward we returned for inspection. Chief Rose strode toward us with that same smile. He inspected our log from one end to the other. He paused at the far end and smirked. "What do you call this?" He found three tiny pebbles.

Mr. Plumb was quick with his wit and challenged Rose. "Chief, I know that, but we felt that when the sun beats down and dries them, those three pebbles will just fall off!"

"Good idea, Mr. Plumb, but we just don't have the time. Hit the surf!"

Hell Week was a test to see one's limits. Looking ahead was a sure way to fail.

One foot after the other, one step at a time, for as long as it took.

Surf passage followed, and our boat crew dug paddles to conquer eight- to ten-foot waves. The afternoon waves were not as big as the ones from the previous night, but they were sizable.

I was up front on the left. Jim Gore was on the right. We both grinned from ear-to-ear. We loved those winter waves.

We all chanted in unison, "Dig! Dig! Dig!"

Our oars cut into the milky foam, looking for solid water. The rip had increased its power. Another wave broke in front of us, sending new foam and current our way. We dug deeper and harder to hold our place, fighting the ocean, physical exhaustion and a night without sleep. We made it through the first and second surge, but the further out we went, the bigger the waves.

We saw a whopper forming ahead of us. Building. Bigger and bigger. We hoped it wouldn't break on top of us. No such luck.

The huge monster dropped its load straight down on our boat and we all went flying.

Paddles ripped from our hands, and our boat tumbled back toward the beach. I caught my breath and looked for Gore, my swim buddy for the day. We found each other and swam to shore with the rest of our boat crew.

Our paddles lay on the beach. Now all we had to do was dump boat and try again. We walked toward them, teeth chattering. The wind whipped my wet clothes. I tried to control my shaking, but my body wouldn't listen. When I attempted to speak, my words slurred.

Before I reached the paddles Olivera was on our case, this time spitting black tobacco juice. Our turn for a little motivational counseling.

"What kind of sailors do you guys think you are? If you can't get your boat out through the surf, how do you expect to escape from an enemy beach on a recon? Get your feet up on the tube and push 'em out!"

"Hooyah, Olivera!"

It's no fun being a loser.

Walking with a heavy boat on my head was impossible. But with help from my teammates it was doable. We learned to shuffle our feet in unison, rather like line dancers. We developed a technique by trial and error—miles and miles of it. The constant bouncing of the boat on my head compressed the bones in my neck. My life jacket straps rubbed my thighs raw. I was miserable. I was glum. But I re-minded myself I was on my way to becoming the Navy's best.

Near the end of chow that evening, two more chose to DOR. Chief Rose took them aside.

"You know what you're giving up, don't you?"

"Yes, Chief."

"Are you sure you want to do this? Do you want to go back to the gray Navy and ride ships?"

"Yes, Chief."

Edwards looked on; by appearances, questioning his own reason for being there.

Thirty-six remained.

Hell Week was weeding out the weak.

After chow, the instructors ordered our class back into the water for more surf torture. We now called it "getting sandblasted." Lying in the surf filled our pants with sand and grit.

The sun had set and the air had grown colder. We sprawled under a layer of punishing waves. A long night stretched out ahead of us.

Traversing the obstacle course was nobody's favorite. It challenged the best athletes, made fools out of some and mush out of others. But what they wanted us to do next was sheer insanity.

"Okay troops, listen up. You are going to go through the O-course tonight by boat crews, and you are going to take your boat with you."

During our training briefs when we were told we would be doing things we never thought we could do, this had not been one that came to my mind. I never imagined we would have to lug an IBS through that huge playground.

We pulled. We shoved. We pushed and we lifted. And with sheer guts and determination we managed to complete our mission.

We had been awake for almost twenty-four hours. The sky was dark. The night air cut through my wet shirt. An instructor ordered us into the freezing ocean, for more of what he called "surf appreciation." To us it would always be torture. We lay on the ocean floor as wave after wave of ice water swept over us. A wave retreated and cold air swept across my body. I didn't know which was worse—the freezing water or the punishing breeze.

We were pulled out every twenty minutes and harassed in the sand, and then we were ordered back into the waves for another bout of surf torture. This continued for two hours. My body cried out in pain. My mind said I was crazy. I told my mind to hush.

The moon shone down on us, but it didn't give off any heat. We were wet and sandy. Grit was in my shirt and down my pants. My legs were chafed. It was hard to walk. My inner thighs burned with each step. I could hardly keep my eyes open. I was beyond miserable.

I grabbed my partner's legs and lifted them to my waist, then I pushed him through the sand.

The instructors called this "wheelbarrow races." I called it *stupid*. But the strenuous movement helped to warm our bodies.

Tuesday 1:15 a.m.

The "Base Tour" was supposed to simulate a UDT/SEAL operation. We ran around the base carrying our IBSs, pretending we were on a dangerous operation, except we had no weapons and no ammo. All we had were tired bodies and lethargic brains.

It was becoming difficult to stay awake. I had to consciously keep my eyelids open. We wandered around the base for more than an hour at the whim of the instructors, frequently pausing from our simulated operation to do hundreds of push-ups and enduring the leaning-rest on our arms. We didn't accomplish anything except getting more tired. My arms finally gave out. Chief Rose screamed at me, so I struggled to lift my body off the ground.

Next we were ordered to tread water in the bay. It was said to be warmer than the ocean by a few degrees. I couldn't tell. Cold was cold. The instructors played with our minds. Someone said the water temperature was fifty-seven degrees. The air temperature was in the high forties. The water started to feel warmer than being out in the air.

Maybe I was losing my mind. We swam in place until we were numb. Fortunately we enjoyed a few chuckles when someone started up a song they must have heard in church:

Give me oil in my lamp, keep me burning, burning, burning,
Give me oil in my lamp I pray...Hallelujah!
Give me oil in my lamp, keep me burning, burning, burning,
Keep me burning till the break of the day.

Cold water and lack of sleep relentlessly invaded our minds and bodies until every nerve was exposed, every emotion was raw. The job of each instructor was to see how each of us reacted to extreme stress and unbearable conditions.

"This is a frogman's way of life, tadpoles," one instructor reminded us from the beach. "Frogs are cold and they are tired. Do you really want this? Is this something you want to do for the rest of your Navy career?"

The instructors watched us shake and convulse. I think they enjoyed this. Corpsmen watched us closely for stress and hypothermia. They knew the danger signs—severe pain, heavy shivering, slurred speech, confused responses to questions, then sluggishness, semi-consciousness, a core body temperature ninety-one degrees or below. They didn't want any fatalities. All instructors looked for signs of uncertainty in the class and were quick to pounce on the victim. Weeding out time again.

"All of you are staying in there until someone DORs," the instructor said.

Two men swam to shore. One of them was Edwards.

Thirty-two were left.

The sweat and mildew odor we gave off was putrid. We stank so fiercely we could have qualified as a biological weapon. Trainees' eyes teared when we were in the same room together. Instructors only approached us from upwind.

Our worn bodies became breeding grounds for germs and bacterial infections.

San Diego Bay was always cold. But the steel pier was worse. It added a new dimension to the word *frozen*. The instructors herded us like cattle onto the steel surface and ordered us to strip down to our skivvies. Without the cover of our long sleeved shirts and pants, the elements struck with a vengeance. We were instructed to lie down on our backs.

The cold steel instantly froze my skin wherever it touched

me—the backs of my calves, my buttocks, the backs of my arms, my shoulder blades. I remembered a grade school classmate who stuck his tongue on a flagpole one winter. When he removed it he screamed for a very long time.

Chief Allen switched on the pump. Cold water blasted out of the fire hose onto our exposed bodies. It was so cold it almost felt hot. Gallons of water struck my face. I bit down hard and struggled to dredge up my inner resolve. I wasn't sure I still felt sane. The hose moved on, and I could finally hear my thoughts.

You idiot! What in the world are you trying to accomplish? Why put yourself through this torment? You have three more days of this to go yet!

The instructors knew the battle we were facing. They'd been here themselves. Yet they continued to freeze us and scream at us without mercy. They searched through our sprawled out bodies looking for evidence of weakness.

"Come on, someone. We know you're hiding. You can't fool us. You don't want to do this for the rest of your life, now do you? This isn't who you are. Why don't you do the smart thing and get a warm shower, a hot meal and go sleep in a nice comfortable bed?"

Thirty minutes went by. It seemed like hours. Finally we were told to stand.

We left the steel pier. Then were ordered to jump back into the freezing bay. We were still in our skivvies.

Mind over pain, I told myself. I had to block out my misery. Students who couldn't filter out the pain were doomed.

All but one trainee went into the bay.

Hell Week was a contest of the will. It brought each student face-to-face with his breaking point and challenged him to push beyond it. Those who couldn't find that inner resolve DORed.

Thirty-one pressed on.

An hour before sunrise we were allowed to put our clothes

back on. This helped take the chill off, but our body temperatures were so low that we all shook. *Jerry Lee Lewis* must have had us in mind when he sang his 1957 hit, "Whole Lotta Shakin' Goin' On." It was certainly true that night.

A Base Tour followed complete with push-ups and leaning-rests; then an elephant walk. We looked like walking zombies. The only thing that kept us going was that we all wanted to become Navy UDT/SEALs.

One hour later, back to the bay. We lay down on the base's boat ramp in six inches of water and did flutter kicks and rocker chairs.

Caterpillar races in the water were next. Everyone sat down facing the back of the person in front of us, then anchored our legs around his waist. We had become a long water-going caterpillar. Our kapok vests kept us buoyant. It was impossible to kick, so we paddled backward with our hands. Our awkwardness must have amused the instructors. They laughed among themselves.

The red-orange canvas kapok vests we had to wear were torture in themselves. Kapoks were different than our lightweight black swim vests. These were very heavy vests that had been used by the Navy since before World War II. They could keep a man afloat in the roughest seas, but they were uncomfortable. The straps rubbed our legs and crotches raw, removing chunks of skin. Some men were scarred for life after Hell Week.

During breakfast I realized I had done strenuous activities without sleep for thirty-two hours. My body had never done this before. My brain tried to send messages. I refused to listen. I put all self-defeating thoughts in a separate compartment, forced my eyes to stay open and my body to stand.

Another elephant walk followed, then a four-mile run. Surf torture. Obstacle course. Bay boat paddle. The steel pier. IBS surf passage. Boat races. We had a meal in there somewhere. Maybe two—outside was dark.

We sat side-by-side at the pool, breathing mist into the air, trying to absorb as much body heat from one another as possible. It was time for us to amuse the instructors and add a little humor to our long day—the officer flip contest.

Each officer was given three chances to make his best dive or belly flop off the three-meter board.

Some of them had never done a flip from that high, and it showed. We watched one belly cracker after the other and occasionally a decent dive. We applauded and yelled to cheer them on.

The enlisted men were next. We made a long line up the ladder. Everyone had to either do a front or back flip. Some of the guys had diving experience and performed smooth flips. Others like myself, improvised. I chose a running backflip and landed halfway on my stomach. Everyone cheered. The flops got the most applause. After our initial dive, we had to choose one representative from each boat crew for a diving contest to see which boat crew had the best diver. This time the instructors judged.

Winners were rewarded. Losers paid. Our team's representative didn't win, so along with the other losers we had to swim two laps by doing the butterfly.

Even so, in the past few weeks, perhaps in past few days, the sense of brotherhood and mutual respect among us had become forged into something rock solid.

After a few push-up sessions and flutter kicks, we swam relay races across the pool with each boat crew as a relay team. Each team was given two towels. We had to swim down and back holding heavy, wet towels, then give them to the next man.

The towels stretched out behind us and dragged through the water. It was almost impossible to stay afloat, let alone swim. The strenuous swim drained what little energy we had. After our turn we collapsed at the wall.

During World War II, UDT swimmers had to swim ashore carrying five or six demolition packs connected in a long chain. To simulate this, the instructors had us complete more relays, each of us swimming with a brick, then a bucket. The bucket quickly filled with water, and we had to find a way to drag that along with us. Some did so by walking on the bottom of the pool.

These simple challenges not only caused us to experience hardships, but helped us to become innovative as well.

We broke for midrats. We ate like garbage cans, yet we were losing weight.

Wednesday 1:00 a.m.

Our night's mission was nothing more than to float aimlessly in the San Diego Bay until some sorry soul quit. Because our training emphasized teamwork and pulling together we were instructed to get into four long columns, one man behind the other, with our legs and arms wrapped around each other. This not only encouraged solidarity, but also proved to keep us a little warmer by absorbing each other's body heat.

As always, we sang songs to help keep our minds off being so cold, and constantly encouraged each other to hang on. Since the task was to endure the freezing cold until someone decided to quit, it only made us wonder how long we would have to hold out for this experiment. What if no one quit? We might be in this ice bath all night long.

We had been taught to compartmentalize our pain, which meant to isolate it in a room all by itself, then lock the door and pretend that it wasn't there. When the singing stopped, I played the same "elimination" game I had played as a child.

After forty-five minutes of floating motionless in that liquid freezer, someone finally cried out, "I'm out of here. This is insane. I quit!" Thankfully, his exit was also our ticket for a reprieve. We scurried to the beach.

Whenever someone DORed, there were usually others thinking about it, those who would cave if they were given a little nudge. The instructors were aware of this, so they messed with our minds.

"All right, gentlemen. Who wants to get back into the water?"

Our bodies shook so hard they could be used as vibrators. The brisk wind off the bay made it worse. I was thinking—we were all thinking—*What on earth am I doing out here? What does this have to do with fighting the Viet Cong? Have the instructors lost their minds?*

Our instructors went in for the kill. "I think it would be good if all of you enjoyed another swim."

That was all it took. Just the thought of having to go back into the simulated ice melt was unbearable. The contemplation of it was worse than the actual water itself. Some guys had all the heart they needed, but they just didn't have the body for that level of cold.

Another trainee DORed.

For the rest of the night, distance swimming in the bay, boat drills, running and harassment all merged into a big mass of ice cold misery, muscle cramps and exhaustion.

Wednesday 1:30 p.m.

It was near impossible to stay awake. Everyone was dead meat. The instructors added a little humor to our schedule again. They called it "hydro recon." The twenty-nine of us still left in Class 44 lined up waist deep in the Pacific with our paddles.

"All right, tadpoles. Start paddling toward Mexico."

Our legs strained to move through the stubborn water.

Though the instructors continued to demand we perform, evolutions gradually became less complicated, primarily because lack of physical coordination meant higher risk of severe injuries.

The cold water, physiological torment, and agonizing exercises took their toll. We were becoming numb to our misery. Everyone functioned on instinct alone. We spent a good half hour on "whistle drill," responding to Olivera's whistle. One whistle meant hit the deck. Two whistles, crawl. Three whistles, stand up. We responded to the shrill sound like robots.

Thursday 12:45 a.m.

Many deliberate and well thought out reprieves were built into the curriculum of Hell Week—brief moments of respite carefully designed not to give us rest, but only to test us. For a moment, the hectic whirlwind of activity stopped, and the pressures and discomfort of being constantly wet and cold were temporarily suspended.

After long hours of shivering in wet clothes and in freezing, waterlogged boots, we were allowed to take hot showers and put on dry clothes and socks.

Fitted with clean, dry clothes, minimally refreshed, we headed outdoors.

Olivera immediately ordered us into the surf.

Finally after seventy-five hours of no sleep, we were allowed to shower and go to bed. It wasn't real sleep though. We lay down, but our minds kept racing. Our leg muscles twitched and jerked involuntarily.

Like hot shower "reprieves," short bouts of sleep were carefully planned, not so much for us to get any real rest, but to find those who were willing and had the endurance to jump back into severe conditions at a moment's notice.

The entire BUD/S course was the means the Navy used to locate men to do the impossible. The selection process was critical, because those men could one day be the difference between lives lost, or saved.

"Get up! Get dressed! Muster in five minutes!"

Twenty-nine of us sluggish trainees did our best to mobilize after our one-hour nap. We moved slower than a tree full of *sloths.* After a little warmth, a little sleep, a little bit of relief, it wasn't easy to get back up and go outside to the cold air and mean-looking taskmasters.

For me this was the most difficult part of Hell Week. A brief moment of rest was worse than not getting any at all.

My body rebelled. It cried out for relief—comfort. Once again I had to force myself to block out all messages that would cause defeat. The best thing that could happen to me now was to get wet and cold. My instructors didn't let me down.

The "mud flats" weren't just any kind of mud. This mud was particularly nasty—gray-black silt that had built up for decades.

The mud reeked of rot and decay. The methane and sulfides that lay beneath the surface of the mud bubbled up in spots.

We spent much of Thursday in this slimy pit, performing caterpillar races, relay races, wheelbarrow races, swim races, belly crawls and backstrokes. We even played king of the IBS. The last man standing was the winner.

By turning our boats upside down they became springboards for a diving contest. It's surprising how much bounce you can get off one of the tubes.

"Hey, John! Match this." Frank Sparks did a full flip with a half twist. He excelled at this. His gymnast ability made him look like a star. His short frame was doing the impossible. A couple of guys came close to matching him, but most of us stuck with the swan, jackknife, backflips or belly flops—lots of belly flops. No one could compete with little man Sparks.

The instructors wanted us mud-covered from head to toe. Those with skin showing on our noses or chins were ordered to lie down face first in the mud. I happened to be one of them. Olivera walked on the backs of our heads to ensure our faces were completely covered. I braced for the jolt but still my nose almost broke. Pain surged through my head and mud jammed up my nostrils. Every inch of my face screamed for relief.

"Get up! Let me see your faces!" he ordered. Finally, he was satisfied.

At mealtime we obediently rolled over in the mud and faced the instructors.

"Anyone hungry?"

Suddenly box lunches came flying from every direction.

"That's mine!"

"No, it's mine," bellowed Solano.

"No, I've got that one!" Gore insisted.

In the end it didn't matter who got what. Most of us chose

not to eat. The putrid smells and the unsanitary conditions made it unbearable.

Corpsmen watched us for signs of bad infection. Some trainees had entire patches of skin missing due to the abrasions of the sand and kapok life jackets.

Thursday 2:00 p.m.

By now we were all on autopilot. The rest of the week was pretty much routine. "Camp surf" was backbreaking but doable. Each team dug a hole in the sand using our boat paddles. After two hours we were judged to see who had the biggest hole in the sand. Winners were rewarded. Losers paid.

For the next hour we filled up our holes. Our boat crew was performing very well. We were ahead on points. One of our original guys quit, so they gave us Rocky thinking he might slow us down. But all Rocky needed was a good leader, and Paul Plumb was the best. He knew how to get the most of his team.

Friday, 1:00 a.m.

After days without sleep, we began hallucinating. As our bodies went deeper into shock, we saw warm beds, hamburger stands, flying saucers, and even creatures from outer space, just like the instructors predicted. Friday's all-night boat paddle was the worst.

"Rocky, where are you going?" I asked.

"I'm going to get something to eat from that restaurant over there."

"What restaurant? Are you sure? I don't see it."

"Yeah, it's right over there," he insisted.

He already had one leg over the tube and into the water. We fought to bring him back into the boat before one of us had to go in and get him.

"Now stay put."

I saw my share of weird things too. Objects bounced off the bay like a thousand *Tinker Bells* in *Neverland*. My body and mind were out of sync. Unidentified objects appeared. The boat crew played along. "Sure, we see them too."

Friday 7:30 a.m.

The instructors' challenge now was to keep us awake for another twenty-four hours. To keep us busy we played simple games and relays on the parade field. Our voices were hoarse and some of us could only whisper. A few had coughs. Surprisingly, no one had caught pneumonia.

Friday 1:30 p.m.

To observe us under fire during extreme battle fatigue, our instructors waited until the end of the week to take us to the demo pits.

We ran, crawled and rolled in mud and sand for hours through simulated shellfire, hand grenades, detonated mines and machine-gun fire.

Ear shattering noises affected people differently, though explosives blowing up nearby stressed all the trainees. Startling blasts created shock waves that slammed into us. The closer we were to the explosion, the more terrible the pain. Our equilibrium vanished. We were affected so much that our ability to walk, run, and even crawl was hampered. Dirt, sand, mud, and other debris rained down with each explosion, and we smelled and tasted gunpowder. Learning how to think, react, and follow orders under those conditions wasn't easy. Soldiers often die when panicked. Indecision and carelessness can be deadly. The demo pits gave us a sampling of a combat situation.

It was early Saturday morning and we were plugging along on what would prove to be our last evolution. I think we were just killing time. Our bodies had all but given out. Our minds were dingy. We had been cold for so long that we were starting to feel warm. Everybody's skin had turned an eerie gray-tan, wrinkly and leather-like from the water, sun and wind. We looked like death warmed over. Ghouls from the abyss.

We had been constantly wet and freezing for a week. If it wasn't the ocean then it was the bay, if not the bay it was the pool, if it wasn't the pool it was the mud flats, if it wasn't the mud flats it was the water hose. It would be over soon.

We were on what I think the instructors called a "scavenger hunt"—going from point to point following clues, lugging our IBS around, which by now seemed like 400 pounds. Chief Rose approached our boat around 3:00 a.m. on Saturday.

"Congratulations!" He grinned. "You've been determined the best boat crew of Class 44's Hell Week. Go ahead and secure."

What a sweet, wonderful word, *secure*. Never had one word sounded so beautiful.

Rescue—salvation—liberation—emancipation—add all those up, put them inside a little box with a ribbon and bow, and you have the perfect gift—the end of Hell Week.

Chief Rose was our *Santa Claus*, *Easter Bunny* and *Tooth Fairy* combined. He was the bearer of good tidings. He was Michael Anthony, the man who delivered the checks on the '60s TV show, "The Millionaire." It was New Years and the Fourth of July with fireworks exploding in the air. It was our V-Day. For us Hell Week was OVER!

Unfortunately we were in no condition to celebrate. Our minds were not the sharpest, and our backsides were dragging somewhere on the road behind us.

Mr. Plumb was the first to come alive. "You heard the chief. It's over. Congratulations! We made it through Hell Week! I am proud of everyone one of you. We worked well as a team. We're number one. Let's hit the hot showers!"

Because we came in first place, we had the luxury of the showers one hour before the others secured. Winners were rewarded. Losers paid.

Hell Week took its toll. We all looked like zombies. Hardly anyone could wear boots, shoes, or sandals for days. Several guys' eyes were bloodshot or swollen shut in puffy faces. Nerves were frayed and many were irritable. Our minds were groggy as we slowly came out of the haze.

We were encouraged not to leave the base right away because it would have been dangerous for us to drive, or even walk around traffic.

Several had oozing sores, and as a result cellulitis (infection and inflammation of the tissues beneath the skin) set in. Our hands were club-like with fingers too swollen to function. Our inner legs and crotches were cut and bleeding from the straps of the kapok vests. We walked like cowboys, slightly bowlegged to relieve the chafed skin of our inner thighs. Our feet were sore, swollen and bruised from the constant jogging around the clock.

The corpsman gave us a complete medical inspection. He looked for signs of flesh-eating bacteria, pneumonia or other respiratory problems. Trainees in the worst shape were those with cellulitis and iliotibial band tendonitis, or IBT. IBT is an inflammation of the long tendon that runs the length of the femur to the knee, and is extremely painful. A few had problems with their hamstrings and hip flexors. The overworked muscles now quivered from inactivity.

Our class had dropped to twenty-nine. Over fifty young men had either quit or were set aside on medicals. If someone was dropped for medical, he could return to another class if he wanted to. One of the guys who would return another day was a guy by the name of Trigg. Cellulitis had set into his leg. He had a large, festering hole about the size of large hen's egg. It was red and swollen and full of puss. He along with a few others like Mike Anderson, Eric Echerman and a Hawaiian guy by the name of Kaneakua (Pineapple) would be back to try again. I later learned they all made it into the Teams by going through another class. Echerman almost became a full-time BUD/S student. I heard he went through three classes before graduating.

Throughout the weekend we dozed for as many sleep sessions as our bodies and minds would allow. Some fell asleep immediately. Others had fought to stay awake so long their bodies refused to turn off. They lay in their beds staring at the ceiling. Between sleep and chow, we took long, hot showers, basking in the luxury of being warm again.

Completing Hell Week was a proud time for me. I beat the odds. I had made it through the most physically and mentally challenging week of my life. Two thousand men were screened before our class started. Seventy-nine started. And after Hell Week, my original class had shrunk to twenty-nine.

The belief that BUD/S is only about a person's physical strength is a common misconception. In actuality, it's 90-percent mental and 10-percent physical. Trainees just come to the conclusion that they are too cold, too sandy, too sore or too wet to go any further. It's their minds that give up on them, not their bodies.

It is not the individual, physical trials of Hell Week that doom a candidate. It's enduring the continual, nonstop 144 hours of physical feats while being deathly cold.

One thing for sure: Hell Week turns up the pain level several degrees. Being cold, wet, and exhausted is what a future UDT/SEAL will have to endure for his entire career. If he can't hack it during training, he certainly doesn't belong in the Teams. For many, just the thought of having a career where you are often cold and miserable is too much of a commitment.

In the beginning it's hard for some to see BUD/S for what it really is—an introduction to continuous physical demands as a way of life. They have only looked at BUD/S through the eyes of theatergoers or as some college fraternity hazing. The training is the beginning of a career as a warrior.

That endless week was a defining moment for me. I would never be the same. To this day, I look back on it as a benchmark whenever I face a situation that seems overwhelming.

Through those six seemingly unending days and nights, we learned to rely on one another to keep awake and stay motivated. Periodically, we'd tap one another on the shoulder or back and wait for a reassuring pat in response. It meant, "I'm still hanging in there. How about you?" We cheered loudly when we noticed a mate struggling to complete his mission, and relied on the same fuel when we ourselves felt drained. We learned to continually silence that inner voice that urged us to give in and bang our helmets on the doorpost. Those who couldn't train their minds to shut out the pain eventually succumbed to it and quit. That was why on the average 60 to 70 percent of those who began BUD/S training failed to make it to the end of the first phase.

Quitting was never an option for me. I can't say it never crossed my mind, but when it did I slammed the door shut before it could get a foothold. I knew before I went in that barring any broken bones or illness, I would be standing with the survivors at the finish. And I was.

I came into the Navy looking for direction. I was looking for a challenge and found the ultimate by going through Hell Week. I found a new beginning and another family to belong to. These brave and valiant men would soon become my very close friends. As for the Navy, it was the open door for new adventure, exciting travel, unique experiences and the chance to be a member of Naval Special Warfare's UDT/ SEAL Teams.

— Chapter Seven —

Bring on the Big Toys

Our whittled-down class made it easier to get to know each other at the beginning of Phase Two. Our Hell Week party helped. A couple of officers rented a huge house in Coronado right across from the beach. We celebrated our accomplishments until dawn.

At the end of working days, Gore, Durlin, Solano, Bracken, Harness, Wolf, Lang, Sparks and I hung out at the barracks talking about our individual philosophies and goals. On weekends we bussed over to San Diego, went to Tijuana, Mexico or met to explore some-place we hadn't been before. A couple of us attended the base chapel once or twice. We were young, optimistic and shared a craving for adventure. We were each other's family.

We painted our green helmets blue, leaving the green color for the upcoming class.

The first two weeks of Phase Two, the dive phase, was more mental than physical, to give our aching bodies time to mend. We wore flip-flops instead of boots while our blistered, swollen feet healed. In swift BUD/S fashion, subjects like mathematics, physics, chemistry, physiology, hydrography, and underwater navigation were crammed into a tight schedule. Before we got into the water with our scuba gear, we spent several days in the classroom.

The first week we learned Boyle's Law and Charles' Law—the relationships between temperature, pressure and volume. The test at the end of the week was timed, so we had to know it cold. By the end of the second week we had to pass exams in diving physics, diving medicine, and diving decompression tables.

Almost immediately our instructors informed us that our physical performance standards from Phase One were no longer good enough for us to graduate. Now we had new standards. We had to complete our four-mile run in thirty-one minutes or less. We had to finish our two-mile open water swim in less than eighty minutes. The obstacle course times, previously eleven minutes, was cut to ten and a half. If we didn't meet the standards, we'd be dropped.

Oxygen tolerance tests were given to us in small groups. We were taken down to sixty feet in the recompression chamber where we had to breathe pure oxygen. A small percentage of the population has a toxic reaction to oxygen under pressure. Our instructors needed to find out if we were among that group.

Just before "pool comp" week, we were introduced to free-swimming ascents, or FSAs. In San Diego Bay we made one FSA from twenty-five feet and another from fifty feet. We entered a diving bell at each depth, breathed air under pressure for a few minutes, and then made the FSA. Breathing air in the bell at twenty-five feet left our lungs with twice as much air as we had at the surface—close to three times as much at fifty feet. As we swam to the surface, we had to continuously exhale—blow bubbles—or risk overexpansion of air in our lungs, which could be fatal. On future UDT/SEAL missions, we may be in situations where we would need to abandon our diving rigs. If so, we knew how to get to the surface safely.

Dive training started with a two-hour presentation on open-circuit scuba (self-contained underwater breathing apparatus). Our dive tanks were called twin 90s because ninety cubic feet of air were compressed into each tank. We used a two-hosed scuba regulator during training but later used a single-hose regulator, which was simpler, safer and easier to maintain. Our first dive took place in the deep end of the pool where we were taught three important object-tives: familiarization, buddy breathing, and student gear inspection.

The next day was "ditch-and-don" day. While underwater we practiced taking off all our gear and arranging it on the bottom of the pool—ditching. The last item to come off was the face mask. We secured our gear with our weight belts and made an FSA to the surface. After an instructor critiqued our skills, we swam back down to our gear, reestablished our air supply, and donned our rigs. Once we had this down, we did the whole procedure with our masks darkened to simulate a night ditching. Next we did a gear exchange, which was nothing more than a ditch and don that we did while buddy-breathing. Durlin and I teamed up. He removed his gear, I put it on, then we switched roles.

One of my most difficult pool comps was a drill called "pool skills." This was a problem-solving diving evolution. One instructor shook me to simulate turbulence while another instructor tied a knot in my air hose, turned off my air valve, undid my weight belt, released my scuba tank straps, ripped off my face mask and pulled off my fins. My task was to handle each problem with calm, by doing first things first. The challenge was, whenever I fixed one problem, they created another.

The open-circuit portion of Phase Two ended with a 120-foot bounce dive (down and up) off Point Loma and a FSA from a submerged submarine. We also learned a neat method of *drop and pick up* (delivery and retrieval of us future UDT/SEALs) out in the ocean. While we sat in two IBSs connected by a line, the submarine's telescope caught the line and pulled us along. Big toys. Big fun!

Being diving qualified had other perks. I would now receive an extra $55 dollars a month for hazard duty.

If they had taught drop and pickup in grade school, I would have signed up. BUD/S training was becoming seriously cool. We were taught to execute different types of drops and pickups with IBSs, sleds, fast boats and helicopters. Jumping off the back of high-speed boats was dangerous and hard on the neck and back. It was also a blast.

During World War II a reconnaissance mission was normally carried out four days before D-Day, up to dawn on D-Day itself, and occasionally during a volatile mission an hour before H-Hour. Destroyer escorts were converted to become Attack Personnel Destroyers to transport the UDT. For training purposes, our transport boat was a LCPL (Landing Craft Personnel-Large) and we were in friendly waters. But we could make believe.

Just like WWII recon maneuvers, our transport boat heading toward the beach made a fast turn to port (left side when facing forward) and ran parallel to the beach at high speed, keeping its starboard (right) side to the shore. The craft was now on its "splash run."

We slung a seven-man rubber boat over the concealed port side and waited for orders.

Chief Allen screamed over the roar of the boat's diesel engines, "Go! Go! Go!"

One at a time we dropped into the rubber boat, in preparation for entering the water. We hugged the rubber bladder as it bounced wildly through the waves, and waited for the next signal. Salty spray stung our faces and the engines blocked all other sound from our ears.

My eyes were glued to the chief. His arm jerked downward.

I rolled into the icy water. Salt water filled my wetsuit and mask. I cleared my mask and waited. My place on the rubber boat was immediately taken by the next man who, in turn, waited for his signal to enter the water. This way, a line of swimmers was quickly dropped at predetermined intervals along the entire length of the target beach. With our heads barely showing, we were almost impossible to spot from shore, even through binoculars.

During World War II the frogmen rarely were fired upon. Once in the water, they swam toward the beach and surveyed their assigned sections while writing the details on plastic slates. When the survey was complete they swam back out to meet their fast-moving boat with the rubber raft. For now we only practiced drop and pickup. Beach reconnaissance would come later in the training.

We formed a straight line, twenty-five yards between one man and the next. The transport boat circled, then came hurtling back toward us for pickup.

Chief Mack knelt in the rubber boat, holding out a large padded loop as a snare. He picked up one trainee after another. Then the coxswain aimed the speeding boat at me. My first instinct was to move away but I steadied myself, knowing I'd have to trust the guy.

When the raft was right on top of me, I extended my arm, and Chief Mack held out the snare. When the snare hit my arm, Mack immediately pulled his hand to his chest, locking the snare between his upper arm and forearm. I gave a hard kick with my fins. The momentum of the speeding boat snatched me from the water. I flew up over the side and into the rubber boat. I released the snare and quickly climbed into the transport boat, leaving room for the chief to snare the next swimmer.

This was why I joined the Navy!

During actual combat, if a swimmer was missed—and this was rare—he would have to wait until the boat finished picking up the remaining line of swimmers, then it would return for him. No one liked second runs. During a second run the boat was usually receiving enemy fire because the enemy would have had time to determine the boat's range and speed. That day, two people in my line were missed. It took a few more runs for everyone to get the hang of it.

If this had been a real mission, our job would have only been half-finished. Once the intelligence information gathered by the swimmers was assessed, the boats and swimmers would go into operation again—this time for demolition and clearance.

During demolition and clearance drop-offs, items such as marker buoys and explosive charges were dropped off with the individual swimmers.

Swimmers on the extreme ends of the beach would run a long line of detonating cord along the full length of the beach. Other swimmers placed charges on individual obstacles then carefully attached their detonating cords to the main line.

When all charges were placed, the swimmers, except for those who set the fuses, were picked up. When the signal was given, the fuses were connected and set on time delays. The remaining swimmers quickly made their way out to sea for pickup. When the fuses detonated, a series of rippling explosions cleared the entire area within half a second.

In time, I would get my chance to blow things up.

My favorite drop and pickup was called The Fulton Recovery System, which we practiced on the waves of San Diego Bay. The

Fulton System used two six-foot-long pods or sleds that looked like small, flat boats and were made of buoyant foam. A two-hundred-foot polypropylene line connected the two pods at their bows. A long float at the center point held the line above water.

The LCSR (Landing Craft Swimmer Recovery—the drop-off and pickup boat) had a long rod attached to the bow just below the waterline.

To do a drop-off (called "casting"), the LCSR made a high-speed pass across the drop-off location. When the signal was given I jumped off the stern. Others followed me one at a time. To keep from getting whiplash I braced my head with one of my hands. I landed on my rear and skipped like a rock over the water.

If we were part of a UDT/SEAL Team performing recon, we would have partnered up and swam toward shore, then back to sea for the pickup. Today, however, we were just practicing how to be dropped off and picked up.

To pick us up (called "retrieval"), the LCSR made another a high-speed pass by us and dropped off the pods (sleds), then circled around to pick us up. We'd have to swim to the pods and maneuver them apart by kicking hard with our fins so the line connecting them was taut and the float in the middle of the line was visible to the pickup boat. Each pod could hold six men, three on each side.

The LCSR blazed toward us. The coxswain aimed the bow rod on the front of his boat at the float so it would snag the float line in the water. He caught it.

A guide moved the line up from the water to a winch on the bow. The sleds jerked and whipped toward each other. We were dragged forward, bouncing over waves in our pods. As the LCSR sped away from the beach (performing evasive maneuvers), the pods (and us) were winched in closer to the boat. When the sleds finally hugged the boat, we climbed aboard. Recovery was complete.

Hydrographic reconnaissance and cartography began in the 1940s when the Navy frogmen were in their infancy. The basic tools are a lead line (a length of cord with a lead weight attached to one end, used to measure depth and gradient in the ocean floor) and a Plexiglas slate. We practiced hydrographic surveys by first dropping groups of ten men off a boat. Next we swam to fifty yards off the beach and formed a line perpendicular to the shore, each man about twenty-five feet apart, with the first man in the surf zone and the last man out to sea. We kept the line of swimmers straight by watching two men on shore with flags, one standing behind the other. As they moved down the beach at twenty-five yard intervals, we moved with them and took soundings. When the men on the beach saw that our line was straight, they'd wave a flag for us to take the next sounding with our lead line. We marked the depth on our slate for each sounding.

After the operation, the slates were handed to the cartographer who drew up a map of the beach gradient, marking any obstacles, taking into account high or low tides.

"Underwater compass swims" sounds tame. Had Ian Fleming been a U.S. Navy SEAL, James Bond would have originated right here.

For the underwater compass swim we used an "attack board." An attack board is a plate-sized Plexiglas board with mountings for a compass, a wristwatch, and a depth gauge. We took turns *driving* on compass headings as if we were doing a live demolition mission on an enemy ship's hull.

Underwater navigation is similar to using a map and compass on land, except your vision under water is limited. The San Diego Bay had one- to three-foot visibility in the day and almost zero at night. As always, our underwater swims required a swim buddy. One swam above the other. The man below was the navigator.

These swims were thrilling at night. The attack board's watch and compass glowed in the dark, a welcome but eerie contrast to the murky, gloomy water. In order for the safety boats to monitor us, each swimmer attached a nylon line to his tanks with a marking buoy and Chemlite attached. Our white lights flickered on the surface, allowing the safety boat and instructors to see our location.

We quickly learned to trust the compass. Those who didn't often ended up going 180 degrees in the opposite direction. It's a strange feeling relying only on an illuminated needle twenty-five feet below the surface in pitch-black conditions. My human compass rebelled, telling me to disregard that silly bright green metal indicator. But experience was a good teacher. I knew all too well to disregard my senses and rely on the tried and proven. In this risky business I would have to put my trust not only in technology and gadgets, but in the expertise of those individuals who would be rigging our parachutes, filling our scuba tanks with the right mixtures and other people further removed, whom I had never met.

—Chapter Eight—

Demolition and Commando Training

C harley Free, a holdover from the previous class, joined us for Phase Three, making our Class #44 an even thirty. Our helmets were now painted red.

Phase Three emphasized demolition handling and tactics. Along with the explosives, booby-trap and small-arms techniques, we were also taught basic commando techniques such as reconnaissance patrolling, river and stream crossing, ambush techniques, unarmed combat and sentry disposal.

Before we could fire a weapon or learn demolition, we were drilled for safety and had to memorize this set of rules and regulations:

1. Consider all weapons loaded all the time.
2. Never point a weapon at anything you don't want to put a bullet through.
3. Never put your finger on the trigger unless you want to shoot.
4. Know your target and know what's behind it.

BUD/S demolition training included fixed ordnance like claymore mines and hand grenades. We also worked with illumination and pyrotechnics such as pop flares and 40-mm grenade-launched parachute flares. But the heart of demolition training utilized C-4 satchel charges, Mark-8 hose, and Bangalore torpedoes. We also became familiar with electric and non-electric firing devices, charge initiation, blasting caps and the safe handling of all these.

A Mark-8 hose looks like a fire hose and is filled with PETN, an explosive used to dig trenches and blast channels in coral. Bangalore torpedoes are long metal tubes filled with an explosive called

Composition B. These tubes could be connected end-to-end to form a long train of explosives. We would use these often in Vietnam to widen small rivers and deepen canals.

San Clemente, one of southern California's Channel Islands, is rugged with patches of scrub grass and rocky terrain. The northern tip of this island is reserved for BUD/S training.

On San Clemente, John Durlin and I shared a small cabin with two bunks. John was a genuinely nice guy. He wasn't one to pry into people's lives, but we had some serious talks—mostly about girls, our families and our outlooks on life. Both of us had been raised in homes where we attended church at one point or another. While on San Clemente, I received news that my grandmother had died. I couldn't make it to her funeral because of BUD/S training. I shared my grief and anger with John.

I told him how my grandmother would recite, word for word, dozens of nursery rhymes when I was a little boy. Memories of her frugal Christmas parties, the times she took me to an early sunrise Easter service and breakfast at church brought a smile to my face. Then the sobering truth set in: I would never see her smile or hear her encouraging words on this earth again. We agreed that my grandmother was now in a much better place, which I found comforting. The death of a close friend or loved one had always made me reflect. But now I had to refocus my mind on training.

Swimming around the little island brought all kinds of surprises. Curious but playful porpoise often joined us. Less entertaining were the sea lions that nipped at a fin or ankle as we traversed the choppy seas. Most of the sharks we swam among were Leopard sharks, known to be harmless as sharks go. But occasionally a more menacing variety showed up.

During one three-mile swim I heard a blood-curdling scream.

"Shark!" Roger Warner yelled—my most outstanding memory of him (except for when I knocked him down three times in our boxing smoker).

"Over here! There's a shark circling me!" Roger thrashed and wildly waved his hand in a distress signal to the safety boat. "Hurry!"

We had been taught to be calm if we encountered sharks. Sharks can sense human fear. It excites them. We were no longer in the classroom.

"I want out of the water! Now!"

Instructors had no choice but to pull Roger into the safety boat to be calmed down. It wasn't just for his wellbeing, but also for ours. It took a little extra self-motivation and self-talk for the rest of us to ignore the big fellow and continue our swim around the kelp beds.

"You better pull yourself together, Roger," I heard one instructor say. "You're halfway through Third Phase. It would be a shame for you to botch it now because of this."

After a few minutes, they coaxed Roger back into the water. He could have been dropped, but after discussing the matter, the staff felt Roger would overcome his fear of sharks in time.

The kelp beds were thick and treacherous. Their long winding tentacles tangled in our knife sheaths and fins, so we kept our distance. No one wanted to get enmeshed in that jungle. To make matters worse we were swimming against a stubborn current and through thousands of floating jellyfish. Roger had reason to be unnerved.

While on San Clemente Island, we conducted simulated land and sea reconnaissance missions. These were extremely dangerous because of live explosives and the free-diving methods used in laying demolition fields. Underwater obstacles had to be blasted away along the landing beaches, and some obstacles were set deep enough to afford concealment, but most were in the raging surf with the usual barrage of explosives to simulate enemy fire.

We swam out to our obstacles in the surf zone, towing our demo packs behind us. When we reached our targets, we knifed the bladders that floated the haversacks and followed them as they sank to the bottom of the ocean. Due to high tide, the obstacles sat twenty feet below the surface.

My swim partner for the day was Frank Sparks. He and I

were assigned the row of obstacles in the deeper part of the cove. We had to free-dive (mask and fins only, no air tanks) eighteen feet down and secure C-4 demolition packs against concrete obstacles. After securing the packs with ropes, they had to be tightened with a tourniquet. I could comfortably hold my breath for a minute and a half while working strenuously, but this exercise would still take several dives to complete.

While Frank and I worked, other pairs swam along the width of the beach attaching a detonation cord line from obstacle to obstacle. Down at the bottom, I winched the rope to make our charges tight.

I stayed down way too long. When my lungs felt like they were going to burst, I knew I only had a few more precious seconds to get to the surface before blacking out.

As I kicked toward the surface to get air, the K-Bar knife on my web belt got tangled in the detonation cord that had just been laid. At first I didn't notice, but as I was surfacing the line became taught, holding me under.

My lungs were out of breath. The oxygen was sucked out of my entire body, leaving me light-headed and weak. I was seconds away from blacking out.

Two men in Class 42 had drowned during a similar exercise. The swimmer who got hung up in the cord grabbed the fin of his buddy above him and they both died.

Panic was my human reaction. Staying calm was learned. My training paid off. *Think, John. Check out your environment. What's the problem? Okay, my knife is caught in the trunk line. Just undo your belt and you'll be free.*

Fortunately, my swim buddy was doing his job. He'd been keeping an eye on me, so he was aware of my predicament. I was in the process of releasing my web belt to free myself, when Frank simultaneously cut the line.

I broke the surface, took one huge gulp of air and hyper-ventilated. I had nearly drowned. I hadn't had a near-death experience since I was a child, but I shook and had that same warm, sick sensation in my stomach. I remembered the feeling all too well.

As it turned out I was able to free myself, but Frank's actions reassured me the buddy system works.

The demolition was laid and everyone was on the beach, and accounted for. Two swim pairs remained in the water with two instructors and the firing assemblies. On the signal from the officer in charge, the trainees tied their double waterproofed firing assemblies into the trunk line.

Waterproofing a non-electric firing assembly dates back to World War II. Early frogmen discovered using water-proof neoprene cement and condoms—actually two condoms for extra protection from the saltwater—worked better than anything else. That technique is still used today.

"Fire in the hole!" Mr. Plum yelled from the right flank of the field.

"Fire in the hole!" Mr. Hollow echoed from the left flank.

The two trainees in the water pulled the rings inside the double prophylactics and triggered their fuse lighters.

"Smoke!"

The swimmers headed for the beach. The obstacle field was dual primed with two fifteen-minute firing delays. We waited. *KA-BOOM!* The charges exploded, taking several hundred gallons of water and a bunch of fish with it. We called that DuPont fishing, after the manufacturer of the explosives.

Now that I was demolition qualified, I earned an additional $55 dollars a month as an enlisted man. Added to my dive pay, I now made an extra $110 a month. Officers received $220. We fondly referred to it as double hazard duty pay.

We spent the last week of Phase Three at a training facility in the Laguna Mountains, three thousand feet above sea level, eighty miles east of San Diego. We were introduced to land warfare, taught patrolling, how to apply camouflage and set up ambushes. With a map and compass, we negotiated different courses set up by our instructors.

We experienced what it was like to walk into an ambush with guns blaring (instructors used blanks).

"Bullets don't care if you were born stupid," yelled Chief Sick. "The only virtue of the stupid is that they don't live long. People who get killed have so many things on their minds that they forget to stay alive. Stay focused on what you are doing at all times."

Basic UDTRA/BUD/S training was over. We graduated from being "tadpoles" to full-fledged "frogs." I had made it.

During the graduation ceremony, it was a proud moment when I stood face-to-face with the base admiral to receive my diploma. I remember him looking at me with a twinkle in his eye.

"Son, how old are you?" he asked.

I answered, "Nineteen, sir."

Below are the tenets of the Naval Commando:

1. We commit to the Team and its mission.
2. We persevere.
3. We prize victory.
4. We excel in ambiguous environments.
5. We keep one foot in the water.

BUD/S training was just the beginning. Further training was paramount for the Navy frogmen and SEALs. Once we were assigned to an Underwater Demolition or a SEAL Team, our training continued. We were required to go to jump school, SERE (survival, evasion, resistance and escape) school, and after that there were various diving, judo, weapons, survival, HALO (High Altitude-Low Opening), language and academic schools to choose from. Likewise, a career Navy SEAL today is constantly schooled in the latest technology and equipment and is kept on the cutting edge of specialized warfare.

Toward the end of training we were given a questionnaire. Our instructors needed to fill the billets across the street at the SEAL and

UDT compounds. We were given a choice as to which Team we wanted to join. Tom Bracken, Forrest Harness, Steve Wolf and I were among those who wanted to belong to UDT-11. Jim Gore, John Durlin, Richard Solano and Frank Sparks, chose SEAL Team One.

—Chapter Nine—

Airborne!

"Get Ready!"

"Get ready!"

"Stand up!"

"Stand up!"

"Hook up!"

"Hook up!"

"Check equipment!"

"Check equipment!"

"Sound off for equipment check!"

"Sound off for equipment check!" "Ten okay." "Nine okay." "Eight okay..." "One okay!"

"Approach the door!"

I stared out the door of a roaring C-130, looking down at the patchwork fields below. I wore a 44-pound T-10 parachute and a huge grin. It was my turn to jump.

Ever since I was a boy I imagined jumping out of a plane and sinking toward earth under a giant, billowing canopy. That day the Navy checked another dream off my list.

A green light flashed. The jumpmaster yelled, "Go!"

I plunged into the sky.

Three weeks earlier I had fought an inner battle to not unbuckle prematurely as our plane touched down at the Fort Benning Army Base in Columbus, Georgia.

Jump school. We had arrived.

Two dozen frogs (my former classmates and some guys from Class 43) stepped off the plane into a sweltering ninety-eight degree June welcome. With the added humidity, we virtually swam in steam. We were eager to become paratroopers, but just as eager to get back to the temperate beaches of California. To Navy UDT/SEALs, jump school was a one-week course the Army stretched into three long weeks. The three weeks included ground training, tower training and jump training.

Landing is the most crucial part of parachuting. For the first part of ground training, we learned the proper parachute landing fall (PLF) so our legs wouldn't break when we hit the earth.

A good parachute landing minimizes the shock of the fall by dispersing the impact among five main body parts: balls of feet, side of calf, side of thigh, side of hip, and side of back. We were to tuck our chins tightly against our necks, hold the risers with our arms protecting our face and throat, and clamp our elbows to our sides.

We practiced dozens of PLFs on land. Then we jumped from a mock door one-meter high into a sawdust pit.

During the second half of ground week, we learned how to exit an aircraft. Our new mock door stood atop a thirty-four foot tower.

I was fitted with a harness contraption that looked like something a mother would put on a hyper child to restrain him in the mall. After climbing the stairs to the top I waited in line to reach the open door. A few wary soldiers took one look down and decided being a paratrooper wasn't for them. They returned to the ground via the stairs. Thirty-four feet doesn't seem that high, but when you lean over the edge and look down the length of the tower your mind tells you you're about to fall five stories.

My harness was attached to a pulley. At the command of a Black Hat (Army Airborne instructor), I jumped. I endured a short free fall, then felt a reassuring jerk. The pulley swept me down a long cable. I landed in a huge mound of dirt where I was unstrapped from my harness. *Hooyah!*

Hot adrenaline shot through my veins.

I wanted to go again.

Week two, "tower week," had three phases: the *swing landing trainer* (SLT), the *suspended harness*, and the *two-hundred-and-fifty-foot tower*. We applied the traits learned during week one and improved them. Mass exit drills from the thirty-four foot tower helped us to learn how to work as a team and prepare for a group to jump from a plane as quickly as possible.

At the beginning of week two, I found myself strapped into a new contraption—the swing landing trainer, or SLT. I was harnessed to risers on a platform about ten feet high, then swung down to a meter above the ground, where I hung until a Black Hat released me to fall. Not only did the SLT allow me to practice my PLF, but it also gave me practice pulling the correct risers. Yanking the correct risers helped slow the parachute by making the parachute draw in.

The second session of the week, the suspended harness session, prepared me for emergencies like landing in a tree, water, power lines and on highways.

The two hundred-and-fifty-foot tower should be a theme park ride. I was put into a parachute harness with the chute already open, then lifted crane-like to the top of the two-hundred-and-fifty-foot tower. Then I was dropped. The Black Hats below coached me down, reminding me to pull the proper risers and to keep my feet and knees together.

This was my first real taste of what it felt like to sink to earth. Only one weekend separated me from the actual plane jump.

Week three at last! This was what I'd been waiting for! The third week was devoted to our five qualifying jumps. Along with PT and rehashing techniques learned during weeks one and two, we also reviewed malfunctions that could occur and how to safely deal with any adverse situation.

A "Mae West" is when your canopy turns partially inside out, making two chutes instead of one. To solve: be prepared to use your reserve chute.

The "horseshoe" is when your chute wraps around your body. Pull your reserve immediately without cutting away your main chute.

A "barber's pole" is when your lines get tangled up behind your head. Cut the lines and activate your reserve chute.

The "streamer" is a long, thin looking silk object above you and mother earth is coming at you a hundred miles an hour. Hope you paid attention in class. Activate your reserve chute.

A "jumper-in-tow" is when your static line fails to disconnect and you are flopping alongside the plane. Pray for a miracle.

Then of course there is the "full canopy." That's when—unless you break an arm or leg—you have made a good jump.

We also went over basic introduction to the aircraft, seating, static line connections, donning the parachute, and the commands we'd be hearing from the jumpmaster.

We strapped into our parachutes, and were ready. A Jumpmaster Parachute Inspection (JMPI) was next. First our reserve parachute was checked to make sure it was in proper working order. Second our static lines were inspected. Third our parachute harness was examined. The fourth and final inspection was the overall look of the equipment.

We boarded the C-130 and lifted off.

Our groups were divided into lines (sticks) in the order we would jump. Soon the plane neared the drop zone.

The jumpmaster screamed above the roar of the engines the sequence of readiness. "Get ready! Stand up! Hook up! Equipment check! Sound off for equipment check! Approach the door!"

A green light flashed. The jumpmaster yelled, "Go! Go! Go!"

I was conditioned by now to just jump. I followed the man in front of me out the side door of the C-130 without thinking. This first would be a twelve-hundred-foot jump.

A one-hundred-mile-an-hour wind shoved me toward the tail of the plane. Then I fell through the sky.

I counted, *One thousand, two thousand, three thousand...*

I heard rippling as the green silk unfolded. The wind caught the canopy, and I was jerked upward. I sighed a quick, "Thank you, God."

After relaxing a second, I took in the view. What looked like a hundred Army-green jellyfish—some below, others still above—all drifted down. I heard someone yell, "If only my mother could see me now!"

I tipped my head back and looked up into my canopy. Someone was walking on my chute—I could see the indentations of his feet. He finally escaped and dropped past me, falling fast until his canopy caught air.

A different guy to my right had slipped through another paratrooper's lines. The two of them were hanging together. They would have an interesting landing.

On a twelve-hundred-foot jump, the ground comes up fast. I grabbed hold of my risers, pulled my elbows in tight and braced for landing. I hit the ground hard. Landing with a T-10 parachute is like jumping off a one-story building. I applied my PLF and rolled in the direction of the wind.

I hit a button on my harness releasing the canopy. I chased the silk, stuffed it into its bag then jogged toward the bus, eager for my next jump.

My face still felt the rush of the wind.

UDT and SEALs had a reputation of being mavericks, especially those of us straight out of BUD/S—we were down-right cocky. Jump school was a breeze compared to what we had just gone through—almost boring—so we decided to give the Army a dose of Navy attitude. We turned jump school into a playground.

Army instructors split us up to try and bring order, but that didn't work. They threatened us, coaxed us, begged us, and finally gave up on us. We had a fun time, though I'm not sure anyone else did.

One morning a frog we called "Happy" tossed some Army guy

out of our barracks. The dude had entered, screaming it was time to get up. He was only doing his job. But he never bothered us again.

On the Fourth of July we tied several sheets together and hung our homemade UDT flag on the parade field, to the disdain of the Fort Benning command.

We volunteered for the front row on runs in order to speed up the pace until other less physically conditioned troopers bent over from exhaustion.

When the Army instructors dropped one of us UDT frogs for push-ups, we all fell to the ground as a group, and did them as a unit. We were one. We were macho. We were the Navy's best!

When it came to push-ups we went the second mile. We did the ten that the Army required, and then did an extra ten for the Navy. When we finished we'd holler a loud "*Hooyah!*" The Army recruits who witnessed our bravado couldn't understand why we did more than was required, but we enjoyed showing off the great shape we were in.

One drill sergeant decided to make an example. He separated me from the group and said, "Okay, trooper, give me ten." I did ten for him, then another ten for the Navy. He dropped me again—then again and again for almost an hour. He thought he could wear me out, but I could do push-ups all day long by doing twenty at a pop. He finally became the nice guy and begged me to cooperate. "Hey, guy, help me out here. I'm only trying to do my job. Make life easy for me, will you?" I almost felt sorry for him.

The Army was stingy with their food portions compared to the Navy. I recalled hearing a song when I was a kid that went something like, "The Navy gets the gravy but the Army gets the beans, beans, beans." So when it was our turn to serve lunch we filled the Army food trays with "Navy" portions. Only half the troops ate that day, but those who did must have thought it was Thanksgiving. The rest of the troops didn't completely miss out. They got to watch a screaming lady cook play baseball with our heads, wielding a wooden spoon like a bat.

After two weeks, instructors gave Tom Bracken a blue helmet.

That meant he didn't have any demerits and was among the few being considered for Distinguished Honor Man. Now instructors watched him closer than ever. Once we found out he was on the short list, we all pulled together to help Tom keep his slate clean.

The instructors kept a chart and marked off any demerits they found during inspections. We were graded on presentation, coordination and style. We sheltered him from our bad behavior and pretended he wasn't one of us to help him win.

During muster one day, Tom noticed he forgot to put on his dog tags, which would have given him a demerit. He was in the second row. The drill sergeant was already half-finished inspecting the first row.

Tom whispered to a frog behind him, "Hey, got a dog tag I can borrow?"

It was passed up to Tom just in time. Tom passed that inspection without a bump.

"And the Distinguished Honor Man goes to..."

It was jump school graduation day, and we had sat through several boring speeches listening to Army bull, when we finally heard the announcer identifying the class Honor Graduate.

"... T o m B r a c k e n."

We jumped to our feet, interrupted the ceremony and yelled one of our hardy UDT cheers that ended with a big, *"Hooyah!"*

Several Army instructors snapped around to look our way. By appearances, they were in shock. They mustn't have realized Tom was a frogman.

We Navy frogmen got them twice. Not only did we get away with being mavericks, we walked away with the Distinguished Honor Man trophy as well.

That might have been the last big hurrah, though. The next class of UDT/SEALs wasn't as fortunate. They were all kicked out and had to go through jump school in Okinawa. The Army evidently had enough of our shenanigans.

—Chapter Ten—

SERE School—Survival, Evasion, Resistance and Escape

I will never surrender of my own free will. If in command, I will never surrender the members of my command while they still have the means to resist. (Article II, U.S. Military Code of Conduct)

I lay tied to a board, feet in the air, a dark cloth over my head, an interrogator screaming at me. Soon buckets of water poured onto my face. I held my breath as long as I could, but the water kept flowing. I coughed, then choked. There was nothing I could do.

I was going through SERE school, a requirement for anyone who had greater than normal risks of being stranded behind enemy lines or captured by the enemy. The fact that the Navy even had such a school might seem barbaric to those not being sent off to war. But for those who were already sitting in small dingy cells at the *Hanoi Hilton*, SERE training proved to be invaluable. Unfortunately, every war has its share of casualties and prisoners of war. The Navy wanted to make sure we were prepared.

Just a week earlier, I had taken a seat in a briefing room on Coronado's North Island Air Base in San Diego, California, with thirty-five of my teammates and a few hundred other Navy personnel. During this, our first class, we were briefed on military code of conduct in the event we found ourselves in the hands of the enemy.

A poster on the wall spoke volumes: *If I am captured, I will continue to resist by all means available. If senior, I will take command. I will make every effort to escape and aid others to escape.*

The brief ended. We were told we had just eaten our last meal. From now on we would have to forage to survive.

SURVIVAL

Our first night, we camped in makeshift tents made out of palm branches and driftwood found on the beaches of North Island Air Base. If we wanted to eat, we had to find things near the seashore. Our instructors walked along and pointed out different plants we could eat to survive. Not many of us were hungry enough to eat the bugs, snails and slugs we found. A few playful types tried to trap a seagull and to fish with their hands.

Remember Forrest Harness? He was up to his usual self. He told a few of us he was going on a clandestine mission around the fence that separated the naval air base from the civilian Coronado beach. He was off to the local store. "Anybody want some snacks?"

The next day we boarded a bus to Warner Springs, California where the Navy had a remote training area in the desert. Once we arrived we attended another briefing, and Navy corpsmen told us they were available to treat any bruises, cuts or snakebites, but couldn't help us with our hunger pangs. The camp, we learned, had boundaries marked with cautionary fences to keep students from going off course. They had very strict rules about safety, and any violations could be cause for dismissal. Contraband items were identified—knives, lighters, matches, tobacco, flashlights, and food of any kind. All students were given a grace period to place our prohibited items into a large bin provided by the camp staff.

We were divided into small groups with an instructor. The UDT guys were integrated into the general population, but some of our groups still had five or six fellow frogmen. For the next four days, we wandered the desert looking for edible plants and bugs, and conducted compass navigation. Our survival lessons were not much different than those in an advanced Boy Scout handbook—fire building, making shelters, trapping, and living off the land.

EVASION

Everyone was ravenous. Bugs and worms started to look good. On one long compass course through the desert, fellow teammates Fred Lang, Forrest Harness and I devised a covert plan. We knew a major road had brought us to this camp. If we could locate that road, we might find a ranch house or something. We crossed over the forbidden fence and headed toward the highway. After following the highway for a couple of miles we saw an orchard. Crunchy, sweet apples were a far cry better than snails, grubs and roots; believe me. We made it back undetected, and our stomachs felt a whole lot better. Compass course was paying off.

It was pitiful to watch two hundred starving men wander around the desert looking for lizards and snakes to eat. I don't remember who came up with the idea but as night came on, some of us thought, "Hey, if this is really a survival course, and if we want to be realistic, we need to do whatever it takes to survive, even if it means breaking the rules." We planned a nighttime clandestine mission to slip into the instructors' compound and break into their mess hall. After all, that was what we'd do if we were behind enemy lines.

We drew straws to see who would go.

An hour later, we feasted on crackers and a five-pound canned ham.

The next day, we had more energy than most of the troops. We kind of felt bad that everyone couldn't have shared the ham with us, but if we'd told too many people, we would have gotten in trouble. We did share the ham with the airmen who were in our group. They seemed very appreciative.

On our third night, camp instructors made a stew out of one rabbit for a couple hundred people. It was basically just greasy water with small bits of rabbit meat, including the rabbit's head, eyes and internals floating around inside the huge pot.

Instructors offered everyone a cup. They asked for a volunteer who might be hungry enough to enjoy the rabbit's eyes. Surprisingly, several starved men raced to the pot for the delicacy. I suppose that was a lot better than eating bugs and lizards and sucking on cacti.

The guys in my group took one look at our sorry cups of soup and dumped them out on the ground. We already had a plan—another chow hall raid. Two different UDT guys were chosen to raid the instructor's mess hall. Their raid yielded canned Spam and cookies.

The fourth night, the camp cook discovered his canned ham was missing and notified the instructor staff. They set a trap. Unfortunately two frogmen were busted, kicked out of SERE school and sent packing back to Coronado. Back at the base the guys got some extra duty, but unofficially the UDT command was elated. This was the kind of stuff that separated the men from the boys, and we were the men.

RESISTANCE

After four days of wandering the desert learning survival techniques we began to anticipate the next event. This was the dreaded part of SERE—the prison of war camp.

We were set off on a compass course with orders to locate "Freedom Camp." No one ever makes it. It's a trap. As we traversed the sandy ground toward our destination, "enemy" instructors bore down on us from every direction, in trucks, in jeeps and on foot. We were captured, roughed up, then marched or trucked to a prison camp with high barbed-wire fences and watchtowers. It looked and felt authentic.

Our captors spoke in an accent, dressed in Communist garb and were mean. The prison PA system played loud strange music. After five days of our barely eating and being tired, the prison truly became one. We milled around the camp doing odd jobs. We were screamed at, and we were interrogated.

Instructors had informed us that if we escaped, we'd be rewarded with a sandwich. I was up for the challenge. *I'll never have a chance to play this game again*, I thought. I tried unsuccessfully to convince a bunch of guys to do a mass escape. "Hey, if we all escaped at once, going in different directions, they wouldn't have enough guards to catch all of us," I coaxed. "It would cause absolute chaos." No one accepted the challenge. I would have to have some fun on my own. *After all, this is just a game of sorts, and besides, there are no real bullets in those guns*, I mused.

For several long minutes, I covertly observed the guard on the north watchtower. Every so often he turned his head away from the compound. My heart was pounding. The next time he looked away, I made my move.

I bolted for the fence, dropped, and crawled under the mesh of twisted wire, ripping my shirt as I inched my way through to the other side.

A siren went off and machine guns blasted. I ran.

A horde of Red guards swiftly gave chase in jeeps and on foot.

I found a thicket of bushes and dove for cover.

Barking dogs, human voices and running feet closed in. It didn't take them long to find me.

I was taken into the interrogation building and assigned to a crazed, dangerous looking man who tore into me.

"You are American spy!" he ranted. "You kill our women and children!"

"My name is John Wolfram. I'm a Navy seaman. My serial number is B52-87-23."

He snarled. "You are not prisoner of war. Your government has not declared war on our peaceful country. You are war criminal, no protection by Geneva Convention. You tell me information about mission and I be good to you. If not, you have hell to pay. Where you come from? Where is unit?"

When I wouldn't give him any more than my name, rank and serial number, he slapped me hard across the face.

My veins pumped blood hot with rage. I said nothing. I did nothing.

He screamed and slapped me a few more times, pulled me outside, then forced me into a short, narrow box under the desert sun. I couldn't sit, stand or lie down. I had to squat. Time passed. My legs trembled in pain. One thin hole was cut into the box for me to breathe. It wasn't enough. I poured sweat from the hellish heat and started to think I was going to suffocate.

An hour or more later, I was dehydrated and weak. Someone approached, unbolted and threw open the door then dragged me out. The same man took me into another room and interrogated me some more. We had been taught that we didn't have to John Wayne it. But we were told that we should resist as much as we could. This time they gave me the waterboard treatment. I had more fight left than I expected. It didn't matter. Strapped to a board, my blood throbbed in my head and barrels of water struck my face. I tried to breathe but couldn't.

Afterward, I was led back to the general population.

I discovered later that one of my friends had gotten a tooth knocked out during his interrogation. The officers had it worse. There were a few regular Navy guys who broke under the pressure and started to cry. I heard that the senior-ranking officer of our group (who wasn't Special Forces) broke down like a baby. Not everyone was made to handle such stress.

ESCAPE

Then there was Forrest Harness. To him this was just cowboys and Indians. He probably broke the camp record for escapes. All we knew was he escaped so many times that he became friends with the instructors. They finally told him he couldn't have any more sandwiches, but if he promised not to escape anymore he could sit in a special room until the evolution was over.

Nonstop harassment continued through the night. We could hear the sounds of others being slapped around by screaming interrogators. Never had I experienced more respect for the men and women in our military who are captured by the enemy.

We looked at each other in the dark, each of us silently hoping this would all end soon.

"Air raid! AIR RAID!" the commandant screamed over the PA system.

Confusion erupted throughout the camp. We were told the camp was under attack.

All prisoners were herded to one corner of the grounds behind a dirt hill to take cover. Machine guns fired and noises and explosions of a battle surrounded us. Then it turned quiet.

At the flagpole near the far end of the compound, someone began hoisting a foreign-looking flag.

"You see? Your planes could not destroy us. We are still alive!" an enemy soldier screamed. "Stand up and honor our flag!"

They played what must have been their national anthem over the loudspeakers. We stared at the banner being hoisted, full of resentment and disgust.

Halfway up the pole, the flag stopped and headed back down again. Another flag was hoisted in its place.

When the loudspeaker released the first notes of "The Star Spangled Banner," we recognized our American flag.

Everyone including the guards snapped to attention and saluted.

Some teared at hearing our national anthem and seeing Old Glory.

We shook hands and slapped shoulders, overjoyed. SERE training was over. But more importantly, we were fiercely proud to be Americans.

UDTRA Class 44

Front Row (kneeling): First from left - Harnes, Wolfram; third from right - Bracken, Sparks. Second Row (standing): Fourth from left - Durlin; fourth from right - Gore. Third Row (standing): Fifth from left - Solano.

UDTRA Graduation 1968 / UDT -11

*John receiving his diploma
from the Admiral.*

Chapter Eleven: First Tour to Vietnam

I asked for it. When I volunteered for BUD/S, I knew the intense training wasn't just for a friendly football game. Yes, Vietnam was the main topic of the day, but at 8,000 miles away, it wasn't much of a threat. Even after SERE school, my nineteen-year-old mind didn't fully grasp the seriousness of what would follow.

Then they handed me an M-16. I knew I would be aiming it at other men. And they would be aiming their rifles at me.

I was a hippie at heart. Once, while growing up, my brother Gary and I took off with his BB gun and we went to a local park. He shot several robins in a tree, then encouraged me to shoot one. I took aim but missed on purpose. I didn't enjoy killing.

Though I valued life, BUD/S had trained me to be a warrior during combat situations. I was honored to serve my country, and I would defend my life and the lives of those beside me.

My Vietnam was unlike that of most who served there, because the Teams had six-month tours, not twelve. Since we were a specialty group, our assignments varied depending upon the particular needs of the Navy. Some of our Team members spent all six months in country, while others had assignments that were not Vietnam related. In 1968 I made my first West Pac tour, which included a stint in Nam. We headquartered out of the Philippines.

The Philippines was the perfect place logistically to base our operations. Subic Bay had a deepwater port ideal for the U.S. Navy to moor their huge ships. Vietnam was just a few short hours away by air, and the jungles and beaches of the Philippines provided an ideal environment to conduct training exercises.

My first tour in Nam was split between riding ARGs (Amphibious Ready Groups) like on the USS *Ogden*, a transport ship, and others, and actual combat duty in the Mekong Delta—the southern tip of (South) Vietnam—full of winding rivers and rice patties.

My first thought as I stepped down onto the tarmac in Vietnam was, "Ah, so this is hell." It was too hot and too miserable to be anything else. The air was foul—filled with rancid odors of who-knew-what. I gagged. The humidity was far worse than Fort Benning, Georgia in July—even worse than the Philippines. The heat threatened to stifle the life out of me.

While riding the ARGs, nine of us frogs led by Lt. (jg) Wes Chesser patrolled the coast of Nam, transporting troops and supplies. We provided security for the flotilla and were on standby for emergencies.

I took a liking to Wes. He was from Arlington, West Virginia, a good six feet tall, medium build, dark brown hair—the average GI Joe by appearances. His character was anything but average. He was good-natured, fun to be around—the guy you want with you when you're at war in Vietnam.

Another of the nine was Mike Mallory from Washington State—six-foot-two and as massive as a rock wall. Everyone literally looked up to him, around him, and often amiably ducked the camera he always held. Mike's love for photography would help to land him on the primary Apollo 11 recovery team along with Wes and me.

After eighteen weeks of BUD/S, Jump School, SERE School and advanced diving courses, riding ARGs was dull. Both detachments—Echo and Foxtrot—had the tedious job of being prepared for action, but rarely did we see any. We circled the coast of Nam, and waited, and then waited some more. This was a ready group. We frogs were ready. The Marines aboard were ready. The ship's crew was ready. But until orders came in for an operation, all we could do was wait. To be ready and never be called upon was frustrating. But someone needed to do it.

Unfortunately that *someone* included me.

The huge walls of ocean rolled the *Ogden* right then left, up then down, or a sickening combination of those directions. The constant pitch and roll had some new arrivals hanging over the rail hollering Eureka.

In time we would get used to it—we always did. Meanwhile those who needed time to adjust found an empty bucket to be very handy. Being housed in cramped quarters, one bunk on top of the other wasn't ideal, but doable. We'd soon adjust to that discomfort as well.

Being a Navy frogman did have its perks, even while enduring boring assignments like riding the ARGs. Besides getting in a good hour of PT each morning, Wes told the captain of each ship we were on that it was mandatory for us to get at least two hours of sun bathing each day to keep our skin tough. The captains bought it hook, line, and sinker. We sun bathed on the flight deck every afternoon. That didn't go over well with the rest of the ship's crew who were forced to carry on with their monotonous duties, especially when we brought out lawn chairs and beer coolers.

Another perk was conducting our weekly swims. The ships shut down their engines long enough for us to jump overboard and swim two miles. Different ARGs even provided a safety boat to follow us. A handful of frogs commandeering a whole ship was heady.

The Marines we transported were treated far worse. I watched without envy as their NCO hounded them like they were still in boot camp. They were screamed at, drilled, and made to strip and clean their weapons several times a day. I heard a couple of them cursing under their breath, threatening to take care of guys like him 'once' they got in the jungle.

To keep our double hazardous duty qualifications current, we dug out the C-4, detonation cord, blasting caps and set off charges from the fantail of the ship. After the ARGs traveled up the larger inlets to unload supplies and troops, we were called on to dive under the ships to check their hulls for mines.

That would normally be considered an easy job. However, the water was dark and overrun with flotsam. For all we knew, VC frogmen were swimming up beneath us. A few minutes into our first dive, a teammate I was paired with—who normally had more grit than industrial grade sandpaper—lost his nerve.

There was nothing anyone could do but leave our teammate alone. Fear had paralyzed him. That was exactly the kind of weak point our BUD/S instructors watched for during training. But you never knew how someone would react in each situation. Mallory went in his place.

Even I felt uneasy as I dove back into the murky water.

Something evil lives down there, I thought.

I compressed my fear of being blown up into a tiny ball in the back of my mind, and I ignored it. I kept hearing the words of my BUD/S instructors, "If you don't mind, then it don't matter."

Mike Mallory and I continued our underwater search for mines, feeling with our hands, inch by inch, from bow to stern of the huge underbelly of the ship since the water had practically zero visibility. We found none.

Eventually my teammate was able to overcome his fears and became an excellent operator.

I'm certainly not qualified to explain the complex mind of man, but I do know that it is vulnerable—fear has to be controlled. The mind can be an instrument for torment and defeat, or it can be used as a powerful tool. Fear has to be conquered. It is contagious.

One of the ARG ships we occupied docked at Da Nang to unload supplies. We looked forward to seeing our teammates who were stationed there. But the officer on deck refused to let us off the ship. "No one gets liberty while we are here, including you," he said. "Everyone is confined to the ship."

We were going stir-crazy and desperately needed to get off the ship, even if only for a few hours. Not ones to be told no, we contacted our Da Nang friends who found a boat to come pick us up. Again the officer on deck refused to let us disembark the ship. Honestly, I'm not quite sure what happened next. The lieutenant claimed he was tossed off the gangplank into the water below. I must have been looking the other way. We boarded the boat and headed to shore.

On the truck ride to the UDT-11 compound we passed a Navy shipyard. Our friends told us that the night before a sapper had blown a huge hole in the side of an LST (Landing Ship Tank). When we saw it, we could hardly believe it. Military police and hordes of Navy and Marine personnel surrounded the area. I was beginning to understand how Charley worked—he did his dirty deeds at night then ran for cover. Even a huge Navy and Marine base like Da Nang, full of soldiers and sailors, wasn't immune to the cunning of VC sappers.

I took in the sights. Vietnam was definitely Asian, but different from the Philippines. Maybe it was the intensity of the war, but the locals seemed more distant. Everywhere I looked, I saw military— ships, boats, trucks, jeeps, soldiers, sailors, gates, fences and weapons of every kind. Somebody here was serious about killing or being killed.

The truck ride—no air-conditioning, just hot humidity pushing the sweat across our faces—was my first encounter with the culture of Nam. I soaked up every detail. Little ladies gracefully balanced a long wooden stick across their shoulders with what seemed to be a tree full of bananas in two baskets hanging from the ends. They walked about in a rhythmic bounce. Motorbikes, bicycles and cyclos transported hordes of men and women up and down streets crammed full of people. Many walked. Little shops sparsely filled with staples such as rice, spices, herbs, fish, shrimp and chicken sat out in the open air. Rodents, roaches, bugs and flies competed with the locals for samples.

When we arrived at *Frogsville*—the name given to our Da Nang compound—we found a million-dollar complex complete with air-conditioning, hot showers, kitchen, bar and—luxury of luxuries— flush toilets. Detachment Delta frogs were in the process of converting two Quonset hut shells into an elaborate R & R center, a side project, while they went about doing other UDT business in the area. The frogs had just returned from removing an underwater I-beam the old-fashioned way—blowing it sky high with C-4. After the explosion they retrieved several huge sea bass floating on the surface. They kept one for themselves—it was a beauty—and donated the rest to an orphanage on their way back to Frogsville.

It was good to be off the ship and on land for a change, but the best part was joining our fellow teammates. Our Da Nang brothers introduced us to Tigre Biere, the local brand of booze. The next couple of days we shopped the Navy exchange, did odd jobs and played hours of volleyball on the white sand around the beach complex. A few of us dove on a sunken LST out in the harbor. R & R was fun while it lasted. But then it was back to the boring ARG.

Or so we thought.

Remember the lieutenant? He hadn't forgotten about us. He reported our insubordination toward him to the ship's captain and the bunch of us were called in for a *Captain's Mast* (a session with the captain of a naval ship where he hears and acts on the case of an enlisted man charged with committing an offense).

The lieutenant was furious. The captain sent him and the yeoman who was transcribing the proceedings out of his office. Come to find out, this captain was a former UDT guy who had been stationed on the East Coast of the United States years before.

"Okay, guys. I'm going to tell you this once. You can't be tossing officers into the ocean when they are following orders. I'm going to let you off the hook this time, but if you mess up again I'll have your hides. Understand?"

"Yes, sir!"

I always suspected he enjoyed a good chuckle after we left.

The second three months was a little more challenging. I became a part of Detachment Golf. I joined a Mobile Flotation Group in the Mekong Delta, where we patrolled hundreds of miles of winding rivers throughout Viet Cong-controlled areas from the Cambodian border to the far south of the Ca Mau Peninsula. Our new home was a barracks ship in the middle of the Bassac River. The carefree days of riding ARGs up and down the coast of Vietnam were over.

It didn't take long for things to liven up. The last time I'd been shot at was when my cousin Bobby and I raided a farmer's berry patch back home. The farmer's shotgun pellets had stung and bruised. The Viet Cong were trying to kill me. We were not in Wisconsin anymore.

The VC frequently launched surprise attacks against our river flotilla. Since the VC's modus operandi was ambush—hit and run—we never knew when their next attack would come—unnerving, to say the least. Suspicion became a living part of us. We were wary of every movement and every person. Never was I more thankful for my BUD/S instructors who trained us to keep calm even when our nerves were on edge.

I was also thankful for our forest-green flak gear—two-piece, fiberglass layered, supposedly bulletproof body armor. The jacket weighed a ton and was hot and sweaty—a small price to pay for protecting my heart and lungs. Helicopter pilots were known to sit on theirs to protect them from a dose of hot metal in their backsides. It also made a decent pillow at night.

Years before, the UDT and SEALs surveyed Vietnam beaches, and all the charts were up to date, so we moved inland. We now manned guns on boats and were assigned to any job that demanded diving, demolition, or salvaging personal effects off sunken vessels. On occasion, we patrolled with the ARVN (Army of the Republic of Vietnam) troops. Sometimes Navy brass just created things for us to do.

Then I was asked to change a Tango boat's screw (propeller), which I had never done before. What was more, the Tango (a dark green, blunt-nosed boat) had drifted backward into the wall of the dike and sat in six feet of mud. I am not the most mechanically gifted person, and this seemed impossible. Ahhh, a challenge! An EOD (Explosive, Ordinance, Disposal) chief volunteered to help, and in we went.

Within moments our *challenge* turned deadly. The waves of passing boats drove the Tango on top of us. We were literally entombed in thick mud.

It took forever to get that monster off of us and for our teammates to dig us out. If it weren't for the scuba gear I had on, and the tight grip on my mouthpiece with my teeth, I would have been a goner. I had never been more shaken. An hour or two later we completed our mission.

That evening the two of us dug mud out of our ears, still waiting to laugh it off.

In the Mekong Delta we came across vast areas of forest that appeared to have been burned, leaving the trees bare of any leaves. For miles all I could see was dark brown dirt and defoliated trees. It felt eerie, as if I were on another planet. Years later, I found out about Agent Orange, the deadly herbicide.

After unnerving days of waiting, we were ordered on a mission. We boarded the Tango with our M-16s, nine-millimeter side arms, grenade launchers and several boxes of ammo. The engines throbbed with the same discordant rhythm that wore on us all day long. Spewing a gray cloud of diesel exhaust, the boat left the dock and joined other boats in one long line. The Tango cut a foaming wake through the foul, cocoa-colored water.

The engines droned on through a convoluted maze of rivers and canals. Mile after mile of lush green jungle glided past, broken only by the occasional grass hooch, grazing water buffalo, passing sampan and drooping banana tree. Vietnam's Mekong Delta region was breathtaking—absolutely beautiful.

Eventually the engines slowed, and then idled. We came to a place of rice paddy dikes lined with palm trees and bamboo. I hurried topside to the helicopter landing pad to better take in the scenery. Wild parrots and other colorful birds sang and chattered, gliding from tree to tree.

Barefoot children from a nearby village gathered on the embankment fifteen yards off our port side yelling, "You numba one, GI. You numba one."

Wes lugged a case of C-rations to the landing pad and we started throwing the meals one at a time to the kids. Soon children appeared like swarms of pigeons at a park chasing birdseed. Other sailors joined in, and a throng of laughing kids got a pretty good lunch for the day—and several dozen sailors got to dole out happiness and feel like Mother Teresa.

We spent the night on the flight deck on top of our blown-up air mattresses slapping mosquitoes. Our only cover was a camouflaged poncho liner. The evening breeze was much better than the stuffy quarters below decks. We counted stars to fall asleep.

The next morning we were off on our caravan again. Traversing rivers with forty or fifty armor-plated Monitors, Zippos, Alpha and Tango boats was reassuring. We had enough firepower to win WWI—or at least that's how it felt to me. Days went by. Then one afternoon we passed a village and saw no children playing.

We exchanged looks, donned our flak jackets, and set our M-16s with several magazines nearby. I also placed an M-79 grenade launcher with several bandoleers of grenades within arm's reach.

It was painfully quiet as we stood rigidly at our positions. We scanned the jungle, waiting in anticipation. Adrenaline burned through my veins. I held my M-16 butt against my shoulder, ready to shoot.

The Tango's radio came alive. An excited voice reported movement to starboard.

Suddenly I heard the *whooosh* of several enemy B-40 rocket-propelled grenades, followed by a *boom!* as they hit some unlucky boat.

It was only a matter of time until the VC directed their rockets our way. The masses of incoming ordinance pounded my ears. Enemy bullets zinged and pinged all along our starboard side.

Our riverboats fired back with a vengeance—105-mm howitzers, 40-mm grenade-launching machine guns, 20-mm aircraft cannons, and .50- and .30-caliber machine guns shredded the tree line and foliage.

I let loose one clip after another until my gun barrel was flaming hot. I couldn't see if I was hitting anything, but it didn't matter. I was more concerned with putting a bullet next to every speck of dirt on the bank.

Then I grabbed my M-79 and launched grenade after grenade into the jungle. We pulverized the beach along a three-hundred-yard swath while we glided forward at five miles per hour.

Someone screamed, "Cease fire! Cease fire!" Two Cobra

helicopter gunships swooped down and showered deadly Mark-19 grenades, rockets and mini-gun fire onto the enemy positions from above. It was over.

Now all we frogs had to do was wait for damage reports and be ready to be called on to dive down to any sunken boats, or worse, to retrieve a dead body. Fortunately today there were neither.

As the choppers disappeared over the tree line, I heard the order to "Insert troops." The forward ramps fell to the ground, and a dozen ARVN troops walked into the thick brush.

The South Vietnamese troops were young. I read where some twelve-year-olds were in uniform. I often wondered how the South Vietnamese felt fighting their fellow countrymen. Those I worked with never seemed to be overly motivated or gung-ho. The ARVN troops were a unique bunch. Many were forced into the army for indefinite periods, sometimes with a deadly lack of training and battlefield preparation. Before the war was over, more than 250,000 ARVN troops would be dead, and well over a million wounded.

The Vietnamese disciplined their soldiers differently than Americans. A couple of days before, I had set my M-16 up against one of the walls of a Tango boat while talking with a team member. When I picked up my rifle to move to another location, I noticed the barrel had been switched. This one was dented and rusted. My senior officer, Wes Chesser, confronted the Vietnamese officer about our suspicion that one of his soldiers had replaced my barrel with his. A quick inspection of all M-16 rifles found the culprit.

The Vietnamese officer ordered the Tango docked, then ordered his troops off the boat. They made a huge circle. The thief was thrust into the center. With his walking stick, the officer flogged the young soldier. I assumed this was partially done for our benefit, but it also served as a warning to the others: if they got caught stealing, this was what would happen. The key word was "caught." I believe if I had not discovered the switch, the young soldier would have been commended for his cunning.

Riding ARGs we got plenty of showers and clean sheets and clothes. But riding with the Riverine forces for days on end had left us all smelling like rotting eggs. Now, having sweat through a tense skirmish, we were worse, and there was no place to shower or take a bath except the river. Flesh-eating bacteria, microbes and sea snakes didn't make the muddy waters inviting. We didn't bring a change of clothes along, as we didn't have lockers or a storage place for a lot of excess gear. The only thing we could do was pray for rain.

Thankfully, a miracle. At first it was a low rumble off in the distance. Then a welcome thunderhead approached, dropping warm beads onto our line of boats. Then a downpour so thick we could hardly see our hands in front of our faces. Clothes were thrown off, bars of soap appeared, and a couple hundred naked men boogied in the rain.

It felt great sluicing off all the mud, crud and filth that had accumulated during long, anxious days filled with suspense, disgust and anger. In some ways it was symbolic. I would have equally welcomed the chance to wash off the frustration and millions of questions that dogged my mind while I tried to understand what this mad world had come to.

~

Christmas without being surrounded by family just wasn't the same. This was my first one away from home, and my first ever without a yard full of white snow. My mother sent me a care package full of homemade fudge and chocolate-chip cookies. It didn't matter that it took three weeks to reach me, that the fudge had turned semi-white, and it was no longer soft and chewy. Nor did it matter that the cookies were hard and stale. My friends and I gulped them down with Christmas cheer.

A Navy chaplain flew in from Saigon by helicopter and conducted a church service for whoever wanted to attend on the flight deck of the barracks ship. It had been a long while since I had attended any church, so I hugged up to a horde of others in order to hear what the preacher had to say. He was soft-spoken and read the Christmas story from Luke 2:8-14. Once again I learned about the One who came to this earth to bring peace. As he read his text, I listened intently.

"'And there were shepherds living out in the fields nearby,

keeping watch over their flocks at night. An angel of the Lord appeared to them, and the glory of the Lord shone around them, and they were terrified. But the angel said to them, 'Do not be afraid. I bring you good news of great joy that will be for all the people. Today in the town of David a Savior has been born to you; he is Christ the Lord. This will be a sign to you: You will find a baby wrapped in cloths and lying in a manger.' Suddenly a great company of the heavenly host appeared with the angel, praising God and saying, 'Glory to God in the highest, and on earth peace to men on whom his favor rests.'"

Peace? That word sounded so surreal in the context of this strange war. The country of Vietnam was supposedly observing a Christmas truce. I never could figure out if governments could formulate a ceasefire for a holiday, why couldn't they just end a war? I was still getting used to the idea that people were killing people. I wasn't the brightest student in class, but it seemed to me the world needed help.

I was young, impressionable but mostly lonely. I was serving my country 8,000 miles from home. As much as I didn't want to admit it, I was homesick for the things that made me feel secure. It was Christmas Eve, after all, and I missed being with those I loved, the familiar surroundings, the Main Street Christmas lights, carolers, the manger scene in front of the churches and my high school buddies who were waiting for my return. *I should be home surrounded by the people who care about me and who I care for*, I thought. As I was leaving the church service and heading down the ramp to our hooch, I passed a sailor whose radio was tuned to the Armed Forces Radio and Jackie DeShannon was singing a seemingly odd, but appropriate song for this bizarre setting, "What the world needs now, is love, sweet love..."

A few of us ended up sitting out on the pontoon gazing up into the night sky, taking in the Christmas carols playing on my Sanyo radio. A blackout order was in effect, so the sky popped with trillions of blinking stars above us. We admired their beauty and discussed the birth of Christ and what Christmas meant to us. In the midst of war, it was a perfect night. It was about to get even better.

Suddenly the Christmas carol we were listening to was

interrupted for a live feed from Apollo 8 astronauts who were circling the moon:

William Anders: "We are now approaching lunar sunrise and, for all the people on Earth, the crew of Apollo 8 has a message we would like to send to you.

"'In the beginning God created the heaven and the earth. And the earth was without form, and void; and darkness was upon the face of the deep. And the Spirit of God moved upon the face of the waters. And God said, Let there be light: and there was light. And God saw the light, that it was good: and God divided the light from the darkness.'"

Jim Lovell: "'And God called the light Day, and the darkness he called Night. And the evening and the morning were the first day. And God said, Let there be a firmament in the midst of the waters, and let it divide the waters from the waters. And God made the firmament, and divided the waters which were under the firmament from the waters which were above the firmament: and it was so. And God called the firmament Heaven. And the evening and the morning were the second day.'"

Frank Borman: "'And God said, let the waters under the heavens be gathered together unto one place, and let the dry land appear: and it was so. And God called the dry land Earth; and the gathering together of the waters called he Seas: and God saw that it was good.'

"And from the crew of Apollo 8, we close with good night, good luck, a Merry Christmas, and God bless all of you—all of you on the good Earth."

First Vietnam Tour - 1968

DET Echo

Da Nang Vietnam - John, third from left

John aboard helicopter   *Riverboats, Mekong Delta*

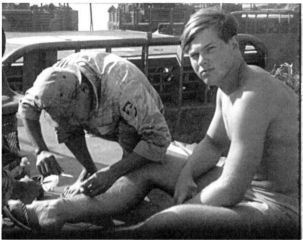

John, receiving first aid after diving on a sunken boat.

Demolition Loading

Mekong Delta

Mekong Delta - Riverboat

John, leaving for Saigon

—Chapter Twelve—

Apollo

My Vietnam tour ended and I arrived back in California. I learned UDT/SEAL volunteers were needed for a special mission: to recover the astronauts and command modules of Apollo 10 and Apollo 11 from the sea. The command modules would splash down less than two months apart—Apollo 10 on May 26, and Apollo 11 on July 24, 1969. The Apollo 11 mission: To walk on the moon.

I immediately volunteered.

Twelve frogmen were needed. There would be a primary recovery team, chosen during the training process, along with two complete backup teams. Since the whole world would be watching, the U.S. Navy didn't want to make any mistakes or come up short.

Each volunteer was given the opportunity to earn a coveted spot on the primary team. We competed against one another, as certain skills were required for each job. One of these jobs demanded a fast swimmer who would jump from a helicopter into the ocean, swim to the wind- and wave-tossed capsule, and attach a sea anchor to secure it. Though I posted the fastest swim times during tryouts, a guy named Louie Boisvert, who was an E-6 rank to my E-3, was awarded a spot on the primary Apollo 10 recovery team. He had been around a long time and had earned his dues. Louie had participated in the last Gemini space recovery as well as two other Apollo space shots.

I would serve on one of two backup teams in place to assist the primary team. We were the guys who would make sure the space capsule didn't sink to the bottom of the ocean and lose its precious cargo—chiefly, the astronauts. The recovery of the Apollo 10 capsule and crew was a success.

It had been over a year since I took a leave. I surprised my mother by walking in on her while she was napping on the sofa. She awakened but her legs were still asleep. "John!" She crawled to me on her hands and knees. I was even happier to see her.

Another reason I went home was to attend the funeral of Larry Smith. He and I had been close friends through the years. We'd been on the same basketball team in grade school, played drums in band and ran track together throughout high school.

When we were kids, Larry and I made a daily summer trek to Cambridge—a good ten miles from Fort—to enjoy the lake. His mother dropped us off at the edge of town and we'd stick out our thumb and have a ride in no time. Once a car stopped, and I quickly jumped in the front seat, and Larry followed. After a mile or so I felt a sharp jab to my right side. It was Larry. His eyes were as big as saucers. He was as animated as he could be without speaking, and he was pointing in the direction of the driver. I looked to my left and discovered our host was stark naked! We laughed over that for years.

And now Larry, another friend, was gone. I couldn't believe it. Like Terry Beck, Larry's funeral was a closed casket—I heard he arrived in pieces. I visited his grief-stricken parents and they gave me a picture of him that had been taken in Nam. He was in country the same time I was, but we were at least seven hundred miles apart. We corresponded, but were never able to get together.

Then another shock: I received a phone call from a buddy in San Diego. My Coronado housemate, Bill Threet, an Apollo 10 team member, was killed on Memorial Day while out riding his motorcycle. My return to Coronado was depressing.

After the Apollo 10 recovery, while the nation became caught up in the moonwalk hysteria leading up to the Apollo 11 launch, twelve of us Navy frogmen again underwent extensive training on the Naval Amphibious Base, Coronado. Several men were new to the Apollo project, but a few had been trained for Apollo 10. As before, there would be a primary team, along with two complete backup teams.

I had experience as backup for the Apollo 10 space shot, and again posted the fastest swim times during tryouts.

I earned the coveted place on the primary pickup team.

When I was nine, Bill, my swim instructor encouraged me to join the swim team. He had no idea what wheels his encouragement would set into motion, and the thrill of a lifetime that it would bring. God bless all Bills.

The Navy had made sure we could do our jobs backward and forward. Houston Space Center provided us a boilerplate (a mock-up that resembled the actual space module) to rehearse with. We honed our skills by going through the recovery process dozens of times, step by step, which included jumping out of a low-flying helicopter, attaching the sea anchor and collar, and maintaining all equipment before securing for the day. This also provided the helicopter pilots and their crews a time to train.

During classroom sessions we learned procedures for all possible scenarios, and were briefed on safety hazards such as locations on the space capsule that housed explosives to deploy the parachutes and flotation bags. The twelve of us also discussed how to improve our performance, save time and best work together as a team.

What we dreaded most in each training evolution was the tedium of maintaining the equipment. Cleaning, drying and repacking the flotation collar and sea anchors were boring jobs, but important. If not packed precisely, the accordion-folded rubber collar wouldn't fit into the carrying bag for smooth transport from the helicopter down to the command module. A poorly packed or improperly folded sea anchor could become useless once in the water, and the command module—and those in it—could potentially be lost.

While we trained, various military, civilian, and NASA personnel likewise drilled. Since the success of all space missions depends on cohesive teamwork between all participating affiliates, numerous conferences took place in many locations with the goal of successfully recovering the space module and astronauts. Representatives from NASA, NELC, GE, Western Union, Affiliated Press, ABC, the *Hornet* and capsule recovery teams had to blend their individual skills and contributions into a very complex operation in which they were highly dependent upon each other.

MEET THE FROGS

The group of twelve frogs who volunteered for Apollo 11 was an assortment of men from both UDT-11 and UDT-12. Four of us—Lieutenant (jg) Wes Chesser, 3rd Class Mike Mallory, 2nd Class Mike Bennett and I—were the only holdovers from the Apollo 10 recovery. Wes Chesser, Mike Mallory and I made up the primary capsule recovery team, designated Swim 2.

Bennett was a seasoned sailor with some years under his belt. He was one of the few guys who had a full chest tattoo—an American eagle, kind of fitting since the lunar landing craft was called the *Eagle*. Bennett would be the backup BIG swimmer.

Wes Chesser and I had spent six months together in Vietnam and developed a mutual respect that only comes about by being in combat. Wes went through OCS (Officer Candidate School) in Newport, Rhode Island. Most of his friends in OCS wanted to drive ships—mostly destroyers—because that was supposed to be a good career move. But that didn't impress Wes. He thought UDT would be more "fun" than the fleet and went to Coronado, California for a screen test. Wes willingly admitted he wasn't in the best of shape when he arrived, but he was determined. Fortunately, he got there early enough for several weeks of pre-training before Class 40 commenced, and courageously pushed through to graduation. Wes was the senior officer among the three swim teams, and second in command. He had been one of the primary rescuers of Apollo 10.

Mike Mallory, if you recall, was a six-foot-two rock wall and had a deep baritone voice. He spent three months with me riding ARGs in Vietnam. Like so many of us, Mike decided to join the Navy instead of being drafted. While talking with a Navy recruiter, he was shown a pamphlet about UDT. He was hooked. Mike was a skinny kid going in, but BUD/S training put forty extra pounds on him. When he went home after graduating from Class 39 his mother hardly recognized him. Mike had been transformed into a Johnny Weissmuller, Tarzan-like guy. He was a powerful swimmer and a good long-distance runner.

Mike, like Wes, had been one of the primary rescuers of Apollo 10.

Lieutenant Clancy Hatleberg would be the senior officer in charge of the entire group of us UDT frogmen. During World War II, Clancy's father joined the U.S. Marines and served his country as a doctor, saving many lives. He served in Iwo Jima at a field hospital and patched up scores of wounded Marines. Clancy wanted to be a Navy pilot but failed his eye exam. While paging through his father's military yearbooks, he saw a photo of a frogman on one of the beaches. Impressed and intrigued by the kind of work frogmen did, he volunteered for UDT and graduated with Class 39 alongside Mike Mallory. Clancy would serve his country for twenty years and retire in 1985 as a commander. During his illustrious career he would also serve as captain of UDT-11 from 1979-1981.

ABOARD THE HISTORIC USS *HORNET*

When the *Hornet* arrived at Pearl Harbor, Hawaii, the MQF (Mobile Quarantine Facility) was carefully loaded aboard. It would isolate the astronauts once they returned. The MQF was a modified thirty-five-foot long, eight-foot-seven-inch tall commercial Airstream travel trailer, a self-contained, germ-proof facility built to assure the general public that they wouldn't be contaminated by any microbes (moon germs) brought back from the lunar surface. Once the astronauts arrived, NASA physician Dr. Bill Carpentier and engineer John Hirasaki would join the three inside the *MQF* to provide medical attention and conduct tests.

As the time for the blastoff grew closer, a commercial jet flew us to Hawaii to board the *Hornet*. Boarding her was a great honor. The *Hornet* served our country during World War II and was credited with destroying 1,410 Japanese aircraft. She came under attack fifty-nine times, yet was never hit. She spent sixteen continuous months in the forward areas of the Pacific combat zone and became one of the most highly decorated ships in the Navy. The pilots that served aboard the *Hornet* were some of the best in the Navy, downing seventy-two enemy aircraft in one day, and 255 in one month. Ten *Hornet* pilots attained Ace in a Day status. The *Hornet's* creed was "A Heritage of

Excellence."

While aboard ship, everyone continued to rehearse his jobs. We frogs assumed the role of the astronauts to allow helicopter crews to practice hoisting us up in the one-man Billy-Pugh nets. Boatswains honed their skills retrieving the bobbing capsule from the ocean. Radiomen fine-tuned their communication equipment, and quartermasters practiced their navigation skills.

When we felt we could do our jobs expertly, the ship returned to Hawaii for a little R & R before the actual recovery. The Navy put us up at the Reef Tower Hotel on Waikiki Beach in Honolulu.

R & R TURNS DEADLY

Being in the Navy had great benefits—big toys, fascinating people, incredible experiences. At twenty-one, I had already been to Vietnam and enjoyed a West PAC tour which included visits to Hong Kong, Tokyo, Okinawa and the Philippines. And now, a luxury vacation in Hawaii. Ever since I could remember I longed to see what life was like outside of Fort Atkinson, Wisconsin. My boyhood dreams had become reality.

The ship docked at Pearl Harbor. We listened to our radios for events to amuse ourselves. We heard it at the same time: the surf was up. Sandy Beach had massive fifteen- to twenty-foot waves. Outside was a bright sunny day. We determined to conquer the waves.

Mallory, Bennett, Via, Free, a couple of others and I checked into our hotel, rented a car and headed to Sandy Beach. The waves were the biggest we had ever laid eyes on. We knew this beach could be treacherous for body surfers due its gradient, especially for novices like us. When a wave broke, it rapidly sucked most of the water back. However, we were powerful swimmers in top-notch shape.

Bennett's grin practically dared me. "What do you think, John? Should we see what big waves feel like?" We were used to the waves around the UDT compound on the Silver Strand. There, eight- to ten-foot waves were huge. These were gigantic!

"Hooyah!" I said. "We may never have another chance like this. Let's go!"

The day was going well. Then someone came up with the idea of playing chicken—seeing who could ride a wave the longest without pulling out. The potential danger was falling off the wave as it broke. Up to this point, we had been playing it safe by getting a good ride and then pulling out before the crash.

We all caught the next huge wave at nearly the same time and were immediately hurtled toward the beach at breakneck speed. It's an amazing perspective on top of a twenty-footer—you look at the beach below as you rapidly approach, frightfully aware of the distance to the bottom of the wave if you fall.

Then it happened. The wave broke suddenly. I plunged headfirst through the air and landed into two feet of water. Several tons of water crashed down, knocking the wind out of me, pinning me to the bottom for a minute or more. Before I could get a breath, the suction pulled me out to sea.

My lungs felt like they were going to burst. I struggled through the foam and was able to grab a small bite of air just as the next big wave buried me.

With my head above water again, I fought the pull of the first two sets of waves, but the third and fourth left me exhausted. The lack of oxygen caused my arms and legs to go weak, and it dawned on me that I could be drowning.

I noticed a lifeguard at the water's edge, watching me struggle. He stood ready to assist, but played it safe by only observing my plight. I surmised he was weighing out the risk of jumping into the rip current to help me or waiting to see if I could save myself.

"Hey, coach," I screamed, "Cordele is drowning!" We were in gym class swimming laps when I saw a twitching body beneath the water. Cordele had epileptic seizures. This one had taken him to the bottom of the pool. I was nearest. "I'll get him!" I dove under the water, grabbed hold of him and pulled him to the edge of the pool. He was still convulsing. I used the techniques I learned getting my Life Saver Merit Badge in Boy Scouts and rolled him out of the water onto the pool wall. "Hurry, coach. I don't know how much water he swallowed." As the coach hurried around the pool, I placed Cordele on his stomach, positioned his arms, pushed down hard on his upper back, then pulled his arms back toward me. Water came out of his mouth. When the coach arrived we felt Cordele needed mouth-to-mouth because he wasn't breathing. Since he was still in full seizure, I let Coach do the drill. Water gushed out of Cordele's throat and he started to breathe.

Now it was me who needed saving. The brute force of the monstrous waves and rip were much stronger than I was. *Is this how it feels just before someone dies?* I thought.

A dozen scenes flashed through my mind. I was a little boy in Sunday school where the teacher was telling me about Jesus. A semitruck was coming at me fast. Smoke from burning leaves filled my nostrils. My mother was holding me in her arms.

It was called Sandy Beach for a reason—it was sandy. When I dug my fingers into the beach bottom, there was nothing to grab onto to stop me from being pulled back out to sea to be crushed by the next huge wave. My fingers dug frantically, searching for a hold. Again, nothing. My strength was drained, my muscles powerless. I imagined the headline in the morning paper. "Apollo Rescue Swimmer Drowns While Body Surfing."

I wondered if I would be able to handle another big wave. Suddenly my fingers caught hold of a large rock protruding from the receding sand. It appeared from nowhere. I held to it against the suction of the rip and foam. I gulped air before the next wash of white water hit me. With fresh air in my lungs I was able to kick, pull and glide until I was in shallow enough water to stand and wobble to shore where I collapsed from exhaustion.

I knew I had come close to drowning, but I quickly pushed the thought from my mind. The lifeguard asked me if I was okay, then commended me for putting up such a good fight.

I gradually got my strength back, sat up and stared at the ocean. I needed to face my fears and conquer those huge waves once more or they would always intimidate me.

My teammates looked on with concern from beyond the breakers. I headed back out into the ocean, dove under another set of twenty-foot waves until I made it past the breakers and joined my teammates.

"Man, John, we thought we lost you there. You were in that foam a long time."

My respect for the sea had multiplied. I would never underestimate its power again.

Oddly, a song kept going over and over in my mind, one I sang in church as a kid. It was called "On Christ the Solid Rock I Stand."

My hope is built on nothing less
Than Jesus' blood and righteousness;
I dare not trust the sweetest frame
But wholly lean on Jesus' name.

When darkness veils his lovely face,
I rest on his unchanging grace;
In every high and stormy gale
My anchor holds within the veil.

On Christ, the solid Rock, I stand;
All other ground is sinking sand.

CAPE CANAVERAL LAUNCH

The imminent blastoff mesmerized the world. Endless editorials, interviews, documentaries, updates and specials by the media built a fury of excitement around the Apollo 11 launch. Everyone caught the fever. The overwhelming media coverage generated a contagious groundswell of attention long before the day of liftoff arrived.

America invaded Cape Kennedy. People from all walks of life used every means of transportation to get there. Motels were booked, the airports jammed and flight schedules were full. Campers, trailers, buses, and homemade sleeper trucks all packed into the few square miles surrounding the launch site. For shopping malls and restaurants in the area, business boomed. Beer and soda vendors could hardly keep their goods in stock. By the time the official countdown began, nearly one million Americans were on hand to witness the historical event live.

U.S. embassies around the world set up televisions so people could watch. In Columbia, the government provided televisions in public squares for students to see. Soccer games were called off in countries where soccer was king. Japan sold models of the Apollo 11 in its stores.

On the morning of the launch, people gathered in every conceivable place that had unobstructed views of the site. Much of the area surrounding the launch site was mosquito-infested swamp, but that didn't stop people from gathering in mass. From some viewpoints, the Saturn V rocket and Apollo 11 could be seen as far as eleven miles away. At thousands of homemade campsites, families and friends huddled around campfires roasting hot dogs, grilling hamburgers and steaks, taking advantage of their summer vacations to witness history. People were tuning their radios to hear the countdown, and every American boy with an imagination was dreaming about being strapped in the space module. Grandmas and grandpas fanned themselves as they sat in their aluminum-pipe, plastic-webbed folding chairs, staring off into the distance with a look of disbelief. For those who had been born before the turn of the twentieth century, this seemed like a fairy tale.

The Saturn V was the height of a football field set on its end—as tall as a thirty-six-story building—and thirty-three feet in diameter at its base. It had 5.6 million pounds of fuel inside, and it would take the equivalent of 30,000 strong men to raise it one inch. With all the high explosives inside, it was, in effect, a huge bomb. The power of the explosion would be a force akin to one million pounds of TNT. That could be compared to a World War II bombing raid with a thousand planes each carrying a thousand-pound bomb.

All eyes were fused toward the launch site. No one was going to miss history being made.

Among the crowd was former President Lyndon Johnson, Vice President Spiro Agnew, members of congress, movie stars and a horde of other national and international celebrities.

Jack King's voice rang out: "Forty seconds...thirty...five, four, three, two, one. We have ignition." At that moment, there was a great storm of burning fuel. Orange and red flames thundered inside gray-black smoke, bellowing out of the rocket while 50,000 gallons of water a minute sprayed the rocket. For almost nine seconds, the rockets strained as the Saturn engines built up a thrust more powerful than 92,000 locomotives.

Steel restraining arms held the rocket in place for those last few seconds while a computer system made sure all the engines fired correctly. Nearly eight million pounds of locomotives was needed to get the moon ship off the ground.

At the moment of liftoff, the rocket burned up as much oxygen as is consumed by half a billion people taking a breath at the same time, enough air for twice the population of America. Gulping fifteen tons of fuel per second, the 363-foot rocket lifted off the pad.

Again the voice of Jack King rang out: "We have a liftoff!" For one brief moment, three billion people worldwide were in that spaceship as it lifted off.

Two million eyes strained to gaze through the heat haze to get a glimpse of the monster rocket that appeared to be leaving the ground in empty silence. Gigantic streams of brilliant reds and oranges shot downward as the rocket struggled to overcome Earth's gravity.

Seconds later the noise hit them. At first it sounded like a far off train, then rose to the intensity of the cascading waters of Niagara Falls, to the flapping wings of a thousand pelicans exiting a pond all at the same time. As the thunder rolled toward them, the ground beneath them vibrated and shook. Finally they were struck by a noise as intense as a sonic boom.

Photographers wrestled themselves up wire fences and wedged their bodies into position for one good shot. Some climbed on one another's backs in the hope of getting the best angle as the rocket shot into the sky.

Meanwhile, the three astronauts, firmly strapped to their contoured couches, were hoping that the engineers and scientists had done their homework. There was not much they could do but brace for the powerful thrust of five F1 engines as the surge of power knocked them first to the right, then to the left, as the Saturn 5 rocket strained upward. Less than a minute later they were being hurled through space faster than the speed of sound.

For eight solid days, three men in spacesuits held the world captive. Front-page headlines hogged the news as the media relentlessly covered every step of the journey. Not that the public complained. They had become as addicted as a druggie who craves his daily fix.

Those of us aboard ship were forced to listen to shortwave radios and nibble on tidbits from the *Voice of America* and the *BBC*. Since the *Hornet's* general population had no satellite TV or access to the local newspapers, we depended solely upon our daily briefings for updates.

During mail call, someone would receive his *Newsweek* or *Time Magazine*, or a family member sent a copy of the local newspaper, but old news was about as tasty as stale bread. The captain announced major events over the intercom. We missed not being able to have immediate access to all the hysteria and the gratification of seeing the first moonwalk, but we wouldn't have traded being on the recovery ship and being an integral part of the astronauts' recovery for all the newspapers and televisions in the world. Plus, we were occasionally invited to sit in on briefings that only a handful of special people were able to attend.

MOON LANDING

The Nielsen rating experts estimated that 29,410,000 American households watched the moon landing on their TVs, and millions of households stayed up to watch part of the moonwalk. It was calculated in Japan that as many as seventy million of Japan's one hundred million people watched the lunar landing. Newscasters commented that the older generation was getting more of a thrill out of the landing than the youth. The youth, they explained, were brought up with astronauts and space, while the older population remembered it as just a dream.

Few outside Houston's control room knew that the moon landing almost ended in disaster. With about one thousand feet to go, Armstrong realized that the lunar module's guidance computer was steering the ship toward a field of boulders. Armstrong took manual control of the *Eagle*, and with only thirty seconds of fuel left, found a place to land. Neil Armstrong's heart rate during the powered descent to the lunar surface at the time of the burn was 110. At touchdown, his heartbeat jumped to 156 before edging down to the 90s.

After being on the moon for two and a half hours, but before anyone actually walked on the moon's surface, Buzz Aldrin took a few moments to himself and observed Holy Communion. He would later say, "I offered some private prayers, but I found later that thoughts and feelings came into my memory rather than words. I was not so mindful as to include my family, or so spacious as to include the fate of the world. I was thinking more about our particular task, and the challenge, and the opportunity that had been given to me. It was my hope that people would keep this whole event in their minds and see, beyond minor details and technical achievements, a deeper meaning behind it all, a challenge, a quest, the human need to do these things;" (*First On the Moon, A Voyage with Neil Armstrong, Michael Collins, [and] Edwin E. Aldrin, Jr.*, by Neil Armstrong, Michael Collins, Edwin Eugene Aldrin, Gene Farmer, and Dora Jane Hamblin, Little, Brown and Company, © 1970, page 300).

At 9:56 p.m. Houston time, Neil Armstrong stepped out of the dish-shaped landing pad and onto the surface of the moon. The words he spoke were immortalized in time: "That's one small step for [a] man, one giant leap for mankind."

Armstrong's 9 ½ medium boots only sank a fraction of an inch, dispelling the once widely held theory that the windless surface of the moon was overlaid with a dangerously deep coating of dust. Nineteen minutes later, Buzz Aldrin was walking alongside Armstrong.

During the same day at Arlington National Cemetery, a bunch of flowers appeared on John F. Kennedy's grave. An accompanying note read, "Mr. President, the *Eagle* has landed."

Approximately 500 million people worldwide watched the televised moonwalk. Unfortunately, an estimated 800 million Chinese, North Koreans, North Vietnamese, and Albanians never got a chance to see the moon landing. Their governments deliberately blocked out all news concerning the historical space first. Having no television in South Africa didn't stop twenty businessmen. They boarded a plane and flew to London just so they could watch the moonwalk. And for only the cost of a beer, patrons in a classy beer establishment in downtown Tokyo were able to peer through one of four high-powered telescopes the management installed, with the helpful assistance of a professional astronomer.

A Russian moon probe, Luna 15, landed 100 miles from Apollo 11's lunar module the day after the moonwalk, in a Russian attempt to acquire moon rocks for a return to earth before the Apollo 11 astronauts. But the probe crash-landed into the surface of the moon at 300 miles per hour, and the Russian attempt to beat the Americans failed.

THUNDERSTORMS AT THE SPLASHDOWN SITE

Splashdowns are highly dependent upon good weather conditions, and the weather had been acceptable until Tuesday, July 22, when the *Hornet's* radarscopes picked up a number of thunderstorms. On Wednesday the situation grew worse. The forecast for the splashdown showed that the module would land amid scattered showers in winds up to fifteen knots (seventeen mph) on one- to three-foot waves and five-foot swells.

In a quick decision on the eve of reentry, Houston's Mission Control changed the splashdown site. Now splashdown would be 250 miles from where the USS *Hornet* was positioned Wednesday afternoon, 950 miles southwest of Hawaii. Turbulence and thunderstorms at the original landing site could have caused structural damage to the spacecraft. However, the weather forecast for the new splashdown site wasn't much brighter for us frogmen. No rain was expected, but the winds were sixteen- to twenty-four knots (eighteen- to twenty-eight mph) with potential swells nearly as high as a man, making the seas notably rougher.

The 250 miles wasn't a problem for the aircraft carrier *Hornet* which could travel at a speed of thirty-three knots (thirty-eight mph), and everything could still be coordinated with the other communications ship. The President of the United States would still be flown in.

Bottom line, everyone could tolerate the last-minute shift, but up to this point we had never rehearsed in seas as high as the one forecast.

Though we'd practiced rescuing the command module and astronauts until we could do it blindfolded, we didn't want any mistakes. High swells would complicate everyone's job. We would be thrown around in our rafts—a greater challenge in getting the astronauts out of the module and into a helicopter. The boisterous seas would hamper the entire water sequence.

While NASA officials were worrying about the weather, the astronauts were busy preparing the spacecraft for a return to earth. Mike Collins grabbed a manual and meticulously reviewed flight procedures for the delicate task of reentry. Armstrong and Aldrin carefully removed forty-seven pounds of rock samples from the lunar excursion module (LEM), the *Eagle*, to stow in the command module.

JULY 24, 1969

At last! After staring at the bunk above me most of the night, my alarm clock sounded. I fumbled around in the dark, found the 'off' button, and reached for the light—2:00 a.m. I don't think I slept. I doubt my teammates who were sharing this once-in-a-lifetime event with me did either. The moment had finally arrived. This was no drill. It was the real thing. It was July 24, 1969, and the astronauts were just minutes away from splashdown.

Hours earlier I had been surrounded by dignitaries who

attended our final briefing—the ship's captain, senior officers, NASA officials, helicopter pilots and crews, fellow UDT swimmers, and news reporters and photographers. As a twenty-year-old seaman, I was awed to be included in this gathering of seasoned military personnel and scientists. When I graduated from high school two years earlier, it had never crossed my mind that I would be a player in something as monumental as the Apollo 11 rescue. I was *ecstatic*!

"Well, Joe?" I swung my legs over the side of the bunk. "We've trained hard for this. We're in the best shape of our lives. We can handle this." I felt invincible.

Joe Via shot a cocky grin at me. "We've been through Hell Week. Nothing can be as hard as that. Unless the landing site is in the middle of a typhoon, we'll be up for the challenge."

I agreed and jumped down from the middle rack I occupied in our stuffy, barely cooled compartment in the *Hornet*. Our barracks had housed troops being transported to the front lines during World War II, but today they were claimed by a handful of elite members of the United States Navy's Underwater Demolition Teams 11 and 12.

Around us others hurriedly shaved, showered and prepared for the day.

"This is it, John. This is what we've been waiting for," said a smiling Mike Mallory, the second team member of our designated trio, Swim 2.

I grimaced. "I just hope I don't jump into a bunch of sharks."

When we drilled two days earlier, sharks swarmed around us, and one rubbed against my wetsuit. I yelled to the others, "Sharks! Get into the rafts, quick!" Everyone scurried for safety, as sharks are unpredictable.

The media picked up on our dilemma and printed a story that went out over the AP. "NASA officials and swimmers say they've never encountered as many sharks in the area of any previous space shot recoveries."

I was quoted as saying, "The sharks watch us. We watch them.

They've been nibbling away at our gear all week." It's comical how journalists could make us look like idiots. Helicopter crews saw the sharks too. Night ops were the worst. Chopper lights shining down on us attracted the pests. But lately they were drawn to our daylight practices as well. One shark had bitten off a piece of the Styrofoam surrounding the base of the Billy-Pugh net, and another had taken a piece of the sea anchor.

I had to jump into the water first—and alone. I didn't want to be shark bait, but my job was to secure the capsule. That came first. I told myself not to worry about the sharks.

With a resonant, thunder-like sound, the *Eagle* was jettisoned into space while the command module pilot fired small thrusters to carefully maneuver away. The astronauts took a quick gaze through their windows, bidding the *Eagle* farewell. The *Eagle* was left to orbit in the darkness of space while Houston watched its systems slowly fade. The crew took their last photo then stowed the cameras and film.

As the astronauts began reentry procedures, they each swallowed a motion-sickness pill. (Collins later wrote that he feared becoming seasick and vomiting in the isolation garment since it could have created serious complications like choking or breaching the strict germ barrier.) Aldrin carefully marked off each item from his lengthy checklist, while Collins began shutting down the systems. Then all belted in for reentry and splashdown. The noise of power inverters, thrusters, and other equipment slowly faded in the command module.

Once showered, I headed to the rack on the wall where my wetsuit bottom was hanging, grabbed the baby-powder canister and shook it until there was a fine coat of white residue throughout the suit. Then I slipped my legs one at a time into the rubbery holes. After wiggling and pulling, I succeeded in stretching the rubber wetsuit bottom onto my lower body. I repeated the procedure with the top piece and, after a slight struggle, got my arms into their respective openings. I zipped it halfway to my neck and let the tail portion hang for securing at a later time.

I pulled the required life vest over my head and tightened the straps, then checked to see whether the CO_2 cartridge was screwed in firmly, and snapped the tabs that covered the canister. I couldn't help but notice the bright orange and red flower decal I had pasted onto my life vest a few hours earlier. It complimented the other two flower decals I had glued onto the right leg of my wetsuit bottoms. I wondered how the higher-ups might respond, but I didn't pause long enough to let it sink in.

After pulling on coral booties, I slipped a lanyard over my head, and secured my web belt around my waist with a Navy-issue K-Bar in its sheath and a flare secured to it with black electrical tape. I grabbed my face mask and Navy-issue tan duck-feet fins. Everything checked out.

In the chow hall I had a quick predawn breakfast with the other frogs. The cook on duty made an attempt at conversation. "Good luck today, guys! We're all pulling for you. Don't let the astronauts sink to Davy Jones' locker."

I said a quick, "Thanks," and moved on. Afterward we headed up to the flight deck. I'd already forgotten what I ate. I was totally focused on the splashdown.

The ship was surprisingly busy. From the boiler room deep down in the belly of the ship to the quarterdeck topside, all phases of recovery crews readied themselves. The air was damp from the mist and spray coming off the choppy waves as the *Hornet* raced toward the revised landing site.

"It's showtime, guys, let's get moving!" Michael Bennett, the backup BIG (biological isolation garments) swimmer, slapped us on the shoulder. He didn't have to remind us. Nothing could have slowed us down.

I took in the sensations—the smell of salt water and diesel fuel, sailors hurrying to complete their tasks, the whining shrill of helo blades revving up and beating. Over the PA, an announcement blared to clear the flight deck.

Mike Mallory and I hurried over to the Sea King SH-4, our

designated chopper. Wes Chesser, the third team member of Swim 2, was there to greet Mike and me. "Got your act together, guys? This is the real deal, you know?"

We nodded and checked to be sure everything was in place—the package holding the collar, the sea anchor's and mandatory scuba gear we loaded a few hours before—then climbed aboard and strapped ourselves into our webbed seats.

Wes noticed the flowers on my life vest and wetsuit bottoms, but only smiled and shook his head in mock disbelief. He remembered too well the rift he and Mike Mallory caused during the Apollo 10 recovery when they placed a flower decal on the hatch window. *Old Baldy* from NASA had come unglued: "What do you renegades think you are doing? That's federal property you're messing with." You'd thought they committed the unpardonable sin or something. I suppose tampering with highly sensitive government property, especially something that had come that close to the moon was a big no-no. For the probing scientists, that was like tampering with evidence at the scene of a murder. We were warned emphatically not to have any tom-foolery on this recovery. Oh well.

Swim 1 and 3 likewise prepared while the helicopter pilots and crews went through their checklists. Then we anxiously waited for the signal to be airborne.

When the signal came, we lifted off the flight deck and began our mission.

The door in front of us remained open. Beyond it, the ocean called to me.

At 0512 hours, *Marine One* landed on the forward flight deck of the *Hornet*. President Nixon, along with Henry Kissinger, Bob Haldeman, Apollo 8 Commander Frank Borman and their official NASA escort disembarked, and were greeted by Rear Admiral Davis, Captain Seiberlich, and Dr. Thomas Paine, NASA's administrator.

Following Nixon's official welcoming ceremony he was taken to the hangar deck, given a briefing of the quarantine procedures, and shown the Mobile Quarantine Facility that would house and monitor the astronauts when they arrived on the *Hornet*. He was then served a specially prepared breakfast of doughnuts and pastries.

Five thousand miles away in Houston, the controllers who had been working around the clock were now readying themselves for the final critical moments of the eight-day space shot—the reentry. All that remained of the 2,902-ton vehicle that blasted off at Cape Kennedy was the 4.8-ton Apollo capsule, *Columbia*, which was screaming through the atmosphere at close to 25,000 miles per hour.

The astronauts began to feel the effects of gravity as they peered through the windows. The weight of gravity continued to increase until they felt the effect of six times the pressure of normal gravity, driving them harder and harder into their seats. The darkness of space above them was a sharp contrast to the brilliant light show of lucid reds and yellows with bright green edges that surrounded the capsule as it zoomed toward earth.

Just inches away from their backs, protected by their heat shield, a blistering red-hot inferno of flames reached 5,200 degrees Fahrenheit. As they skipped through the atmosphere, the scorching heat shredded the thin gold foil and melted off ablative material from the capsule's housing.

At 0539 hours air support made visual contact of the Apollo 11 command module, and at 0540 radar contact by the *Hornet* was confirmed. The overcast conditions had obscured the breathtaking reentry burn—a flame trail nearly two hundred miles long—from the President and those aboard the *Hornet*. President Nixon was escorted to the flag bridge, where he would watch the recovery.

By 0541 hours, our three frogmen crews had been circling over the Pacific Ocean in our respective helicopters close to an hour. The roar of the engines made our eardrums throb even with the headgear on. For months we had gone through endless rehearsals, and now it seemed surreal.

Because of the change in location, we didn't know exactly where the module would reenter. For our pickup team, that meant that even though we were scheduled to do the recovery, if another backup team arrived on the scene first, they could be given the order to enter the water. Understandably, it gave the two backup teams hope, but made our team a little nervous. With our expectations so high, we didn't want the disappointment of being cheated out of this once-in-a-lifetime opportunity.

"Mr. Chesser, what do you think our chances are of getting into the water today?" I asked.

"Man, it's anyone's guess now that they changed the splashdown location. It will probably go to whoever is closest to the capsule. Let's keep our fingers crossed."

The spacecraft decelerated through the atmosphere. For more than three minutes, the astronauts were separated by a blackout of radio communications due to the generated heat of reentry. The heat shield of the command module was built to withstand this high heat. The radio was not.

I searched the sky through the helo door. Everyone waited in tense silence.

The spacecraft first penetrated the atmosphere nearly 1,400 miles southeast of its ultimate landing point. Its first contact with Earth was about eighty miles above the Solomon Islands. It then flew over Guadalcanal, Tarawa, and the Gilbert Islands. The silence continued until the USS *Hornet* confirmed the chutes had opened.

The astronauts felt a sharp jerk as the sixteen-foot drogue chutes opened to help stabilize the capsule in order for the three main chutes to safely deploy. After a few minutes of radio silence, it was then confirmed by the recovery force that all three chutes were opened and operative.

The astronauts peered through the hatch windows examining the large chutes. They glided gently toward earth, feeling like they were in a state of suspended slow motion. As the spacecraft slowly drifted downward, they saw a blanket of cumulous clouds flowing past the hatch window—a welcome sign of home. They pulled harder against the shoulder straps to catch a glimpse of the ocean. Yes! They were home.

The command module was too far away for the ship's filming crew to cover the actual opening, but the photo helicopter was fortunate to be closer to the action. Gathered around the landing point to greet these space travelers were 9,000 men in nine ships and fifty-four aircraft, all led by the *Hornet*. The *Hornet* ended up being thirteen miles away from the splashdown site, but the communications ship Arlington was only two miles away.

The splashdown was remarkable to me because I had a better-than-good chance of being the first man in the water. Everything in the Navy is done through the chain of command, and our job descriptions were determined long before the actual recovery. That certainly didn't stop a few eager souls from trying to jockey themselves into a primary position. Some tried to use their rank as muscle to manipulate their way through the system in order to oust one of us.

Mike Mallory's hobby of home photography saved him from being replaced. While serving on Apollo 10, he became friends with a reporter in the photo pool and offered his assistance by taking several cameras with him in the water. His photos turned out to be the best of the regress of the astronauts from the module into the rescue raft because of his vantage point in the water. His friend knew that Mike was going to be involved on Apollo 11, so they stayed in touch.

One day back in Coronado, a chief petty officer walked up to Mike and flatly stated, "I'm taking your place on Swim 2 for Apollo 11." Since Mike was outranked, there wasn't much he could do from the Navy's side. But Mike had an ace up his sleeve. He simply made a phone call to his friend in the photo pool.

"Jack, this is Mike from Apollo 10."

"Hey, it's good to hear from you, pal!" his AP friend said. "I'm looking forward to working with you again."

Then Mike laid his trap. "Well, I'm sorry to have to tell you this, but an eager chief wants in on the mission, and he told me today he's replacing me. It's really too bad because he doesn't know beans about photography."

A couple of days later Mike was back on the primary team, and the chief was reassigned to another detachment that wasn't Apollo related.

The bottom line, though, was that our senior officer, Lieutenant Clancy Hatleberg, had already determined who he wanted in the water with him to do the recovery. He later told me he had gone to Commander Jones, the senior in command of the helicopter crews, and requested that Swim 2 be placed in the primary drop recovery helicopter, #64. He felt our team was the most qualified and proficient of the three crews and therefore wanted us in place.

Clancy was the BIG (Biological Isolation Garment) decontamination swimmer, and was in Commander Jones' helicopter, #66, that was designated as the primary pick-up chopper.

Wes and Mike Mallory had hands-on experience since they had been the primary rescuers of Apollo 10. Since I was the sea anchor swimmer assigned to complete Swim 2, if all went well, we would be in the water at splashdown. But the safety of the astronauts was paramount, so any one of the three teams could end up in the water if deemed necessary. We knew there was no guarantee.

At 0546 hours, VHF voice radio and recovery-beacon contact was made. Four minutes later at 0550, the command module splashed down into the choppy Pacific Ocean at twenty miles an hour. Collins and Armstrong had bet a beer as to whether, when they hit the water, they would land upright in Stable 1 position or not. To ensure this would happen, Aldrin would have to push in a circuit located beneath his right elbow in order for the chutes to be jettisoned from the capsule. But when the crew splashed down they hit with such force that his hand jerked away from the panel, and by the time he was able to regain his bearing it was too late. The command module was dragged across the waves by the chutes and was turned upside down.

The crew hung suspended by their bench straps while Collins engaged the air pumps by flipping three switches. Once again, radio communications were interrupted since the communications antenna was submerged under water. The pumps slowly inflated the small airbags.

Our helicopter crew, Swim 2, was ten miles away. Swim 1 was

located almost directly over the landing site. We felt sure the recovery would go to them, and no doubt they were salivating at the opportunity. However, since the space module was in Stable 2, which meant that it was upside down and had to right itself, it gave us hope. Swim 1 was only seconds away from deploying their swimmers.

We raced toward the drop zone at full throttle, the bulkheads shaking and vibrating like they were going to split in two. Undoubtedly, the helicopter pilots were in direct contact with each other, discussing the module's Stable 2 position, the safety of the astronauts, talking Navy protocol, and exercising the chain of command to its fullest authority. The photo pool had placed all bets on Swim 2 (which was us) because we had their cameras. We held our breath.

Air Boss One carrying Squadron Commander Colonel Robert Hoffman, reported: "It's still in Stable 2. The bags are inflating."

Armstrong added: "Air Boss, Apollo 11. Everyone is okay inside. Our checklist is complete. Awaiting swimmers."

Hornet: "Air Boss One, this is Hornet bridge. Say when it is Stable 1. Over."

Air Boss: "...[static]...stability above the vertical axis is approximately thirty degrees."

Hornet: "Air Boss, Hornet. Recovery 1 is ready to deploy swimmers in one minute."

Chesser, Mallory and I waited in suspense. We had trained a long time. This was supposed to be our day. Hatleberg wanted his best team in the water. We wanted to be in the water. The helicopter crew wanted us to be in the water. Unfortunately, our bird happened to be in the wrong place. Our chopper became the little engine that could. "I think I can, I think I can." It screamed toward the spacecraft.

Swim 1 would be deploying in sixty seconds. Come on chopper, hurry. I was counting: Thirty seconds...twenty seconds...ten seconds.

Air Boss: "The capsule is in Stable 1 position."

Swim 1 stood in the door, ready to deploy their first swimmer.

Then, a miracle.

Air Boss: "Swim 2, start recovery at once. You are cleared."

Recovery 1 moved away, and Lt. Richard J. Barrett piloted our helicopter close to the bobbing space module. I unstrapped from my seat and stood in the open door, hoping I wouldn't make any mistakes.

I reminded myself, the United States' military had given its all to prepare me. I was a Navy UDT frogman.

Aware of the world's eyes upon me, I leaped into the choppy ocean alone.

—Chapter Thirteen—

In the Sea

I landed almost on top of the wind-tossed module. *Wow, I did it. I'm making history this morning,* I thought. *If only the gang back home could see me now.* What I didn't know was that ABC was covering the event live, even though they weren't able to get the close-ups they coveted. My family and friends were superglued to their TVs.

"Hey, Mom, they just mentioned John's name. He's the first frogman to enter the water. Hurry!" Tom yelled. At twelve he was my youngest brother and he wasn't about to miss one second of the recovery.

"Really," Mom said, "can you believe this? Who would have ever thought that one of my boys would be involved in something as big as this?"

The phone rang. It was Aunt Vicky. "Are you watching TV? They just mentioned John's name. He's in the water right now. You can see the tiny capsule."

As soon as she hung up, the phone rang again. This time it was a reporter from a TV station in Madison, Wisconsin. He wanted to confirm with my mom that it was, in fact, her son who had just jumped into the water. Mom was going to have a very busy day.

As I hit the water I had sharks on my mind. I took a quick look around. None. *Great!* I thought. *Now let's get down to business.*

From the hatch window one of the astronauts gave me a thumbs-up. *They're okay. So far, so good.* I signaled the observing helicopter to let them know.

The magnitude of what I was doing hit me. *Wow! These guys just walked on the moon! A billion people around the world maybe watching us by television right now. Thank God they made it back in one piece.* I set to work. *The astronauts. They're probably praying right now that I don't botch my job.*

Before NASA required flotation collars, a Mercury space capsule was lost. When Gus Grissom's hatch door flew open, a wave of water sunk it to the bottom of the ocean. That's why we frogmen were here—to make certain we didn't lose the men inside.

Waves pulled at me as I kicked my way over and looked for the O-ring underneath the hatch window. Good—it was in the same place as the mock-up we trained on. The capsule bobbed violently.

The sea anchor was a small parachute about twelve feet in diameter that I had to open underwater. It would be tethered upwind about fifteen yards. The parachute's purpose was to cause a much-needed drag on the capsule, to prevent it from skipping across the water and, therefore, help to stabilize it so we could attach the flotation collar.

I grabbed hold of the ring. The tossing capsule flung me right out of the water. Still holding on with my left hand, I managed to snap the anchor on with my right. Then the capsule slammed me back into the water, and its weight pushed me below the surface. *This may not be an easy day after all,* I thought.

I used my fins to surface, then kicked hard upstream ten yards and shook the nylon parachute loose from its bag. The current opened it. Perfect. Apparently I'd folded it right. The parachute shot forward until the line was taut. The capsule jerked, and then settled down. *Whew! The astronauts' bobbing should be minimal now.*

I gave a hand signal to the hovering helicopter. Wes and Mike joined me in the water at about 0604. They swam up to me with the flotation collar that had been dropped from the helicopter downwind. We were required to breathe on scuba because of the moon germ quarantine, so we wouldn't be able to talk. Our only communication would be through hand signals and mumbling.

They guided the collar, still in its housing, to the rear of the command module, opposite where the crew hatch was located. The mark point was the umbilical housing where a few wires were left dangling. Mike and I each pulled half of the collar and its bungee cords from the housing. One of us swam to the right and the other to the left around the capsule. Under the crew hatch window, we secured the collar on the sea anchor ring. After we secured all the bungee cords above and below water, Wes pulled the release to inflate the collar. Success!

After another hand signal, a helicopter crewman dropped a small cube-shaped package that contained a rubber raft. We inflated the raft and hooked it to the module alongside the crew hatch. This would be used for the recovery of the astronauts.

A second raft was dropped, inflated, and tethered to the module on a line twenty-five yards long. The three of us waited with this raft. The helicopter hovered close above. Hatleberg jumped into the water and swam over to us. Once he had climbed into the raft, several containers of decontaminate, along with biological isolation garments (BIGs) for Hatleberg and the astronauts, were lowered to him from the helicopter. These special suits were dull-green overalls topped by hoods and face masks—a part of the quarantine program designed to protect the world against the unlikely possibility of contamination by lunar organisms.

I left the second raft, swam to the first one that was attached to the capsule, and waited. Hatleberg donned his BIG suit while sitting in the second raft. After he was in the special suit, we pulled from both sides of the tether line until the second raft was alongside the command module. Hatleberg climbed onto the floatation collar and I climbed back into the second raft. I handed him the decontamination containers, which he secured to the side of the command module, and he began the decontamination procedure. I went back to our previous position, upwind of the space capsule, for safety measures.

Hatleberg closed the command module vent valves so the atmosphere inside the command module stayed there. At 0621 he signaled the astronauts to open the hatch and take their isolation suits.

After the astronauts had donned their BIGs, the hatch opened again. They climbed out of the command module and into the decontamination raft. Each was wearing inflated orange life preservers similar to water wings. Then a problem arose: Hatleberg was unable to get a lock on the hatch.

Strange. The night before, Hatelberg had experienced a restless night. His birthing area was too hot to enjoy sleep. When he finally dozed off he had a dream. The capsule had landed, the collar had been attached, and the astronauts were in the raft. When he went to shut the hatch door, it wouldn't close. An open hatch door would negate the quarantine. When his 0200 alarm sounded, the dream lingered.

Now, in the middle of his predicament he remembered his dream. He thought, *My God, everything is falling apart*. Armstrong came to his aid, but he also struggled with the hatch. He returned to the raft and Collins came to help. Finally, after a little negotiating and repositioning, Collins was able to get a lock on the door and get a proper seal.

When Hatelberg returned to the raft the astronauts were scrubbing each other improperly. The method had been changed since their rehearsal months before so he had to stop them and start over. To make matters worse, all of their face masks on the BIGs were clouding and it was hard to see. Hatleberg sprayed the astronauts one at a time with sodium hypochlorite and, using a lamb's wool carwash glove, scrubbed the astronauts' suits. Colonel Aldrin in turn washed Hatleberg down.

During the entire procedure, a doctor in one of the helicopters observed us closely. If the doctor thought we violated any of our instructed procedures and were exposed to the astronauts before they were decontaminated, we would be required to go into isolation with them.

When the astronauts had been washed, we again brought our raft near the decontamination raft and attached it to the module. We served as lifeguards while the astronauts were hoisted up into the helicopter one by one, sitting in the Billy-Pugh net. Wes stayed in the water to help catch the returning net and tow it over to the raft if needed. Mike had initially jumped into the water with five cameras. Two were personal and the other three were from the photo pool and NASA. Once in the water, he gave me one to help take pictures. I hugged the front of the raft, both of us taking as many pictures as we could without compromising our lifesaving responsibilities. All media photographers were required to submit their pictures to a photo pool, and NASA would approve what would go out over the wires for publication around the world. Mike had instructions from NASA to take pictures of the underbelly of the capsule, plus other pertinent areas once he had completed his other duties.

Armstrong was hoisted aboard first, then Collins, then finally Aldrin.

In the operations room at Mission Control in Houston, ecstatic people waved small flags and smoked the traditional splashdown cigars. Above them, a big television screen displayed a picture of *Columbia* bobbing about in the Pacific Ocean. Another screen flashed up *TASK ACCOMPLISHED—July 1969.*

The Apollo 11 command module had traveled 952,700 miles in eight days, three hours and nineteen minutes and landed just ten seconds behind the flight plan time within one mile of its target point.

When the astronauts were safely inside the helicopter, they complained of being overheated in their sealed rubber garments. The first person who greeted them was their physician, Dr. Bill Carpentier, who helped to pull them in from the Billy-Pugh net along with the helicopter crew. He warned them not to remove their BIGs until he was able to swab for microbiological cultures. Each member gave him a thumbs-up, indicating they were otherwise okay and could manage to sweat it out for a few more minutes.

In the helicopter, Armstrong chose to buckle himself into his seat. Aldrin and Collins, however, both still a little unsteady from nine days without gravity, opted to walk back and forth inside the helicopter's cabin to gain strength in their legs for fear that they would step off the helicopter and fall flat on their faces in front of the President and the whole world via television.

Collins said he felt strange when he first stood up in the helicopter as his body struck gravity again. He felt tired and light-headed and his body seemed heavy, especially his legs, because the blood was pooling in his lower body. It would take a while for the cardiovascular system to adjust to pumping blood uphill again, having become used to an easier life in space with no up or down.

ASTRONAUTS ARRIVE ON THE USS *HORNET*

The flight to the *Hornet* was brief. As the helicopter descended to the carrier, all took their seats in preparation to land.

At 0653 (1753 GMT), helicopter #66 arrived safely on the *Hornet.* President Nixon watched from the bridge. The ship's band played "Columbia, the Gem of the Ocean." By the time they reached the carrier, all three astronauts were feeling the effects of the heat caused by their BIG suits. The helicopter was quickly moved onto the ship's mid-deck elevator and lowered into the hangar bay. As they were being lowered, they removed their Velcro-affixed Apollo 11 patches and handed them to the helicopter crew in appreciation for their help. Once the compartment door was opened, the crew led by Armstrong was greeted by Dr. Stuliken (NASA's project officer) and a hangar deck full of cheering and awestruck sailors.

The crew hurried to the MQF so they could remove their hot, sweaty suits. The *Hornet* had realized its temporary motto: *Hornet Plus Three,* signifying that they successfully completed the goal of their mission to recover and bring the astronauts safely aboard.

President Nixon arrived with astronaut Frank Borman, peered into the back window of their trailer and spoke to them via microphone.

"Neil, Buzz and Mike, I want you to know that I think I'm the luckiest man in the world. And I say this not only because I have the honor to be the President of the United States, but particularly because I have the privilege of speaking for so many in welcoming you back to Earth. I called the three of, in my view, three of the greatest ladies and most courageous ladies in the whole world today, your wives. And from Jan, and Joan, and Pat, I bring their love and their congratulations. And also I've got to let you in on a little secret. I've made a date with them.

I invited them to dinner on the thirteenth of August, right after you come out of quarantine. It will be a State Dinner held in Los Angeles. The governors of all fifty states will be there, the ambassadors, others from around the world and in America. And they told me you could come too. And all I want to know is, will you come?"

"We'll do anything you say, Mr. President," Armstrong replied, "Just anything."

President Nixon went on to say, "One question I think all of us would like to ask. We saw you bouncing around in that boat out there. I wonder if that wasn't the hardest part of the journey."

Armstrong answered, "It was one of the hardest parts."

WAITING FOR RETREVAL

We were left out in the middle of the Pacific Ocean, standing on the collar attached to *Columbia*. Hatleberg washed down the command module, flotation collar, and decontamination raft with Betadine. Betadine was not used on the isolation suits, as it's a wetting agent, which would have made the suits permeable to a lunar pathogen. Then, following orders, we used our knives to deflate the decontamination raft, which held Hatleberg's BIG suit, washing glove and decontaminate containers, and sank it to the bottom of the Pacific. All we had to do next was to wait until the *Hornet* arrived.

A small whaleboat approached us with a sharpshooter aboard, prepared to shoot any sharks that might appear while we were waiting for pickup. We put our tanks, weight belts and regulators inside the boat and waited.

"Man! Am I ever glad to get this rig off me," I sighed. Inwardly I was thrilled at how well it had all come together.

Mike was the first to answer. "Yeah, is it ever hot!" The July sun was well above the horizon now, turning the waves a brilliant blue.

"Too bad you guys have to wear those wetsuits," Clancy teased. He had gotten to dump his BIG suit to the bottom of the sea and was wearing only his Navy-issue swim trunks. "Great job, guys!" Clancy added. "I wouldn't be surprised if we completed our part in record time."

Wes energetically treaded water nearby. "I think we all should get at least a 'well done' from NASA and the command. Perhaps even a medal."

We were in a great mood. In fact we were euphoric. We had pulled our part off without encountering one major problem—everything had gone like clockwork. Plus we had the satisfaction of knowing we were the guys who helped the very first men in the history of mankind who walked on the moon, out of their returned space capsule, and into the safety of the hovering helicopters above. Dreams really do come true.

To pass the time, we played "king of the mountain," knocking each other off the collar, and took pictures of one another standing on the capsule with Mike's cameras. Clancy called a truce and we all took a breather.

He said, "This is something to remember, guys. Savor this moment and make a memory. This will be something we can tell our kids and grandkids about."

"If we're smart we'll take a few souvenirs too," I added.

Mike agreed. "If we don't we'll regret it as long as we live."

When the helicopter was out of sight, and while the whaleboat disappeared behind one of the swells, we tore off hunks of the burnt and shredded gold foil that was peeling off the spacecraft from its fiery reentry, and stuffed them down inside our wetsuits. We didn't want NASA to confiscate them, so we did it discreetly.

"I want to take enough to give to my family and friends. Who knows?" I said. "Someday this stuff might be worth something."

"Believe me, when we get back to the ship it will be impossible to get any of this," Mike said. "The big honchos will hog it all. They'll have so many guards posted around this thing it'll be like breaking into Fort Knox."

We all stuffed a few more pieces into our wetsuits.

It's amazing how big an aircraft carrier looks as it bears down on you while you're in the water. From the horizon it looked like a toy approaching. As it closed the distance, its mammoth size was intimidating. From the bottom of the ship's keel to the top of the mast is 225 feet—equal to a 22-story building. The *Hornet's* flight deck is nearly three football fields long—a staggering 894 feet—with a width of 192 feet. The ship displaces 41,000 tons of water and has four separate propellers, each with four blades 15 feet in diameter, with a propulsion of 150,000 horsepower. To those watching us from the tower, we must have looked like thimbles bobbing in the ocean.

The quartermaster's skill was paramount. He had to be an expert pilot to steer the massive ship within a few feet of the bouncing capsule. Too far and the crane couldn't reach it. Too close and he would run us over.

The waves remained unforgiving. They tossed us around, nearly knocking us off the collar. I was given the delicate job of attaching the line and hook to the *Columbia's* recovery loop. I climbed to the top of the module, balancing myself by holding onto the reinforced loop. The choppy waves made it much more difficult, but many months of training paid off.

We waited for a sailor from the ship to shoot us a line by using a "monkey fist"—a knot that looks like a bunched fist, tied to the end of a rope to serve as a weight, making it easier to shoot a line to its target. Shot from a special cannon, the monkey fist carries some force and can be dangerous. Just ask Mike. He had the wind knocked out of him once during recovery training when the dumb thing hit him square in the chest.

As I was steadying myself on top of the *Columbia*, a gunner's mate on the passing *Hornet* shot the line from the cannon out to the capsule. It wasn't his best shot, so Mike retrieved it and Wes handed the hook up to me. I only had a few seconds to steady myself and attach it to the recovery loop. If I failed, the ship would have to make another pass. Nobody wanted that.

Okay, John, you practiced this dozens of times, I told myself. *Don't botch this up. Stay focused.* Fortunately I completed my job on the first run, to the relief of the deck crew and bridge. I attached the hook, the pull of the ship jolted the capsule upward, and I jumped off into the ocean. The deck hands held their breath, hoping I didn't get my hand caught between the hook and the ring. I didn't, and everyone gave a sigh of relief. It was a textbook retrieval.

Always the rebel, as I previously mentioned, I had pasted several flower decals to my wetsuit the night before. Mike had brought them along for pranks, and the guys were eager to do something to live up to our reputation as mavericks. Since the space capsule was off limits, we'd considered placing some flowers on the bottom of the helicopter, but ruled that out. No one would ever notice.

Those with rank and who were career minded were wary of messing around on something as big as the first moon landing. I was a lowly E-3 seaman (not much to lose), and just doing my required four years, so I brazenly accepted the challenge of "being out of uniform" in order to have some fun and perhaps to identify with the hip culture of the day—the flower power, peace, make-love-not-war stuff.

"Let's see, guys. If we're going to get some mileage with these flowers, I probably should stick them onto my vest and wetsuit bottoms. That way no one can complain that we compromised any equipment outside of what belongs to us. And since it's likely I'll be in the water on this recovery, it's only fitting that I be the maverick." Everyone agreed.

When the *Hornet* approached the capsule, hoards of photographers and TV camera crews crowded the deck. I held on to the loop with one hand and with the other gave the notorious 1960s peace sign. A full-page color picture of us standing on the capsule was later placed in *LOOK Magazine*, some encyclopedias and history books. There my flowers were—glistening in the sun! The decals affixed to my wetsuit and vest would forever serve as a memorial to the carefree days of my youth, individuality and the illustrious '60s.

I loved being a Navy frogman. Most everyone in the Teams was a nonconformist to some degree. After all, no frogman wore *skivvies* (Navy lingo for underwear), or was supposed to. I was made for the Teams and the Teams were made for me. Belonging to an elite group was right up my alley—there was nothing regular about being a Navy frogman. I could express myself, keep my individuality and yet be a team player. I had found a home.

The following is the citation I received, along with the Navy Achievement Medal for my part in the recovery:

The Secretary of the Navy takes pleasure in presenting the Navy Achievement Medal to Seaman John M. Wolfram, United States Navy, for service as set forth in the following CITATION:

For professional achievement in the superior performance of his duties while serving as a member of the Underwater Demolition Team ELEVEN detachment aboard the USS HORNET (CVS 12) for the APOLLO eleven recovery operations from June 1969 to 25 July 1969. As a member of the swim team, which performed the actual recovery, Seaman WOLFRAM performed his arduous assignments flawlessly. He executed his tasks in proximity to the command module with rare skill, ensuring that the flotation collar and survival rafts were properly attached to facilitate debarkation of the astronauts and recovery of the module. Seaman WOLFRAM'S resourcefulness, professional skill and devotion to duty reflected great credit upon himself and were in keeping with the highest traditions of the United States Naval Service. For the Secretary of the Navy, I. C. KIDD, Jr., Vice Admiral, U.S. Navy Commander FIRST fleet.

Apollo 11, July 1969

Decontamination

Astronauts ready for pick-up

Apollo 11, July 1969

Wolfram and Hatleberg giving the '60s Peace Sign

Wes and John

*The UDT-11 frogmen: John Wolfram, Wes Chesser,
Mike Mallory, and Clancy Hatleberg*

John on top of the space capsule

The USS Hornet

*President Richard Nixon greeting
the astronauts on the USS* Hornet

—Chapter Fourteen—

Hoopla

When the USS *Hornet* docked in Honolulu, bands played and crowds of thousands cheered. The astronauts, still inside the quarantine trailer, were loaded off first, then others left the ship to join the celebration, including us frogmen. Mike Bennett and I were greeted by two college coeds who we dated during our five days of liberty in Honolulu. They had prepared signs and made leis out of the local flowers to hang around our necks.

We had no idea this was just the beginning of the fanfare that would follow.

Our small part in the Apollo rescue received worldwide recognition. Newspapers from across the nation sent reporters to interview us. Collectors sent envelopes with the Apollo 11 stamp on them for us to autograph. We received telegrams from well-wishers all around the world congratulating us on a job well done.

The most outstanding event, however, was an invitation from Mayor Richard Daley of Chicago to be the guests of honor at their annual water festival. A dozen of us who participated in the Apollo 10 and 11 recoveries were chosen to enjoy this trip.

Mayor Daley flew us to Chicago. We were put up in the Palmer House Hotel, and for three full days we were wined and dined to our hearts' content. Our schedule included several banquets, the dedication of a swimming pool in a new resort, a parade through downtown Chicago, a demonstration of recovery techniques in Lake Michigan, and being the guests of honor in a water festival parade.

My brother Gary, who lived in Chicago at the time, wasn't about to miss his kid brother being wined and dined by the mayor of the windy city. He took a day off work just so he could bask in the shadow of his suddenly "famous" brother. He looked like a little boy in a candy store who desired to taste the goodies but didn't have two nickels to rub together. All he could do was drool. Since he had given me a lot of grief when we were growing up, it was payback time.

"Did you get to do these things when you were in the Army?" I asked. I already knew the answer.

"Naw, it was pittsville all the way," he admitted.

He had been drafted; I enlisted. I got to choose what I did; someone else did the choosing for him. He found his duty boring; mine was full of adventure and excitement. He was fortunate that he went to Panama and not Vietnam, but he would never have any war stories to tell. He couldn't help but be a little envious. His army days were nothing like this. He was treated like a slab of disposable meat. We were treated like heroes. We were given the key to the city; he got to clean latrines. I thoroughly enjoyed rubbing it in.

The entire tab was on the city, so we ordered room service for every meal. Gary enjoyed French pastries, so I ordered twenty-five dollars' worth and had them sent to the room. If he'd been a cat, he would have purred. When the porter arrived, I told him to mark down a twenty-dollar tip (a lot of money in those days) and put it on my room bill. Gary just grinned.

Some teammates headed to the bar and bought drinks for everyone in the place. When the bartender handed them a bill for five hundred dollars, Mike Bennett chased Mayor Daley's PR man down the street to see if he would pay for it. Fortunately, he signed for the tab. Whew!

We had a great time.

A three-hour drive was all that separated me from home, so I took two weeks leave after the Chicago extravaganza. The others flew back to California to take part in California's State Fair.

My father and brother drove me home. Dad stopped at nearly every tavern along the way to brag about me while we all guzzled down another beer. It seemed my father knew every bartender between Chicago and Fort Atkinson. I guess showing me off was his way of letting me know he was proud of me.

At home, local taverns offered to throw parties in my honor, which I turned down. I felt they weren't celebrating the achievements of our men and women in uniform, but were only using me to get customers. The Jefferson County Newspaper did a story, as did the bigger papers from Janesville, Madison and Milwaukee. I donated a piece of gold foil to the Hoard Museum in Fort, and liberally gave out small pieces of foil to all my family and friends.

I received a few memorable letters and cards from my former swim coaches, including Ed Steinbrecher, my high school coach. Though he had moved away at the end of my junior year he evidently had heard of my participation in the Apollo rescue. Ed wrote, *John, I am not surprised. I always knew that you were going to do something special. Congratulations.*

My former high school principal sent nothing. Go figure.

Amid the whirlwind of excitement, fanfare and adulation, I broke up with my high school girlfriend. She wanted more of a commitment from me than I was ready to give. It was a difficult time for me. I was torn between the choice of freedom and someone I cared for, but because I wasn't ready to settle down, I chose to move on with my life without her.

My achievement in the Apollo rescue fulfilled me. Soon it would haunt me.

—Chapter Fifteen—

Vietnam II: Slippery Slope

to Saigon

Apollo was over, I had just turned twenty-one, and my life began to spin out of control—fast. While in the Philippines on my first deployment, I was introduced to amphetamines and barbiturates, better known as uppers and downers or Bennies and Reds. The guys liked to combine them with their drinks. Though I tried them on occasion, I'd had no desire to bring any home with me.

For the first time while in the Navy, I chose to live off base. I roomed with three older teammates in a little corner house at 600 H Street, Coronado, California. They were top-notch operators, and all of them looked like wrestlers. Really cool guys. I looked up to them and was thrilled to share a house with this savvy bunch. But I was in for a big surprise. I had no idea they were weekend drug users. LSD, mescaline, hashish and marijuana were the drugs of choice. I soon discovered that not only these guys but many other teammates were regular users of street drugs after working hours. Living on base had sheltered me. Residing in town opened up a whole new world of adventure, but it was full of temptations. Before long, I too became a regular user.

I knew from my upbringing that experimenting with drugs was morally wrong, but I didn't listen to my conscience. I probably wouldn't have gotten so involved had it not been so popular with the youth culture in southern California. We were surrounded by the "Summer of Love" concept. Most young people were into having good times and promoting peace, which unfortunately included being high on something. We were committed to the Navy by contract, but at the end of the day we centered our free time on partying.

The anti-Vietnam War left-wing society had become a

strong force. Men in uniform were often despised and portrayed as warmongers. It wasn't a popular time to be in any branch of military service, so most of us lived double lives. As soon as we left our duty station, we dressed like hippies—old blue jeans, beads, headbands— and walked around in our bare feet or moccasins. We wore the bright-colored shirts and small beady sunglasses that were the status symbols of the late '60s' drug culture. Those who could afford it bought elaborate stereo systems for their homes and drove around in custom vans.

Partying became the norm where the host usually provided the dope, music and drinks. Drugs were as close as the Mexican border, and we seldom ran out of supply. Eventually, more and more drugs were introduced and I began experimenting with LSD, mescaline, opiates and cocaine. These were fast and wild times and, for a season, seemingly fun. However, they started to have an adverse effect on my personality and attitude toward life.

I had an insatiable desire to find new meaning in my life, because at that time it wasn't making much sense. There wouldn't be any more first astronauts on the moon to rescue, but there had to be something else. Drugs were making me delusional. My dependency made me selfish, and everyone and everything became toys to play with. I became paranoid of all authoritative figures, and in order to pursue my habits, I used my escape and evasion training to avoid being detected by the local police and military types who would turn me in. Life had become a war zone.

The only cement that held me together was family, friends and loved ones at home. Yet my self-centeredness and pride soon ripped apart many of those relationships. A person on drugs is not interested in preserving friendships. He is only interested in the immediate satisfaction of the moment. Needless to say, I made many mistakes along the way. In just a few short months of reckless living, I destroyed intimate friendships that had taken years to build, some going back as far as childhood.

As I continued to self-destruct, my feelings went from extreme highs to depressing lows. Trapped, I watched my life slowly slip away.

Things weren't going well. Though I had people all around me, I was isolated and lonely. Walking along the beach one day, I felt lost, hopeless. Nothing in this world seemed worth living for.

The morale of many of my teammates didn't help. The Vietnam War had become unpopular at home as well as abroad, and it was having a noticeable effect on us troops. Many soldiers including myself were questioning if our efforts were a waste of time and lives, and much of America agreed. I wasn't excited about the prospect of going back to Vietnam. Another hometown friend of mine had been killed, making it three high school classmates who had now paid the ultimate price for their country. Their deaths, added to the drugs, alcohol, love-hate music and the political climate of the day, plus the plummeting attitude of my teammates, was a recipe for despair.

The United States Armed Forces acknowledged it had a major drug problem within its ranks, which prompted a "drug amnesty" program that encouraged rehabilitation without retribution. The downside of this program was that if a person was allowed to stay in the service, and his attempt to shake the habit failed, he was marked and was subject to the full range of punitive actions the next time.

In our case, if we admitted taking drugs and asked for help, we would have been reassigned to the regular "black shoe" Navy. To us, this would have been far worse than a general discharge.

That is exactly what happened to Mr. "B", one of our most popular officers. He admitted to our CO that he had been smoking dope with the enlisted men, and before we knew it, he was no longer among us. He was sent packing across the street to the regular Navy to finish out his term of service. Mr. B's absence left a gaping hole no one else could fill—right before we deployed. His timing couldn't have been worse. It was a big downer.

Something was happening to us guys and it definitely wasn't good. A significant portion of my team was sliding down a slippery slope. Our UDT command showed us anti-drug films produced by the Navy. Nobody took them seriously. They were poorly produced, silly, and unrealistic. We just laughed them off.

We felt invincible. Everything was, "Cool, man." What harm

could a few party drugs do to us? They only helped us to have fun. Besides, who were they to preach? They got high on booze whenever they wanted to, and nobody harped on them. Why didn't they show us films about excess drinking? Smoking? Chewing tobacco? Sleeping around?

We packed our gear, said our goodbyes and departed San Diego on a Navy prop plane that only offered stiff, very uncomfortable webbed seats attached to the fuselage walls. Our first stop was San Francisco—at the Alameda Naval Air Station.

After most everyone debarked and had gone into the lounge, I noticed a very animated Forrest Harness in conversation with a couple of crewmembers in the back of the plane where our cargo was.

"Hey, Fred, what's going on?" I asked.

"I'm not sure. Let's take a look."

Fred and I worked our way closer so we could hear.

Harness was in full panic, practically shouting. "Hey! Listen! I'm telling you, there's a guy buried underneath all of this equipment you folks loaded back in San Diego. He's in one of the boxes!"

The crewmembers were speechless.

Harness had let a guy named "Roach" talk him into loading him inside a small wooden cruise box to be smuggled back to the Philippines. I'm sure the name Roach had something to do with his smoking marijuana—it was the term used for the end of a joint after the rest of it had been smoked. Roach had been a part of UDT-11, but had been recently discharged from the Navy. He thought he could bum a free ride back to Olongapo City where there were plenty of cheap drugs and loose women.

When the crewmembers loaded the box in San Diego, they had stacked tons of equipment on top of his box, covering the air holes. Harness realized that Roach might not be able to breathe underneath all of that gear. Again, he yelled at the crew. "Come on! He might still be alive. We've got to dig him out. Now! Hurry!"

The crew, realizing Harness wasn't joking, started to unload the plane. When they finally got to him and opened the box, steam shot out. Roach was curled up in a ball.

Harness shook him, but Roach didn't respond. "Roach, are you all right?"

Finally—movement. Roach was lethargic, but still breathing. Thank God! He probably would have died had the plane not stopped in San Francisco. The journey was going to be thirty-six hours long.

Roach let out a squeak. "Oh, man, am I glad you got me out of this. I couldn't breathe in there."

As soon as Roach was resuscitated, he ran for cover...just ahead of the base police.

As I mentioned earlier, Forrest was a real character—always up to something. While being confined to the Subic Naval Base on our first tour, he bagged his clothes, swam naked across a polluted river to enjoy the nightlife of Olongapo City, then swam back across the next morning undetected.

Another time back in Coronado, Forrest hid on top of a freezer of the local Safeway grocery store at closing. He planned to fill a couple of carts with food and snacks to share with the guys on a three-day op off San Clemente Island. But unbeknownst to him, the store had scheduled inventory that evening, so he was trapped on top of that cold freezer the entire night. The next morning when the store opened for business, he sneaked down, joined the customers and finally walked out. The only thing he left with, though, was a chest cold, runny nose, and the unforgettable memory of a tense and miserable night.

The Teams were full of interesting people. Like Harness, they came in all shapes and sizes. There weren't many angels, but we were a fraternity of brothers, bonded together by our BUD/S training and surviving Hell Week. We knew how to have fun, but we also worked hard. West Pac especially was a time to let our hair down and party. It was also a time to test our skills in the field.

Once again I was assigned to an ARG (Amphibious Ready Group) for my first three months. This time I saw some action. At midnight, we painted our faces green and black, jumped into an IBS, and stealthily made our way to shore with M-16s and grease guns at the ready. Only, they were not loaded with real bullets. We were part of a huge Navy readiness operation off the coast of South Korea.

A hundred yards from shore we took on live fire from crack South Korean troops. The Navy brass had forgotten to inform them of our practice operation. The South Koreans assumed they were under attack from the North. Suddenly a barrage of brilliant, flaming-red tracer rounds flew at us. Bullets whizzed over our heads and struck the water all around our IBS. We dove for cover in the Yellow Sea until the U.S. Navy could get a message through to the South Korean Army. We were shaken, but unharmed.

Not every day on an ARG was that exciting. We had plenty of days of tedium. But this time, unlike my first tour, besides the occasional skeet shoot practiced off the fantail, sunbathing and swims, we had access to a stash of drugs which we'd smuggled aboard ship.

Getting high on ship was weird, and risky, especially with a gung-ho chief as our NCO. It didn't take him long to realize he was stuck with a bunch of "heads." And it didn't take us long to realize that he was going to try and make our lives miserable. He made sure we got our share of shore patrol while we visited Okinawa and Hong Kong instead of the usual VIP treatment we were used to. He was more interested in making an impact on his newfound friends in the chief's quarters than making our lives easy. It was tug-of-war all the way.

Finally we got back to Subic for some R & R before our next assignments. I envied those detachments that were allowed to stay in the Philippines. They didn't have to ride ARGs or worry about being shot in Vietnam. They worked regular hours, got plenty of exercise, were able to make parachute jumps, went on dives and had access to the nightlife of Olongapo City. I was into bands, and the Filipino groups were some of the best. They were awesome imitators. *This was the place to be*, I thought. And I had a chance to make it happen.

While on liberty in Olongapo, Philippines, I met with some local thugs and concocted a plan. A Filipino would do almost anything for money. For a fee of two hundred dollars, it would be arranged for me to be arrested. The charge: punching the mayor of Subic City in a bar brawl. This seemed a little outlandish, but it would have put me on a legal hold until the Filipino government released my case. When our team was ready to return to the States, they would have dropped all charges, thus sparing me from having to deploy to Vietnam, allowing me to enjoy the bands and nightlife of Subic.

The money in my pocket, I stood outside the meeting place to stage this fiasco. I wrestled with my conscience. If I went through with my plan, a friend of mine would have to go in my place, and I could never have lived with myself if something bad happened to him. So, drugged out of my mind, I boarded the plane that transported me back to Vietnam.

The recent change in military policy in 1970 wasn't reassuring. The government was pulling out U.S. troops and slowly turning the war over to the South Vietnamese. That meant we would be working more with non-Americans—a smaller, less experienced force.

One thing I knew for sure—I didn't want to die. I kept hearing County Joe and Fish's "I-Feel-Like-I'm-Fixin'-to-Die Rag" in my head.

> And it's one, two, three,
> What are we fighting for?
> Don't ask me, I don't give a da—,
> Next stop is Vietnam;
> And it's five, six, seven,
> Open up the pearly gates,
> Well there ain't no time to wonder why,
> Whoopee! We're all gonna die.

My Detachment's orders: three months' duty in the Mekong Delta area of the Ca Mau Peninsula on the Cu Long River. This was as south as you could go in Vietnam before you were in the South China Sea. It was much further south than where I served on my first tour. All we knew about this place was that it was hazardous, and we were to live on a barge out in the middle of a river in an area swarming with Viet Cong. Fun.

Since our detachment, led by Lieutenant (jg) Klinger, had a longtime wait for an available chopper to transport us to the barge, we spent several days in Saigon—a city full of energy. The only time excitement waned was during the hours of curfew, usually between midnight and five in the morning unless there were threats of a coup d'état.

The streets of Saigon were overcrowded, full of refugees and soldiers. TB was endemic and many people were undernourished. The usual means of transport was the cyclo-pousse. Those poor drivers who pedaled away all day had a hard life and usually died fairly young. There was a motorized version of the cyclo that let off horribly polluting fumes. Both were highly dangerous to use although fatal accidents seemed rare. The Honda or motor scooter was another common form of transport and much more practical than a car. There were bicycles by the thousands. A few old Renaults were used for taxis, and I even saw some Volkswagen vans.

There were special hangouts for GIs all over the city. Ours was the Victoria Hotel. The top floor was a nightclub where guys could drink; drug and dance the night away with an abundance of bar hostesses at our beck and call. In the Victoria Hotel I experienced a life-changing event.

Late at night I stepped out onto my balcony over the streets of Saigon. Below, motorcycles whined and occasional taxi horns beeped. Rancid odors of fish, fried pork, pungent spices and human waste rose from the busy streets. Above the city, a parachute flare exploded and tracer bullets cascaded across the sky. A solemn reminder there was still a war going on around us.

A loudspeaker blared jerking me from my thoughts. "Evening curfew is now in effect. All U.S. military personnel off the streets!" The MP vehicle drove on, and the American GI's voice faded as he continued to repeat the announcement.

In the room behind me my radio was playing "Detroit City," and Bobby Bare was singing, "I wanna go home,...Oh Lord...I wanna go home." *You and me both*, I thought. Home would be great, but I would easily settle for jukin' and jivin' to the sounds of the rock bands back in Olongapo. That was definitely more appealing than this rat hole. Until then my trusty Sanyo radio would have to do. I turned it up louder.

The maze of smells and sounds, like bitter bile, brought up thoughts I wished I'd forgotten. Deep inside, I resented what I had become in the past year, and I was filled with shame. The LSD I took earlier started to peak, making me delusional.

Hideous voices screamed at me. Bloodthirsty hounds—no, demons—pursued me. Condemned me. Can anyone help? Can I ever make things right again? Whirling thoughts of Larry Smith, Gary Smith and Terry Beck—my high school friends all recently killed in Nam—haunted me. Killed. Gone. If it happened to them, it could easily happen to me.

Damning voices echoed in my head. "John, just look at yourself. You're no good to anyone. Your life is a complete waste."

Now my mind fought for its sanity. This trip was turning bad, fast. The LSD was taking me on a freakish journey. The walls started to breathe, cockroaches were laughing, and the dripping faucet pinged louder and louder. Adrenaline rushed through my veins.

Calm down, I told myself, but my mind was already on a roller-coaster ride and the brakeman was nowhere to be found. I flashed back in time, relived hundreds of events. Dozens of distorted faces appeared. People I knew. People I hurt. People I shunned. They twirled around me, faster and faster until they were a blur. Then suddenly they stopped.

Voices again: "Look at all the people you've hurt. At what you've done to them. At what you've done to yourself. Look how pathetic you are. You don't want to live like this. You're probably going to be killed anyway. End your misery now. Yes, *end* it."

Arthur Brown's "Fire" blared from my radio. His voice carried me into the womb of hell. He was wailing, "You're gonna burn, burn, burn, burn, burn, burn, burn, burn, burn, burn, burn!"

I couldn't handle the noise anymore. Inside the room I switched off the radio. My 9-mm pistol lay in my luggage on the bed. I walked to the gun, pulled it from its holster, toyed with it. The steel felt cold, clammy. What would it feel like if I pulled the trigger?

The pistol weighed heavy in my hand. Death called to me, yet I resisted. Suicide went against everything that was in me. I gripped the gun, hands shaking, as I struggled for the courage to live.

Then I felt another presence beside me, and I became still. Then, for some reason, calm. I had felt this Presence, and its calm, before. I heard a soft whisper though I was alone in the room.

"John, I love you. I can help you. Trust me."

I cried out into the room, "Lord, if that's you then help me, because I don't know what to do. I hate my life. I hate what I've become. I'm desperate. I've hit a wall, and can't find a way out. Can you rescue me from this hell?"

Suddenly, I was in Sunday school and my teachers were telling me how much Jesus loved me. I was walking with my grandmother to an early Easter sunrise service. I heard the choir singing and little children laugh, and my mother was smiling.

I felt something evil let loose of me and move away. An incredible and indescribable gentle warmth filled me. Around me the room seemed to vibrate with hope.

I wanted to live.

There truly is a God, I thought. *He knows who I am. He knows where I am. And he cares about me.*

Previously I had heard the expression "God is love." But until now I hadn't felt the immenseness of that love. He really did love me; no matter what.

I'd noticed that the Filipinos thought a lot about Jesus. His picture was everywhere, on the wall behind the bars in the clubs, painted with bright colors on their jeepneys and on black-velvet framed pictures for sale on the street corners. Why hadn't I become aware of this before? Was he trying to tell me something?

This experience left its mark. I was touched. I was made aware. He was no longer just a stranger who drifted in and out of my life, but I was beginning to perceive him as an abiding presence. He was becoming a constant confidant that I could talk to every day, someone I could lean on, someone I could share my thoughts and feelings with without fear of being criticized or misunderstood.

I told others about the experience and my new feelings about God. I talked about Him as if He was my friend. He was. I'm sure of it. What else could you call it? I didn't have a Bible with me in Vietnam, so I had no road map to guide me. I only had His presence. But for now that was good enough.

My companions observed me with keen interest, and often questioned me about my newfound faith. No one seemed overly offended when I talked about Jesus. It's no surprise that people lean heavily on God during a crisis. There was lots of "God talk" in Vietnam. Someone fittingly said, "There are no atheists in foxholes." People who find themselves in difficult situations often call out to God, but unfortunately, when things smooth out they also have a tendency to forget about Him. I didn't forget about Him, but my habits didn't change much. I still drank and took drugs with my friends.

—Chapter Sixteen—

Vietnam II: Surviving Sea Float

At the Tan Son Nhut Air Base in Saigon, six of us in Detachment Golf hopped on a Chinook helicopter and flew south toward the Ca Mau Peninsula, a breathtaking flight. Multicolored patches of rice fields whipped by below us as we rattled along. We landed at Can Tho, sweated a few hours in the shade of an oak tree, then boarded another helicopter and continued toward the Mobile Tactical Support Base—our assigned post in the Mekong Delta.

It was unnerving to look down from the helicopter with legs dangling out the open side door. Only my body weight kept me from plunging to the land below, but I would get used to it. The Song Cua Long River (Song means "river" in Vietnamese) eased into view beneath us, bordered by defoliated mangrove forests and massive craters; the result of carpet-bombing. Then we hovered over a barge moored in the middle of the river. Sea Float. It served as a temporary support base for the Mobile Riverine Forces until something could be built on land.

From the air, the barge sitting in the middle of that river appeared oh-so-vulnerable. After we landed, my concerns were confirmed.

The operations officer immediately directed us to a small room for our orientation briefing. On the wall behind us was a large map of the surrounding area, peppered with green and red pins. The green pins, we were told, marked Viet Cong sightings. The red pins marked places where actual fighting had taken place. The rumors were true. We were sitting in the middle of a Viet Cong stronghold.

Our primary purpose for being there: to stop the momentum of the enemy by destroying their bunkers, food and ammunition supplies, securing the waterways, and eventually driving them out of the area.

Serving on the Float was a homecoming of sorts. I was reunited with BUD/S classmates Gore, Durlin, Solano and Sparks who were assigned to SEAL Team One. However, the joy of our reunion was short-lived as the gravity of our situation set in. We went to bed, wondering if that night would be our last. Just before we arrived, three Viet Cong sappers floated down the river with demolition charges strapped to their backs. Alert sentries threw concussion grenades into the water and killed the enemy frogmen, but because of the Float's vulnerable location in the middle of the river, we remained sitting ducks.

The floating base consisted of fourteen pontoon barges welded together with shacks constructed on top. Each wood and corrugated metal structure held bunks for the troops and a small table or two on which to play cards or write letters. On the back end of the Float (depending upon which way the tide was moving) were the communal toilets and showers. The water heater was turned on in the evening, but only the first few in line got to enjoy hot water. On the opposite end there was space for a few storage containers and for two Seawolf helicopters to land. Sentry posts on all four sides guarded us from attack. After the sapper attack, concussion grenades were tossed into the water every half hour. When our riverboats were not patrolling, they docked on the wider sides of the barge.

Sea Float's head (toilet) was much like an outhouse. It protruded out over the stern with an automatic flush system called the Song Cua Long. Late one evening, the captain was in the officer's head when the sentry on duty threw a grenade into the river. He was a new arrival and didn't realize the current had shifted. The grenade was swept back toward the barges and detonated right under the captain, sending a geyser of water up through the five-holer, blowing the "old man" off his seat and out through the door. He survived unharmed except for his dignity.

The Float's chow hall was in the center of the barge and we ate in shifts. The food was the best the Navy had to offer. Steaks, baked potatoes, corn on the cob, apple pie, and ice cream were available every day. We just had to ask. Besides the briefing rooms, various barracks, and offices, there was a separate corpsman's, and doctor's office with an operating table and medical supplies among the buildings. I don't remember a brig.

Camaraderie on the Float was strong, and life was unusually laid back, even for the Navy. Not having to shave, get haircuts, wear regulation clothing or have inspections was paradise. Every evening the command showed films between the hooches (barracks). A sheet was spread across the narrow passageway between two sets of buildings, and men could watch the movie on either side. The pot smokers watched the flicks from on top the tin roofs so the wind could blow away the smell. (I'm sure everyone knew why we were up on the roof, but no one ever said anything.) The pot smokers were pretty bold considering it was highly illegal and grounds for a court martial. But this was Vietnam, and rules were redefined according to the circumstances. The door to the corpsman's office was always open, and everyone had free access to all his pills when he wasn't looking, which seemed to be always. For those who were not into dope, there was a never-ending supply of beer.

Shortly after I arrived I got to spend some time with my former classmates already stationed on the Float, SEALs Richard Solano—we'd hung out in the barracks at BUD/S; Jim Gore—we were in the same boat crew during Hell Week; Frank Sparks—the firecracker gymnast and swim partner who'd aided me when my K-Bar knife got tangled in the detonation cord off of San Clemente Island; and John Durlin. John and I were the closest. We'd been good friends since we talked on San Clemente shortly after my grandma passed away.

"Hey, Durlin," I said, "It's great seeing you again. How have you been?"

"Really busy. We go out on ops almost every day. How about you?" he asked.

"For the past couple of months I've been riding ARGs. I've gone to Korea, Okinawa, Hong Kong and the Philippines. It's been kinda' crazy."

John grinned. "It must have been fun."

"We did the sunbathing ruse—told the ship's captain we

needed at least two hours of sun a day to keep our skin tough. So we'd take our lawn chairs, sit on the flight deck back on the fantail and fly kites. It really irritated him, so he'd call flight quarters every fifteen minutes to make us pull in our kites."

John laughed. He always had a great appreciation for the UDT/SEALs' antics.

I continued, "Some of the guys have been hitting drugs hard too. A few have gotten into heroin and cocaine. They gave me some to sniff in Hong Kong and it sent me flying. I think I'll stick to pot and the psychedelics. Have you ever tried LSD?"

"Once," he said. "You know they give us amphetamines to keep us awake at night?"

"The government helps keep your blood pressure high, huh?" I joked. "Here, when you get some downtime, you can try this." I handed him a tiny white pill. "It's some pretty potent stuff. Make sure your head's on straight before you trip because it could get pretty wild if you're not in the right mood. I almost lost it a few days back in Saigon. I was hearing all kinds of voices and I almost did myself in."

John eyed me in surprise. "Oh, wow."

"Yeah, if it wouldn't have been for the Lord, I'm not certain what I would have done. Do you believe in God?"

He shrugged. "Sure, doesn't everybody?"

"If they do, they're keeping it a secret. I mean, I just don't see it on everybody, you know? But I'll tell you, I've been getting some good vibes from the Man upstairs. It's incredible. I'd like to get to know Him better. I feel His presence so strong at times. What about you?"

"Donnelly's Catholic," Durlin replied, "and he goes to church whenever a chaplain comes around. I went with him a couple of times. We talk a lot about God these days. I don't know when, but someday I'm going to check things out a whole lot more. Maybe when I return to the States I'll have time to do that."

"When I was a kid I liked going to church," I said, "but then it got kind of dry. None of my friends were going and it just got stale."

Durlin nodded. "I can relate to that."

A memory came to mind. "In my hometown there was this woman who I would run into on the street. Some stranger. When she saw me walking she would cross the street just to make sure she got to talk to me. She always patted me on the head and told me that Jesus loved me. I really needed to hear that because I was kind of freaked out as a kid. It was just nice to hear that someone besides my Mom really loved me. You know what I mean?"

"Yeah, I think so," John said.

"All I know is that God is on my mind a lot, and when I think about him I get goose bumps. I think he's trying to tell me something. I talk to him every day. I mean, I don't kneel and all that, I just talk to him. He's becoming a good friend. It's really cool." A radio was playing, and we listened for a few minutes. Then I said, "I know God exists. I just need to figure out how it all fits in with me."

After some news the disc jockey announced, "And now Norman Greenbaum's song that has taken the charts by storm, 'Spirit in the Sky.'" John and I took time to absorb the words.

When I die and they lay me to rest,
Gonna go to the place that's the best.
When I lay me down to die,
Goin' up to the spirit in the sky;
Goin' up to the spirit in the sky.
That's where I'm gonna go when I die.
When I die and they lay me to rest,
Gonna go to the place that's the best.

Prepare yourself, you know it's a must.
Gotta have a friend in Jesus,
So you know that when you die
He's gonna recommend you
To the spirit in the sky;
Gonna recommend you
To the spirit in the sky.
That's where you're gonna go when you die.

When you die and they lay you to rest,
You're gonna go to the place that's the best.

Never been a sinner; I never sinned.
I got a friend in Jesus,
So you know that when I die
He's gonna set me up with
The spirit in the sky;
Oh, set me up with the spirit in the sky.
That's where I'm gonna go when I die.
When I die and they lay me to rest,
I'm gonna go to the place that's the best.
Go to the place that's the best.

"That song is so cool." I exclaimed. "I really love the guitar riffs and those outer space blips they put in there. That song is a real pick-me-upper. I'm going to buy their album when I get back to the world."

"I'm really happy for you," Durlin finally said. "We'll talk more soon. It's great seeing you again, John."

"Hey, they're showing a movie tonight," I added. "A bunch of us sit up on the roof so we can smoke. You're welcome to join us if you want. I'll see you."

UDT duties in Nam were mostly water-related, including checking out the underbelly of the barge every day for explosives. The Song Cua Long was a tidal river with a mouth on either side of the peninsula, so it always flowed at a swift five to ten knots in one direction or the other depending on the flow. We waited for the brief ebb. The river was more dark brown sludge than water. The double tide and murky water made it almost impossible for us to execute our diving duties.

Skimming for explosives was a two-man job—one on the barge and the other in the water. When it was my turn to go in, I secured a line around my waist, strapped a scuba tank on, then jumped into the filthy river. I rolled over onto my back and searched the rough underside with my hands. Visibility was zilch. My partner topside fed the line.

Probing for explosives while bumping into sharp barnacles and other debris clinging to the metal was spooky. If I hadn't been taught how to discipline my thoughts, I would have gone bonkers. This wasn't a job for the claustrophobic or faint of heart. However, it was a necessary precaution to assure the Float's safety against mines placed by VC frogmen. I did my job without complaining.

My biggest fear was that some guard topside would forget we were in the water and not cease from their half-hour grenade toss. A mistake on a sentry's part would have been deadly for me.

Three or four of us were assigned to the Monitor, Alfa or Tango boats when they patrolled the rivers. Sometimes major operations lasted several days while we rode in huge caravans of thirty or more boats. Other times we patrolled remote streams with just two or three vessels, with the Seawolf helicopters on call. "On call" was still too far away for comfort. A few times we tramped through swampy fields with the Vietnamese Biet Hai troops or Kit Carson scouts, as they swept an area, searching for the enemy.

Defoliation of the areas off of the main rivers was a precaution to deny the VC cover. Agent Orange turned out to be tragic for Admiral Zumwalt. Years later his own son, who had been stationed on the Float, died from the effects of the defoliant he had ordered.

Constricted space on smaller, side waterways made river patrolling treacherous. We paid attention to every movement. The VC frequently launched surprise attacks. We never knew who or what was waiting just around the next bend. We always entered a side canal with extreme caution.

A couple of weeks after I arrived on Sea Float, the SEALs came across two signs hanging from wires that were strung across a small stream a few clicks (kilometers) up-river. In English they read, "Stay Out!" Of course, that was like holding a red cloth in front of a raging bull. The higher-ups sent down orders to investigate.

The resultant mission was almost certain to end in a firefight.

The SEALs' intel also noted the sign was across a very

constricted stream leading deep into the marsh and jungle. Klinger, Sobiski and I boarded one of the two boats loaded with Biet Hai troops. Then we set off upriver toward our target.

The Viet Cong in the area was a highly motivated, well trained, but moderately equipped force. Their advantage—they knew the territory, people and waterways like the backs of their hands.

They were like the land itself. They blended in.

Charlie seemed to have magic powers, which allowed him to sink into the grass and disappear. Just under our feet, just behind that tree, just yards away. Like us, they also moved by boat, mainly sampans usually disguised as local merchant and fishing craft. Regular civilians volunteered or were coerced into carrying supplies and equipment for the VC. You never knew who was who.

Mr. Klinger, our UDT officer, scanned the shores, visibly agitated. "If they wanted this area harassed, why didn't they just send in the Seawolfs and fire a few rockets?"

"Then they couldn't justify us being here," I joked.

Our last assignment on the ARGs was a cakewalk. Now we had to depend upon our skills, the support teams around us and, in my case, prayer.

I was still radiating God. The others began to feel I might have an inside track with Him, so on the way, Frank Sobiski asked, "John, you feeling anything special? Do you sense the Lord is with us today?" He was halfway teasing, but there was also a note of seriousness in his voice.

I was a novice at this prayer thing, but I wasn't letting my inexperience get in the way. I raised my eyebrow in a gesture that said, "I'll let you know."

After taking the Song Cua Long for several clicks, we took a sharp right turn up a smaller tributary that narrowed as we went. Another turn, an even narrower canal.

We came upon a small Vietnamese village. Men and women with cone-shaped hats scattered in every direction. I didn't see any children. They looked scared. Something was amiss.

The Viet Cong used these small villages as recruitment centers. They strategically placed their ambushes in line with them because they knew U.S. policy forbade us from using the .50-caliber machine guns when there were known civilians in the area.

We slowly navigated the canal for two more clicks. Then we saw the first sign dangling from the wire. "Stay out!"

The coxswain cut the engines. We drifted up just short of the front wire. The river and the land beyond it were eerily quiet. The worst part of water ops was anticipating when we might get hammered.

The radio crackled. A radioman was speaking in hushed tones to his superiors.

I used the pause to confide in my newfound Friend. I whispered what now seemed to be a daily prayer. "I want to see my mom, my dad, my brothers and sister again. I don't want to be killed in this strange land. Not here. Not now. Not in the condition I'm in."

I knew about heaven and hell. I didn't know how to get to heaven. But I heard you didn't have to do anything to go to hell. I needed time to figure things out. I wasn't living right, and I knew it.

As I was talking to God, His comforting presence swept over me once again. He was still there beside me. "Watch over us, Lord," I murmured.

The engine revved and we moved forward. The bow pressed into the first wire. It snapped in two. We all held our breath behind the sandbags and metal mesh barrier. Nothing happened. We looked over the rail to search the banks of the river. No movement. Twenty-five yards ahead of us was another wire. The coxswain gunned the engines and rammed through it.

KA-BOOM! Ka-boom!

All hell broke loose.

Demolition charges exploded in the water beneath us. The VC knew exactly when to detonate them. Our heavy boat lifted in the spray. River water spilled onto us as the boat rocked and reeled. More mines went off, again and again. Our boat absorbed the shock.

In the tree branches above us claymore mines exploded, firing shrapnel down onto us. B-40 rockets slammed the sides of our boat, their impact driving us to the side of the canal.

From the start we opened fire with everything we had. The air filled with zinging bullets and angry blips of red neon.

The 105-mm cannon mounted on the Monitor boat blasted into the thick brush and tore wide spaces in the terrain. VC soldiers dove into their bunkers. I had an M-79 grenade launcher. I loaded, shot and reloaded as fast as I could. Shrapnel flew everywhere. Dirt jumped off the deck and hit me in the face. Bullets and tracers bounced off trees, metal and rock. Where were the Seawolfs?

A sharp burning sensation ripped into my leg.

Second Vietnam Tour, 1970
Sea Float

John aboard Sea Float.
Effects of drug abuse were
very visible.

John, Sea Float

John, Cam Ranh Bay Hospital

James Gore, Sea Float

UDTs blowing up fish stakes

Small canal, VC ambush site

—Chapter Seventeen—

Twist of Fate

I reached my hand down to feel my leg. It came back red with blood. Keeping low, I expanded the tear in my pant leg. The entry hole had already swollen to a knot the size of a golf ball. My blood streamed from the wound, saturated my pant leg, then began to pool on the deck.

I had been in firefights before, but not at this close range. My training helped, but this was a new experience. Somebody was trying to kill me. With thousands of projectiles and us in the crossfire, we were vulnerable. The noise was deafening.

Two choppers bore down at high speed. Missiles slammed into the riverbanks on both sides of us, uprooting banana trees, coconut palms and everything in sight. Splatters of flame shot twenty feet into the air, exploding huge chunks of field with them. Then, just as quick as the skirmish had started, it was over.

That's how the VC operated—hit and run. Charlie couldn't match our firepower. Their tactic was the element of surprise, setting up ambushes then fading into the forest by foot or underground tunnels.

South Vietnamese troops in the well of the Tango disembarked to secure the beach and to chase down the ambushers. We assessed the damage to our boat and applied first aid to our wounds. Our boat took eight direct hits from the VC's B-40 rockets. With a closer look, a few of us nearly ruined our shorts. A live B-40 rocket was lodged in the deck's protective barrier just inches from where we were crouching. If it had detonated, it could have been fatal.

With all the ricocheting shrapnel and bullets flying during firefights, bizarre things often happened. Bullets hit canteens, cigarette lighters, decks of cards and even pocket-sized Bibles, often saving soldiers. Plenty have mentioned how lucky they were, presuming they were spared by chance alone, but I strongly felt the Lord heard my prayers.

When the Biet Hai troops reboarded, we were slowly towed back to the Float. From there I was taken to the doctor's makeshift office. The doctor probed into my leg for the bullet, frowning. He was young, probably inexperienced. When he couldn't locate the bullet, he simply stitched up the hole.

I'll never know what he was thinking. My buddies and I thought this odd. If there was a hole going into my leg and none coming out, that obviously meant that the lead was still in my leg!

At the insistence of Mr. Klinger, my senior officer, I was transferred to the Binh Thuy Base medical center. When the helicopter landed, I hobbled over to the hospital, which was a good quarter of a mile away.

I was directed to a waiting area that doubled as an emergency room. I handed my medical folder to a young clerk then took a seat against the wall among other wounded soldiers. We watched in amazement as doctors and nurses treated other wounded men before us. Soon I found myself lying under an X-ray machine. My bleeding—but curious—audience silently cheered me on while they waited their turn to see a doctor. The corpsman took several pictures, which revealed where the shrapnel had lodged. From the point of entry, it rested a good ten inches up my leg.

A sour-faced man the nurses called "Doc" appeared. I was helped up onto a gurney and given a local anesthetic. The doctor examined the X-ray for a few seconds then put on rubber surgical gloves. With a long tweezers-like instrument he probed my leg to find the bullet.

He repeatedly ripped out hunks of my flesh, and placed them on a stainless steel tray. Then he went after the bullet. He soon dug beyond the numbing effect of the anesthetic. I gripped the sides of the gurney and nearly pulled it around me. As he tore into my leg, every nerve ending in my body demanded I scream, and I was more than willing to comply.

A female doctor hurried over. "What are you doing to that young man?" she demanded. But after she made her plea, she vanished as fast as she appeared. My nightmare continued without relief.

Time seemed to stop. Finally, he yanked out the piece of twisted lead and placed it on a tray for all to see. Faint-hearted applause erupted across the room from the curious onlookers.

The doctor moved on, and I was turned over to a couple of gentle male nurses. They explained it would take several weeks for my wound to heal. The gaping hole would need to be packed with sterile gauze dipped in a Betadine solution twice a day, and allowed to mend from the inside out.

The two wanted to admit me to one of their many wards. With Doc around, I wasn't interested. I talked them into letting me go back to the Float. With the anesthetic wearing off, and my leg screaming in pain, I limped the quarter of a mile back to the helicopter pad and hitched a ride back.

The Float, it turned out, wasn't an ideal place for my wound to recover, as it was hot, humid, dusty and unsanitary. In less than a week my wound was oozing with infection, and the doctor on the Float was helpless to control it. He warned me that if I didn't get proper care gangrene could set in, and I could possibly lose my leg.

So once again they placed me on a gurney aboard a Seawolf, next to the gurney of a very pregnant Vietnamese lady who needed help in her delivery, and I was flown back to the Binh Thuy hospital. I'll never forget the terror in the young lady's eyes as she stared out the open door of the helicopter. It was probably her first time to fly, and looking down from three thousand feet can be scary.

After another thorough probing and cleansing, I was admitted to a ward. It was pitiful to see so many broken bodies in one long sterile room.

Most of the patients were war casualties, but there were some who were admitted for other reasons, like the guy two bunks down from me. His arm was strung up in traction, the result of a bee sting. The bite area had become infected and swollen to an enormous size.

He received lots of ribbing from us, but it was all in jest.

The hospital experiences I had were priceless, because I discovered something unexpected—compassion amidst a tragedy. Young ladies who worked for the Red Cross and the USO, called "Donut Dollies," occasionally made the rounds with candy, cookies and letters from home. They wrote letters for those who couldn't, took time to talk, and played board games with the guys. I admired them for not only risking their lives, but also for giving up valuable time from friends, family, boyfriends, and in some cases college, in order to make a difference in a distant and unpopular war. Every one of us deeply appreciated these young ladies who reminded us of our sisters or girlfriends back home. Their warm smiles and feminine ways were a very welcome reprieve from the ugliness of war.

On a typical day, my leg was probed and cleaned three times. The medic came by to remove all the gauze with long tweezers. Then he squirted Dakin's solution over the exposed wound. The cold sensation felt good at first then, within seconds, the pain hit. It was like pouring cold water over the exposed nerves of a tooth—only much worse. He stuck out his index finger, rammed it up the hole and turned it around several times before yanking it out. Then, wrapping gauze around his index and middle fingers, he began to rub in all directions around inside the wound. My body heaved involuntarily and I always wanted to ask the corpsman to stop for a moment, but I couldn't breathe enough to get the words out. Tears and perspiration poured down my face.

He repeated the cycle, this time with hydrogen peroxide—also cold. The peroxide, I discovered, sizzled and foamed up. At first it foamed white, then quickly went yellow-brown, then reddish-brown. The visual effects didn't help at all.

My next thought was, *This too will have to be wiped off!* Out came the gauze wrapped around the fingers, then the scrubbing began again. Next came a Betadine solution—a deep-red color and about as thick as blood but cold as ice water. It foamed too, but reddish-brown. By this time I was grabbing and regrabbing the mattress, holding back the urge to scream.

With each swipe of the gauze inside the wound, I grabbed for a new hold on the bed. Lastly, after the Betadine scrub was completed, the wound was washed again with Dakin's. Then, with long cotton swabs, strips of gauze soaked in Betadine were pushed all the way to the end of the hole. This procedure continued until yards of the thin gauze totally packed the wound.

My leg felt like an overnight bag with two weeks of clothes stuffed into it.

I stayed at Binh Thuy two weeks. Then I was transferred via two other hospitals to Cam Ranh Bay Army Hospital. Cam Ranh Bay was the dumping ground for many recovering soldiers. One mile away was a very nice Air Force hospital. I had spent eight days there earlier in my deployment, before being wounded, going through some tests for high blood pressure. While there I became friends with one of the nurses. I asked her how safe it was for her and the others. She said, "I was told Cam Ranh Bay was considered one of the most secure bases in Nam. We were still apprehensive, but the pilots stationed here told us not to worry, that Charlie was a rotten shot. And, for a while, he was. His rockets landed all over the place but never seemed to hit anything. Then he changed tactics and did what Communists do best—fight dirty.

"One night, soon after I arrived, Viet Cong commandos, armed with AK-47s (assault rifles) and satchel charges (homemade bombs that explode into flames on detonation) blew up the Army hospital a mile away and gunned down patients as they tried to escape the inferno. From here we saw smoke block out the stars and watched the lights of rescue choppers rushing toward us over the hospital Quonsets. The choppers were so loaded down with wounded that, as they landed, sparks flew from their skids.

"The crews screamed at us to get the casualties off faster so they could fly back to get more. The choppers' floodlights made the landing area look like that awful scene in *Gone with the Wind*—burned and bleeding kids on stretchers everywhere. Some cried out for their moms. Crisp black skin hung from burned bodies. Like charred meat on a barbecue, it peeled off. It just peeled. The air stunk of blood, burned hair and melted flesh."

That's where I was headed now—the same Army hospital she described.

Cam Ranh Bay was a convalescent hospital, which meant it was usually patients' last stay before being sent back to their respective units. It had an unwritten policy that a soldier didn't have to go back to his unit until he felt he was ready. Because of this, the hospital command made it very uncomfortable for the recovering wounded.

I arrived with others. We were briefed on base policy, then given a lecture on drug abuse.

"Okay, men, listen up. Welcome to Cam Ranh Bay. This is an Army hospital, but we have recovering soldiers from all branches of service. No one leaves here until they're ready for more combat. We have a drug problem on this base. It's out of control. There is also some bad dope being peddled. Just the other day we found an overdose victim in one of the bunkers on the beach. He was dead. Cold dead. My advice to all of you is stay off the drugs and stay off the beach at night. Any questions?"

Drugs were widespread in Vietnam during 1970, but his words shocked me. *Advice?* Nobody was going to bust us for drug offenses? How could that be? This was a U.S. Army base, right?!

I'd assumed the Army would take severe measures to assure a drug-free base. I was dead wrong. Patients strolled about on free time smoking pot like they were cigarettes. When the USO brought in live bands to entertain us or when we watched movies, enlisted men and officers alike walked brazenly through the bleachers in their hospital-issued pajamas, selling dope like popcorn and cotton candy at a circus. Nobody attempted to stop them.

My conclusion: *No one cared if they got caught.* Their reasoning was, "What are they going to do, send me to Vietnam?" Since no one cared if he got caught, the Army had no choice but to ignore it.

I heard horrific stories while in that hospital. Some made the hair on the back of my neck stand up. These were the survivors. Many in their units hadn't made it this far.

A young sergeant shared: "The NVA came at us in human wave

assaults, a swaying wall of massed men, pouring into our wire, spilling into the gaps blown by the sappers. When they're hit, the dying enemy remembers to fall flat across the wire so their friends in the next wave can use their bodies as steppingstones. They pushed through our automatic rifle fire, mines, grenades, and .50-caliber machine guns, through salvos of artillery shells that weighed ninety-five pounds each. The human waves kept coming, crashing into our first line of defense, soaking up our entire ordnance. They were an ocean of highly motivated Vietnamese ready to pay the price."

This was a different war than I was fighting deep in the delta. We rarely fought NVA regulars. Our war was mostly hit-and-run VCs. After seeing too many bloodbaths, battle-weary men like this sergeant weren't in any hurry to return to their combat units.

But the Army knew how to motivate the reluctant—treat them like they were in boot camp. At 6:00 a.m. every day except Sunday, we were herded out of our barracks and told to muster on the grinder for PT. Watching guys with bandages on their heads, arms in slings and legs in casts doing exercises was amusing.

"Okay, men, we're going to do jumping jacks. If one of your arms is wounded, exercise the one that isn't. If you can't use your legs, exercise the upper body. If you can't exercise your upper body, exercise the lower part."

It was stupidity to the highest degree. I couldn't help but think, *This is supposed to be a place to heal. How do they expect us to do that when we're sweating in our wounds and tearing open our stitches?*

After breakfast, we continued the insanity. This time it was to pick up cigarette butts and paper.

"Okay, make one long line. Hurry!" the hospital drill sergeant screamed. "I want you to pick up anything that is not sand and put it into your bag."

By now the sun was beating down on us. Nobody stooped down to pick up anything, but we still sweated like hogs as we hobbled through the hot sand. It was nonsense like this that made the front lines look inviting.

As I strolled along South Beach behind my ward one day, I met a young man who was crying. "What's going on?" I asked.

He pointed to an airplane lifting off the runway. "See that plane? I'm supposed to be on it, going home today."

"Really?" I said. "Then why are you here crying?"

"I've been AWOL for three months. I just couldn't handle it anymore. Friends were getting killed every single day. No one seemed to care and no one could explain to me why. I don't want to die."

He knew that if he turned himself in, he would have to make up that time in a brig without pay. He escaped the war, but not Vietnam.

I also met a twenty-year-old staff sergeant and platoon leader—quite remarkable for his age. "Every time one of my superiors got killed they promoted me up the ladder," he said.

I have often wondered if those two men ever made it home alive.

I learned a lot in that hospital. I came to realize that no matter how hard things seemed to be, there was always someone on this earth that had it worse than me. After hearing their stories, I was so thankful that I joined the Navy instead of being drafted into the Army. At least the Navy tried to get its sailors home alive.

The Army in my opinion really sucked. This infirmary wasn't much better than an animal hospital. It sure wasn't like the Air Force facility on the other side of town. Now that was a hospital. Nice young lady nurses were fun and friendly, and doctors had a personality and a sense of humor. It was like an oasis in the middle of a desert. But not this rat hole—this was like a prisoner-of-war camp.

As far as I knew, no one in my unit knew where I was. I hadn't written anyone. No one had written me. I could have sat out the rest of my war right there, because with their insane exercise program, my leg wasn't healing very fast. I petitioned the Cam Ranh Bay Hospital command to let me go back to my unit. They refused my request repeatedly, stating my leg wasn't healed enough, but I kept insisting. Finally they got tired of my daily trek to their office. I was given several days of dressing and bandages, release papers, and was sent on my way.

What a relief. I felt free again. I hopped the first plane I could find to Saigon—a little one-prop Piper Comanche flown by two civilian businessmen. The air was full of activity that day, and a low-flying jet almost hit us. The pilots dove to get out of the jet's way. It was too close. The incident left me shaken. I kept thinking, *Man, there are so many ways to die over here. I've got to survive. I've got to get home alive.*

Saigon buzzed with activity. Hundreds of narrow streets were filled with vendors. Pretty ladies walked about in their Áo Dàis and white, coned hats. Tasty noodle soups, French bread, frozen bananas covered in dark chocolate stuck on a stick were available on every corner. Thousands of motor and pedal bikes made the city accessible. Bells, whistles and honking horns of all sorts competed with the high-pitched sounds of thousands of one-cylinder engines that crammed the streets. This was the U.S. military hub. It would be much easier to find a ride back to the Float from here. Everything filtered through Saigon, one way or the other.

I spent the first night at a flophouse near the airport because it was too late to go downtown to the Victoria Hotel without breaking curfew. In the morning, I dressed my own leg by removing the old gauze and packing in the new with long cotton swabs. By this time the sensitivity of my wound was bearable. After I wrapped an ace bandage around my leg, I hopped into a motorcycle sidecar and headed downtown.

When I arrived at the Victoria Hotel, I checked into a room, then walked the streets looking for some local dope. After making a purchase, I went up to the top floor of the hotel where the bar and dance floor were, a place where people could sit and relax with a good view of the city. All hotel guests eventually went there to drink and chat, and I was soon joined by a couple of SEAL acquaintances who had come down from Da Nang for R & R. By their faces, I immediately knew something was wrong.

"John, have you heard the news?" Evidently they knew that I'd been recovering in a hospital.

"What news?" I asked.

Their faces were bleak. "Man, we're sorry to have to tell you this. Just the other day we lost five SEALs who were stationed with you on the Float."

"You're kidding." Lord above.

"Sorry. I wish we were. They were onboard a Seawolf after an enemy round hit a rotor blade. The blade later malfunctioned, throwing the copter into a spin. Everyone aboard was killed."

"Wow! Who were they?"

"Jim Gore, John Durlin, Richard Solano, Toby Thomas, and John Donnelly."

"No!"

Hearing their names took my breath from me. I knew them all. I felt like throwing up. I was stunned, and overwhelmed with grief. *Man! They're too young to be gone. SEALs aren't supposed to die. They're supposed to be invincible. This wasn't fair! They had a great future ahead of them. They were so exceptional at what they did.*

Their deaths made me even angrier at the war. I just couldn't make sense out of all the carnage.

When I first arrived on Sea Float, it had been fun getting to know Gore, Durlin and Solano again, reminiscing and catching up on what we'd all been doing the past couple of years. Thomas and Donnelly were also fun to be around. I had especially enjoyed my friendship with John Durlin.

John had come into my hooch on the Float once with a loaded M-79 grenade launcher. An unexpected slip of his finger caused the round to go off. There is a certain distinct "pop" sound when a round is discharged from that type of weapon. Everyone froze. After a couple of endless seconds we realized that the round hadn't gone far enough to explode. We collectively sighed in relief.

There's a safety built into the M-79 round because a grenade going off at a close distance throws off lots of shrapnel. The safety is for the protection of those who are using the gun. It had been a close call for all of us. John hadn't been so lucky this time.

John had talked about his childhood, growing up, and how he looked forward to seeing his family again. Now that was impossible. None of his dreams or aspirations would ever come true. He was going to check out God when he got home, he said. I wondered if my talks with him did any good. How did God see these guys? Where would they spend eternity? Where would I spend eternity if I got killed?

Again thoughts of life and dying were driven home. I spent a long time in deep reflection. There had to be some connection to everything. What was the glue that held all the pieces together? Were drugs making me delusional? No, there had to be a higher force, a supreme being working behind the scenes. If there was no God, then what was the use?

I spent two days with my friends from Da Nang, then I flew back to the Float to join my surviving teammates. My five friends' deaths made it hard for me to return to my unit. I knew morale would be low and I would be lonely without their presence. With death hitting so very close to home, I realized that until I finally left Vietnam I would be in harm's way.

I had hoped I would be sent back to the Philippines since our scheduled rotation time was so near, but that wasn't to be. Even though I couldn't go out on operations, I would have to remain with my unit until they were relieved of their duty. I only had two and a half weeks left in Vietnam, but they were the longest weeks I have ever lived.

Our detachment joined Detachment Delta for three days of ops working out of the Navy base at Can Tho. The base had been hit with mortars a few nights in a row, so the South Vietnamese troops laid a trap. Several VC were killed. Among them was the friendly barber who had been cutting everyone's hair. Mr. Smiley chatted away like a starving cricket during the day. At night he turned into a noxious killer.

Being a short-timer in Vietnam was nerve wracking. No one wanted to take unnecessary chances or talk about it either. There were a lot of superstitions prevalent among those who had only a few days left. We may not like death, but death liked us. After the war, I learned that 1,448 American soldiers were killed on their last day in country.

One of the five SEALs killed wasn't even supposed to have been on that operation. He'd been scheduled for departure, but since there was a delay in his flight he volunteered to go with his friends just to have something to do. Stuff like that really worked on my mind.

The chief corpsman who we called "Doc" seemed to have aged twenty years during the short months we served there. He drank heavily, his face turned a grayish-white, his hands trembled while eating and he smoked constantly. He was consumed by fear. He hadn't gone through BUD/S training, but because he was a Navy corpsman he was assigned to our Teams to help us if we got sick or wounded. He never left the Float, refused to go on any operation with us, and ultimately proved to be no benefit to anyone whatsoever.

The only positive thing that happened on the Float those last few days was the field promotion I received for being wounded. I was also awarded the Purple Heart and the Navy Commendation Medal with a Combat "V." The following letter came from the commander of the United States Naval Forces in Vietnam:

The Secretary of the Navy takes pleasure in presenting the Navy Commendation Medal to JOHN MICHAEL WOLFRAM, Quartermaster Second Class, United States Navy for service as set forth in the following citation:

For meritorious achievement while serving with friendly foreign forces engaged in armed conflict against the North Vietnamese and Viet Cong communist aggressors in the Republic of Vietnam from August to September 1970. While serving with Underwater Demolition Team Eleven, Detachment Delta, Petty Officer WOLFRAM was a platoon member of a team established to determine the feasibility of using demolition to destroy three enemy built dams across the Ba Beo Canal. His demolition handling, expertise and physical stamina were instrumental in expeditious preparation of eight thousand pounds of high explosives for a test demolition on the easternmost enemy dam. Upon arrival at the dam, deep within enemy controlled territory, Petty Officer WOLFRAM searched the area and marked enemy booby traps eliminating a grave danger to the entire team. He worked tirelessly preparing and positioning the charges in a complex test pattern. Although tired and exhausted by the time the test demolition shots had been completed, he once more entered the canal and conducted an underwater demolition operation which opened this vital canal and restored it to government control. Petty Officer WOLFRAM'S exemplary professionalism, courage and devotion to duty reflected great credit upon himself and were in keeping with the highest traditions of the United States Naval Service. For the Secretary of the Navy, J. H. King, Jr., Vice Admiral, U.S. Navy Commander, U.S. Naval Forces, Vietnam.

My leg wound would leave a nasty scar, but I am forever grateful it didn't cripple me or leave me with a limp. I was told I would have to extend one month if I wanted a field promotion. After weighing the benefits, I decided to extend. The extra stripe offered a much better pay scale, higher BAQ (funds to live off base), privileges such as eating in a separate dining area, pulling less duty, more delegation power and generally more respect.

In less than six months, I had been promoted from an E-3 to an E-5. Just prior to going to Vietnam, I had passed my test for Quartermaster 3rd Class Petty Officer. The field promotion, or *Ho Chi Minh* as we called it, made me an E-5, or 2nd Class Quartermaster. That was as high as a Navy enlisted person could go in rank in less than three years' time. I considered myself very fortunate.

Finally, early in the morning of August 28, 1970 our plane took off from Tan Son Nhut Air Base in Saigon heading back to Subic Bay, Philippines. As I looked out my window, I saw a new batch of soldiers disembarking a plane that had just landed. I felt a monumental sense of relief that it wasn't me, but a deep sense of sadness swept over me for those who had just arrived. I could only wonder how many of them would never make it home alive.

THE SEA FLOAT CREED

WE HAVE DONE SO MUCH,
WITH SO LITTLE,
FOR SO LONG,
WE CAN NOW DO ANYTHING,
WITH NOTHING,
FOREVER.

— Chapter Eighteen —

From Hooyah to Hallelujah

Just two weeks after I left Vietnam, I found myself standing on Main Street of my hometown. It was like walking through a door into a totally different world. On one side of the door there had been chaos, constant danger, weird smells, distant gunfire, diesel engines revving up, helicopter rotor blades singing, an alien culture, stress and the constant fear of dying.

On the other side of the door I found the calm and tranquil surroundings of a warm, late summer day, birds singing, a farmer's tractor harvesting hay, a neighbor mowing his lawn, the sweetness of a mother's love and comforting family chatter around the dinner table.

My high school buddies who had escaped the draft, and who obviously hadn't experienced anything more dramatic than the country fair, seemed a bit dull. I was Alice who had just come back from Wonderland and there was no one to tell. They didn't want to discuss world events, especially the ugly war in Vietnam. Perhaps talking about the war threatened their secure world. By keeping their heads in the sand, they could pretend it didn't really exist. Then again, they might have been embarrassed about not participating in Vietnam themselves.

Unfortunately, I'd brought memories from the other side of the door along with me. Loud noises made me jump. I drove around scenic river roads instinctively noting good places for ambushes. When I passed congested wood areas, I couldn't shake the feeling that in any given moment someone could unleash a barrage of B-40 rockets and machine gun fire my way. Inside my head I was still fighting a war, and since my basic instincts were programmed for survival, I was suspicious of everyone and everything. This robbed me of the beauty of my home.

I visited the gravesites of my high school friends who died in Vietnam. I felt empathy for them as a thousand memories raced through my mind of better days and times. I fought back tears as I visualized their mangled bodies beneath me, rotting in the cold, dark earth. I muttered repeatedly, "What a waste! What a waste!" When I visited with the parents of Larry Smith, my close friend who had been killed in Vietnam, it seemed as though his ghost was lingering, crying out against the injustice of a life robbed in its youth.

The only people who understood my feelings were other Vietnam veterans. Everyone else seemed detached, a part of another world that was encased in a protective bubble, perhaps intentionally, not wanting to be disturbed.

It would have been much better if I had more of a cushion between fighting in Vietnam and returning home. The difference between patrolling in riverboats up threatening rivers and walking the docile streets of USA was drastic.

I was fortunate to be alive when so many others weren't. My fate could have been much different. I could have ended up like Larry, Gary, Terry, my hometown buddies; or fellow teammates Jim, John and Richard, or like 58,000 other American soldiers who were killed. This was constantly on my mind. I intentionally counted my joys every day, no matter how small. Doing so began to give me a new outlook on life.

I cherished every breath I took. I appreciated every small thing, big thing—sunrise, sunset, every cloudy, sunny or rainy day. I was just happy to be alive.

In the Navy, I found myself, and I found a place to belong. It rescued me from my early life. Now I found joy in life, but I also carried the nightmares of Vietnam with me. I felt God's presence, but I didn't know what to do about it, and I didn't know what to do with myself.

Once back in San Diego, the drinking, doping and partying continued. The guys were always looking for an excuse to celebrate, so returning to our Coronado base was as good as any. Eventually, the partiers separated into two major groups: the heavy drinkers and those who preferred drugs. An unspoken resentment was developing among us.

On one occasion a bunch of UDT/SEAL "heads" and drinkers ended up at the team bar, The Trade Winds, in Coronado. Words were exchanged which fueled a dual between the drinkers and dopers. My buddy Harness came out of the brawl with his jaw broken in two places.

Tijuana's spell pulled us across the border again and again. Its prisons were full of young Americans who got into trouble one way or the other. We were constantly warned about its dangers, but still crossed over more than we should have. A fellow frogman found out the hard way. He accidentally ran over someone on a busy street and killed him. It cost his family their life savings and many months of negotiation and bribes to get him out of jail.

I woke up alone in a dingy bar in TJ once. I had passed out from too much tequila. An acquaintance from boot camp deserted me while partying. The guy was a jerk. He left me there for all the thugs and gangsters. I was shocked when I awoke at 5:00 a.m., my head lying on a table in a strange bar, while the Mexican band played on.

Another time while returning to the United States' side, I was pulled over by the Border Patrol and strip-searched inside a private room while agents tore through my van. An agent said he found three marijuana seeds. Not enough evidence to make a case so they let me go.

My life was one constant high or party. I wasn't the only one. A lot of the guys hit the booze or drugs pretty hard after Nam. It was affecting my behavior at work. Because of my rank I was given a nice cushy position of being the NCO of the Intelligence Department. Intel was a nice sounding name but had little responsibility. Craig Danielson, one of my BUD/S teammates, Larry Faller, and a couple of new guys and I didn't have much to do except write daily surf reports, get the mail, shop for other departments, deliver secret documents from Special Warfare across the street at the Naval Amphibious Base to our CO, and do occasional cartography. At the time we earned the dubious reputation of being the goof-off department. It was full of "heads." All hand-picked. Mostly short-timers.

We had lots of time to go on jogs down the beach and sunbathe. We'd go on our morning runs and disappear for hours on the Coronado beach with the tourists. We'd take turns covering for each other. When my brother Gary and cousin Bob showed up for a vacation, I snuck off for hours every day to show them around town. We hit the beaches, saw the sites, then I returned to the compound just before evening muster. I developed a system so all of us guys could enjoy the freedom our department offered. We didn't feel bad, because we always got our work done, and doing something fun was a lot better than just hanging around staring at walls.

I had my enemies. A gung-ho chief I'll call "Mouthy," who we deployed with on our ARG detachment overseas, knew a bunch of us were into drugs and despised us—he'd got stuck with a platoon of "dopers." We didn't care for him either. He was a loud-mouthed, arrogant guy who came over from a SEAL Team. Mouthy claimed that he had a bounty on his head in Vietnam when he operated with SEAL Team One years before. He bragged about how many VC he had killed, women he had seduced and ears he had cut off. He also claimed to be a black belt in karate, kung fu or whatever. What I despised most about him was he often gave a friend of mine extra duty so that he could go and sleep with the guy's wife. My friend's wife drove him insane with jealousy. It affected his mind. He eventually tried to commit suicide and was discharged.

Chief Mouthy hated that I came back with war stories, a Purple Heart and a promotion to 2nd Class Petty Officer. He considered me a screw-up. I considered him a fool. He found ways to put me on restriction and treated me like a seaman. He gave me extra weekend duty and placed me underneath another chief who was delegated to give me demeaning jobs like scrubbing and buffing floors—jobs that were never given to someone with my rank.

I kind of asked for it though. One day, the NCO of the UDT-12 Intel Department noticed three Nikonos underwater cameras were missing. In jest I made a comment to my friend Danielson so the frustrated NCO could hear it. I insinuated that I might know where the cameras were. I didn't. I was just playing around, but it got me into deep trouble. The NIS (Naval Investigative Service) showed up and I was interviewed, or should I say interrogated. I had a Team lawyer assigned to me and was under a full investigation, which included taking a lie detector test.

Since I had a house full of marijuana and pills I had smuggled in from the Philippines, I sent Danielson to my house to clean up the place while I was being questioned. I feared they would want to search my house next. They didn't, but it made me very conscious of the contraband I had around my place.

Things calmed down after a few days, probably because my lie detector test came back negative. I wasn't worried about questions regarding the cameras. I didn't take them nor did I know anything about where they were. But I was sure nervous about my drug activity. I was thinking, *Man, if they ask anything about me or my friends taking drugs, I've had it.*

I never could get my command to admit to me that the investigation was over. They just left me dangling. But since the NIS didn't show up any more, and I hadn't received a Captain's Mast or demotion, I assumed I was in the clear.

Eventually my easygoing and fun-loving nature won over the chief who had been assigned to make my life miserable. He was now trying to recruit me to ship over (reenlist). He told me how much he admired my ability to smile and take things nonchalantly and gave me a whole line of bull of how much the Navy and Teams needed me. He said I had impressed him by my good-natured attitude while under his harassment. "We need men like you in the Teams," he reiterated. I was flattered, but not interested.

Not everyone in the Teams was a screw-up. There were some very outstanding guys, both enlisted and officers. However, there was probably a 65 percent turnover every year. Most guys I hung with did their four years and were out. Greg Moore, my good friend, exemplified the feelings of many when on his last day in the Navy he came out of the locker room with his Navy whites painted in black stripes. Not only did he have on prison garb, but he also sported a toilet brush in one hand and a broom in the other. We all got a laugh, including the lifers.

Attitudes are catchy. That was why many of the career guys stayed away from those of us who were headed out the door. We had different ideologies—different goals. Since we were not looking for advancement, we could be freer to express our feelings and take greater risks with our behavior. Some of our attitudes would never have been tolerated if they knew we were going to make the Navy a career. They would have cracked the whip, and hard. From their viewpoint they were probably glad to see my types leave.

In some ways I felt sorry for the career guys because they made so many friends who moved on after their time was up. I admired those who chose to stay in the service, especially during the tough times of the '60s and '70s. Our country needed good men and women to help defend our principles around the world and to keep us safe at home. My hat went off to them. I was proud of them. I was proud to have served with them. But military life just was not for me.

The closer I got to the end, the more eager I was to get on with civilian life. However, I was concerned about what I was going to do for a living when I got out. I only had a high school education and four years of remarkable experiences. My Navy training wouldn't do me much good on the outside unless I wanted to pursue a diving job, work for the police, Border Patrol or the government. Those were the furthest things from my mind. I'd had enough of uniforms.

I loved rock and roll music, and fantasized being in a traveling band. I bought a huge custom set of drums and beat on them by the hour. I already owned a van to haul them in, and figured if I practiced, I could make a living by doing something I really enjoyed. In preparation, I attended local dances and concerts of big-name rock groups. I purchased front-row seats and enjoyed studying the different drumming styles of each performer.

In my apartment, with just my hands, fists and elbows, I pounded out drumbeats that must have come from Africa or maybe the moon. My hands took off as if they had a mind of their own, like an out-of-body experience. At times I even amazed myself. It was like something took them over.

But there came a point in my life when I didn't feel comfortable going to the local hangouts anymore, and gradually began to view things through different eyes. I realized that bars and clubs were hangouts for sad and unfulfilled people. I saw myself as one of them, pathetic and lonely. Like I had as a child, I began to want more.

It was a confusing time. I didn't like being in the military. I didn't like myself. I didn't like what I was observing in other people's lives. I didn't like what was going on in the world. I had already known of two teammates who attempted suicide. I saw too many marriages in shambles. I saw alcoholism, mean tempers, antisocial behavior, drug addictions, ladder climbers, psychopaths, sociopaths, manic-depressives, backstabbers, thieves, liars, pushers, wife beaters, overachievers, and occasionally a normal-looking person.

A new sailor from the Administration Department was sent to work with me. His name was Alex French. He was not an Underwater Demolition-trained man. This made his coming to work for me unusual. To my knowledge he was the first person to be assigned to help in my department from the outside, ever. Other black shoes (regular Navy) worked in the Admin office, we had a few hospital corpsman and those who packed our parachutes, but never anyone assigned to Intel.

Alex was a young Christian who wasn't bashful about his faith in God and found it easy to talk about the Bible and his personal walk with Jesus. We hit it off right away. *Wow, someone to talk to about God*, I thought.

I was impressed with his knowledge of the Bible. He sensed that God was dealing with me, and whenever he could, he talked to me about Jesus.

One of our teammates made a surprise visit. Robbie—"Bluegill" as his friends called him—had stepped on a mine while out on patrol near Da Nang on our last tour. He had been in a hospital for several months. He lost his left leg below the knee, left elbow (lost the bone but kept his arm and was wearing an external elbow) and the right lower jawbone. Robbie still looked pretty battered. Everyone tried to cheer him up, but he didn't look too happy. I sure didn't blame him. But he was alive. Bluegill was very fortunate to have survived that tragic day. After they drove him back to the hospital, I said a quick prayer for him and thanked God for bringing me out of Nam whole. The Vietnam War took the lives of forty-nine UDT and SEAL Team members. The youngest American to be killed in action was only fifteen years old. Twenty-five thousand were under the age of twenty.

Robbie's visit was a sober reminder of the tragedies of war. Thousands of our boys came home with missing limbs and messed up heads. For several days I couldn't get Robbie off of my mind, and I withdrew into my thoughts.

One day Alex invited me to go along with him to his church for a revival service. I brought along several of my UDT friends, including some of their girlfriends. It was an upbeat meeting, and I nudged one of the fellows next to me and said, "This is kind of uplifting, isn't it?"

He said, "Better watch out or it'll grab hold of you!"

I had the feeling he didn't want to catch it. However, I was impressed with the lively singing and fiery preaching and, despite the strangeness there was something about this place, no—this experience, that I wanted. The only other church I had ever attended was a Lutheran one back home and, compared to this, it was dead.

Alex was proud to have a full row of sinners, and it didn't go unnoticed. Afterward some of Alex's friends came up to us to talk about heaven. One woman kept asking me, "Young man, are you really sure you're saved?"

I assured her I was by saying over and over, "Oh yes! I'm sure." However, the more I tried to convince her, the more doubts crept into my mind.

One thing she accomplished was getting me to think about it, plus the revival brought a whole new notion to me about church. Up to this point, I hadn't considered attending a church regularly. I'd been of the opinion that I could walk with God in my own unorthodox way. But now I found myself searching for a local assembly to attend consistently. I visited several churches in the community of Coronado where I lived, and found one that was similar to where Alex attended. The people were friendly, and I finally felt that Sunday was a day I could look forward to.

I sensed a change was coming, something not intellectual or emotional, but something spiritual and positive and inspiring. My appetite to draw closer to God was greater than ever. I went to the local bookstore, bought my first Bible, and began reading the Gospels—mostly about how much God loves us. I can laugh now, but I was so desperate to listen to something Christian that I checked out Christmas albums in May, since that was all the Coronado library had available. What made this even more hilarious was that the LP records were scratchy and ancient, as though they had come out of the '40s big-band era, but I dutifully—religiously?— listened to them.

As my spiritual eyes were slowly opening, I became aware of how much Jesus' name was being used in casual conversation. Most people on the street talked about Jesus in one way or another. I began to ask myself, *Why does everyone use the name of God when swearing? Why is it that everyone attributes things in life to the "Good Lord"?* God had to be close by, otherwise people wouldn't be using the name of Jesus so much in everyday conversation. Everywhere I turned, I heard His name mentioned. It was used on radio, television, in movie theaters, rock and roll records, newspapers and paperback books.

I went to another rock concert with the guys, but for the first time I didn't enjoy it. As I listened to the music and watched the crowd respond, I was awakened to the fact that there was more wrong going on here than right. Most of the young people were high on drugs, and pot was being passed around—little clouds of smoke hovered everywhere—yet the security guards didn't do anything to stop it. Normally this wouldn't have bothered me either, and I would have been right in the middle of it. But I was slowly seeing that some things uplift a person, while other things drag them down.

I felt like an observer from another planet, curiously trying to discern what all the interest was about. Many were simply following the crowd and the spirit of the age. I knew this all too well. I had been one of them. Now I felt foolish, like a con artist had ripped me off. I admitted to myself I had been duped.

After the concert, an intense passion came over me that left me shaking. I never felt anything like it before. It was invigorating. I didn't understand fully what was happening to me, but I just knew that it was of God. It was like catching a wave after swimming by your own strength, and then suddenly being scooped up and carried along by the power of the wave. I rolled down the window and howled, "God loves you! Stop messing up your life, and turn your life over to Jesus!"

I was not only surprising myself, but those in the van with me looked as if they were seeing a ghost. At first they laughed, a very nervous giggle. But then they got dead serious quiet, and listened. Dozens of shocked onlookers stood still and absorbed what was spilling out of me. It was a spiritual rush—a part of me I never knew existed—a rush better than any drug-induced one I'd ever had before.

With that incident behind me, reading the Bible and attending church became a regular occurrence. One Sunday morning, I responded to the pastor's open invitation to come to the altar and to fully accept God into my life. I was the only one who walked down to the front of church that day. I was asked to repeat a sinner's prayer asking God to forgive me for all my wrongdoings and inviting him into my life, and was told that I was saved. As you can imagine, I was very excited about that bold step in my life and found myself rejoicing as I walked home after service.

But halfway home I was confronted with a very familiar, but now unwelcome, inner struggle. I normally would go home and just light up. My drug habit was pulling on me. Getting high was a lifestyle I wanted to be rid of. I felt a powerful urge to get rid of it now. I talked to God about it. "Jesus, if this is all that there is to salvation, I don't think I'm going to make it. I want more than anything to get drugs out of my life, but I can't do that without you. Please help me."

My prayer was sincere. I needed help. I wanted to be set free from the drugs. I always felt God was a miracle worker. After all, He is God, and God can do anything, right? Then why was I struggling? I felt I needed more of him in my life than what I just had received. God was about to answer my request.

When I arrived at my apartment—located above a garage in the back alley of A Street—I saw the weekly *Reminder* paper lying on the ground by the stairs. Normally I just trashed these because they were mostly advertising. But this time I felt compelled to open it. Right there in front of my nose was a small ad announcing a Pentecostal revival. It jumped out at me as though it was a billboard encased in flashing neon lights, and it spoke directly to my hungry heart. This is what the advertisement said:

REVIVAL NOTICE. (Say you saw it in the Reminder)

Pentecostal Church Revival Begins. Reverend Vernon Barkley of Ventura, California will be the principle speaker at the Holy Ghost Revival to be held at 631 12th Street, Imperial Beach.

The event, which was announced by Reverend Allen Picklesimer, pastor of the church, will begin June 20, and continue until July 27.

Each service is scheduled to be filled with "wonderful testimonies of God's great delivering power, and beautiful singing."

Persons interested in the "experiences of tongues" are welcome to find out what it's all about. Everyone is welcome. For a ride or for information call the church at 432-5723.

The sentence that said "experiences of tongues" was what caught my attention. That certainly wasn't something I was acquainted with from my Christian upbringing back home, but it sounded *cool* to me. In fact, I didn't have a clue as to what "tongues" was, but something inside my head said, "Yes! This is where the power is. This is what you are searching for."

I was starved for everything the Lord had for me. I wasn't afraid of the supernatural. I was looking for it. I wanted the thunder and lightning that Moses felt. I remember watching Charlton Heston in the movie *The Ten Commandments*. That's the kind of God I was looking for. Something told me that God had more for me to experience than what I had just received. Deep down I just knew God was still in the miracle business. I was sure he hadn't closed down his shop and moved away.

I made up my mind on the spot that I was going to attend this meeting, if for no other reason than to see for myself what this "speaking in tongues" was all about.

When the next Sunday rolled around, I attended the Coronado

church as usual in the morning and lounged around my apartment most of that afternoon anticipating the Pentecostal meeting that evening. Just before it was time to go to the revival someone knocked on my door. When I opened it two of my teammates sailed in, obviously high on drugs. They invited me to party with them and had an ample selection of drugs to choose from. "Come on, John, let's have some fun. It's party time!"

Surprisingly, the thought of getting high repulsed me. I looked into the mirror that hung in the living room. I was appalled. *That messed-up person glaring back at me can't be me,* I rationalized. *That's not who I really am.* But the sobering truth was, it really was me. In Saigon when I had considered suicide, I had hated my life. Now I hated myself. I hated my glazed, red eyes, my face that looked like I'd just gone through Hell Week. I hated that I had no self-control, that I was too weak to get off the drugs. Too weak to see myself as a complete human being without them. I felt no pride in myself. I felt no self-respect, no honor. No wonder other people didn't respect me.

When I had helped to rescue the Apollo 11 astronauts and space ship, I had stood on top of the world. The media had seen to that. Only two short years had passed, and I had sunk so low. Look at me now.

No more artificial waves of high, I determined, *and no more plummets after.* I had discovered a new wave, a real one. That's the one I would catch—God. I knew His wave would never let me fall.

I said, "No thanks. Not tonight, not tomorrow, never again. I don't want to live the rest of my life drugged out of my mind. It's time to move on, and I'm planning to go to a church revival tonight. Want to come?"

They looked at me as if I'd lost my mind. They said no, made a quick dash for the door and disappeared into the night. I hurriedly prepared myself for church.

God's call was personal. It was my special, divine moment. It was up to me to respond. I couldn't wait for my friends. I couldn't wait for my family. It was my decision, and mine alone. Yes, Lord, I'm coming.

I searched my apartment for the revival notice because I needed the address. I couldn't find it. *My roommate probably threw it out with the trash*, I thought. I hurried down the steps to our garbage can, flipped off the lid and dug through the soggy brown grocery bags. *Rats! It's not here. I've got to find that address.*

Down the alley I went. *Maybe there's one of those* Reminder *papers in this can.* I tore through the bags. Nothing but slop, dented cans and empty food containers. *Okay then—this one.* Nothing. My search continued. I went from garbage can to garbage can. I became aware of some people watching me from their back windows as I tore through their trash, but I didn't care. I must have looked like a beggar to them, frantically digging from one container to the next. In a sense, I was. My desperation was fueled by my unquenchable hunger for God, and something told me I *had* to attend that church revival. Nothing was going to stop me. Nothing!

I rummaged until I found a soggy, half torn copy of the paper, ran to my van, then headed toward Imperial Beach. As I zoomed past the Naval Amphibious base, I was sure I heard the voice of God telling me to turn around and ask some of my friends if they wanted to join me. I did so, but nobody wanted to go.

I returned to the parking lot somewhat discouraged. However, before I reached my van, I ran into fellow UDT-11 teammate Rick Whitcomb. He pulled up next to me and rolled down his window. "Hey, John. What's up?"

"I'm going to church," I said as enthusiastically as I could. "Want to join me?"

"Ah, sure. Okay."

He had just returned from working out. He was in training for the Military Olympics. I had noticed Rick, like me, had some deep needs in his life. He too was searching. Together we located the small Pentecostal church in Imperial Beach at 631 12th Street.

I'll never forget the church atmosphere that greeted us that Sunday evening. There was earnest prayer going on, and people were kneeling, walking and standing with their arms raised toward heaven as they called out to the Lord. Their praying alone was enough to put me under conviction. I couldn't help but notice the wholesome appearance of both the men and ladies. It was a stark contrast to the "free spirit" of the late '60s and early '70s. Everyone was friendly and amazingly uninhibited in his or her expression of love toward God. I had never been to a church service quite like this before.

The main service had officially begun with singing, praise and worship. Everything was so sincere, unrestrained and enthusiastic. I observed that everyone, including the children, thoroughly enjoyed the worship. What I was feeling almost blew me away.

Things got even livelier. The lady in front of us waved her arms in the air and danced. Goose bumps raced up and down my spine as I witnessed her spirited display of animated worship. I looked at Rick, and he looked at me, and all we could say to each other was, "Wow!"

The presence of the Lord was electrifying! Every part of the service built upon the other until I shook with excitement. Then suddenly a few men left their pews, ran down the aisle, and began to circle the inside walls of the building at high speed. As they ran past where we were sitting, we could feel the Holy Spirit sweep over us, just like waves in an excited ocean.

Our eyes locked once again. I don't know if it was fear I saw in Rick's eyes or amazement, but they were as wide open as a human's eyes could be. My heart was pumping, and again tingling sensations like little fingers, thousands of them, ran up and down my neck and back.

I don't think we had anything to compare with this. That is, except maybe what we saw and experienced at some of the rock concerts. But those people weren't there seeking the power of God's love.

Rick had his moments of wanting to slip out, but I had the outside seat and blocked him in. Every time he tried, I became a wedge. There was something about this place, no–this experience, that I wanted.

I did my best to reassure Rick. I even appealed to his manhood. "Listen, we made it through BUD/S training, Hell Week, diving school, jump school, survival school and Vietnam. Surely we can make it through this church service!"

Later on while reading the Bible, I discovered that the Lord encourages His people to worship Him in dance and jubilation. Even King David took off his royal robes to celebrate God one day in Jerusalem and danced joyously before all the people.

I remembered a day I brought a small gift to my then three-year-old nephew, Chad. When I handed it to him, he was so excited that he ran and jumped around my mother's living room. With that memory, I realized why some people get excited in church. They begin to think about the goodness of the Lord and they just can't contain their joy. Both the Old and New Testaments have many examples of worshipers expressing their love and devotion to God in spontaneous ways. This church surely did.

I could hardly wait until the visiting pastor/evangelist, Reverend Vernon Barkley, finished preaching and opened the altar for prayer. My mind was going wild. *Come on, people, how do I get this Holy Spirit in me like you have it? Whatever you have...I want it now!*

The big moment finally came. "These altars are now open for anyone who would like to receive the Holy Spirit, with evidence of speaking in tongues," the evangelist announced.

I briefly pondered that. *That is what I read in the advertisement. That is why I came. This is what I want. I should go down to the front like he said.*

However, my feet felt as heavy as lead and my legs froze. My heart became a machine that pounded nervously inside my chest.

Though at first I couldn't move, the appeal was like a magnet. It pulled at me, encouraging me to walk down that long aisle to the altar. Finally the drawing power became stronger than my fears, and before I knew it I was kneeling at the front of the church. God knelt. I discovered that when I took one step toward Him, He met me there.

My military training brainwashed me into thinking that I was among the toughest fighting men in the world. I was taught techniques to kill, how to block out pain, endure hardships, stay cool under fire, and I had just recently returned from the physical and mental devastation of war.

I almost never cried in those three and a half years I was a Navy frogman. So it was a pleasant surprise to feel warm watery beads streaming down my cheeks. It seemed like God was helping me cry. My chest throbbed and jerked uncontrollably. I wept, told God I was sorry for the awful things I'd done, bared my soul and sobbed some more. My whole being was laid open before God. It was like a river rushing over boulders and rocks, causing silt and scum to float away from me.

The tender, forgiving power of God was a great, welcome relief. I experienced the amazing grace of God that millions before me had experienced. His forgiveness and love became mine that night as my sins were forgotten forever, just as the Bible so compassionately declares.

Several altar workers stood around me, raised my arms upward and encouraged me on. I was oblivious to what was happening around me, except for the sounds of numerous people praying and praising God, which resonated throughout the room like thunder. Suddenly I heard myself begin to speak words that I had never spoken before, and wondered if this was the Holy Spirit they were talking about. Whatever it was, it was amazing. Later, others confirmed that I indeed was "speaking in tongues."

I felt inebriated, except I was sober. I was asked whether I would like to be baptized in water that night. Someone held a Bible in front of me and read from the book of Acts: "Then Peter said unto them, Repent, and be baptized every one of you in the name of Jesus Christ for the remission of sins, and ye shall receive the gift of the Holy Ghost. For the promise is unto you, and to your children, and to all that are afar off, *even* as many as the Lord our God shall call." (Acts 2:38-39- KJV).

They gave me a quick Bible study as they went from Acts 2 to Acts 8, Acts 10, Acts 19 and Romans 6 to verify the importance of being buried with Jesus through baptism.

I was in the mood to do anything God wanted me to do. I figured if it was in the Bible, it had to be good for me. A baptismal tank was kept under a trapdoor on the platform, and someone pushed back the organ to access it.

I was ushered downstairs to a dressing room along with others to put on a blue baptismal robe, and in no time we were all standing next to the tank. Three of us were baptized that night, including my good friend Rick, who also experienced the power of God's nearness and spoke in tongues.

Pastor Picklesimer said, "I now baptize you in the name of Jesus Christ for the remission of your sins." While being immersed, I felt a heavy load vanish. As my body broke the surface, a warm sensation engulfed me starting at my head, surging through my entire body, and ending at my toes. It was like liquid lightening had struck me. My body was burning. I felt fifty pounds lighter and had an amazing sense of floating upward. In characteristic '60s lingo I blurted out, "Wow! Awesome, man!"

A fog I never knew existed instantly vanished. Colors looked brighter, people were clearer, and I felt a part of them, felt physically *alive*, as if I had spent the twenty years of my life walking around with impaired vision, impaired hearing, impaired thought, but never knew it until this moment. Now that distance, that fog, was gone.

I don't believe there is a more satisfying feeling in the entire world than to have your sins washed away. Absolutely nothing can compare with the joy and comfort I felt in that water tank.

Jumping into the Pacific Ocean to rescue astronauts, scuba diving and parachuting out of airplanes was exhilarating to say the least, but it didn't even come close to the experience I had with Jesus that night.

I didn't know it was humanly possible to feel this good. (And to discover this feeling was available without the aid of drugs or alcohol was mind-blowing.) The euphoria of my transformation was incredible, yet inexplicable, as an overwhelming peace and astounding joy overflowed my heart. I wanted to hug every person in sight. I felt as if they were my long lost friends.

I undeniably tapped into what the Bible calls heavenly places. I felt like God was inside me. I was truly born again. Forget *hooyah*; now I wanted to shout *Hallelujah*!

His nurturing had finally culminated in my being born again. Inside I was exploding like a billion shooting stars and a million grand finales of gigantic fireworks erupting all at once. God had rescued me!

"He Rescued Me"—Genelle Tennant

On the stormy sea of sin I was sinking,
Never to rise again;
The wind and the rain 'round me crashing,
Had battered and torn me within.

But he rescued me, Jesus rescued me,
From the cold, dark waters of sin's troubled sea;
Oh he rescued me through dark I can see,
Jesus reached down in love and he rescued me.

I could feel death's storm around me as I struggled for my life,
I could see his anger waiting to claim me for his prize;
Then out of desperation I almost lost my mind,
Somehow I cried to Jesus and he saved me just in time.

Oh he rescued me, Jesus rescued me,
From the cold, dark waters of sin's troubled sea;
Oh he rescued me through dark I can see,
Jesus reached down in love...

Oh he reached down in love,
Yes, he reached down in love,
And he rescued me.

—Epilogue—

As I drove home I was drawn to the innumerable lights across the San Diego Bay and realized they represented thousands of people who were searching for a sense of belonging and meaning just as I had been. I was deeply moved. People who drove by me in their automobiles and those who were walking along the streets seemed to cry out. I was struck by how much concern I had for people whom I had never even met. I wanted to tell the whole universe about Jesus. I sensed it must be the Holy Spirit living inside me, because I have never felt this kind of compassion before. I couldn't wait for Monday morning so I could share with my teammates what had happened to Rick and me.

While home I was compelled to rid my life of the things that would eventually pull me down. I did a little house cleaning. I filled a pillowcase full of marijuana, hashish, pills and drug paraphernalia and with my roommate, Nick, as a witness, took them down to the San Diego Bay and "baptized" them.

The very next church service I brought with me a van full of my teammates. My constant talk about what had happened to me had gotten to them. When my friends realized I wasn't going to take a "no" for an answer, they had agreed to come and "get it over with."

The beauty was that as soon as my friends were exposed to the Spirit of God, they too were drawn to him. All of them expressed afterward that they had never felt the presence of God like that before and were full of questions. The entire first batch of friends said they were looking forward to coming back, and they did again and again until many of them invited God into their lives and were baptized and filled with the Holy Spirit. Others followed.

Years later, I visited the BUD/S training area with a local pastor friend who wanted to see where SEALs were trained. When I entered the quarterdeck I asked the young man on duty if we could get permission for a walk-through of the compound. The CO in charge soon met with us. I gave him a copy of the book I had written about my conversion and when he read the back cover he exclaimed, "So you're the guy?"

"What do you mean?" I asked.

He said, "There's still talk about that around here because it made such an impact on the guys back then. It's like folklore around here."

His comments amazed me. I hadn't known.

Not only had many been touched, filled with the Holy Spirit and baptized, five were called to be pastors. Four of us were ordained through the same church organization. James Ghiloni was the only one who stayed in Imperial Beach. He later became the pastor of that very church. Nick Nicholson became an evangelist and a home missionary before his untimely death. Tom Bracken is presently a foreign missionary to the countries of Taiwan and China. I've lost contact with Ramos Flores, but I remember how anxious he was to share Jesus and God's great love with the whole world. Then there was me. I too was called into the ministry. The odds must have been staggering—the five of us coming from such diverse backgrounds and religious upbringings, and having all been called into the ministry with one broad stroke of the Master's hand. He'd assimilated us guys into the family of God.

Reaching my relatives was a bigger challenge. It took several years to get a breakthrough. My brother Jeff was the first, followed by my Mom, then Pam and Tom. Aunt Vicki and a nephew, Jason, were later baptized. I also saw several hometown friends become baptized and filled with the Holy Spirit.

Just as people have always asked me what it was like to be a UDT/SEAL, they have also asked me how I knew I was called into the ministry. I am not sure it was a one-step event. It started with a burden to share Jesus with my friends and family and evolved into a full-time career. God confirmed each step I took along the way.

The first evidence that God was directing my life was by giving me favor with people around me. Through nothing less than a miracle, I was allowed to study the Bible until my discharge from the Navy. All I was required to do was call in each morning. Believe me, that is not typical Navy policy.

Earlier I had opted to participate in a program the Navy called "Project Transition." You could request up to three months working on the outside somewhere to ready yourself for civilian life. I had chosen to work at a music store, but when I became a Christian I asked for a reassignment. I was allowed to attend summer school at Mar Vista High School to prepare myself for Bible college. The teacher let me study the Bible. After my three months were up, I was supposed to return to the UDT/SEAL compound for the remaining three months I owed Uncle Sam.

After much prayer and fasting, I felt led to ask my executive officer, Mr. Nelson, if I could continue studying the Bible. "Sir, perhaps you've heard of my conversion. I feel like God is calling me into the ministry and I would like to attend a Bible college when I get out of the Navy. Do you think it would be possible for me to continue studying the Bible for the remainder of my obligation to the Navy?"

To drive the point home about my dramatic change, I had brought with me two boxes of items I had acquired from the Navy. Most everyone had apartments full of nonessential *stuff* they accumulated from their UDT offices and departments. He looked at me kind of funny and just shook his head in disbelief. But what came out of his mouth stunned me. "All right, Wolfram, continue what you're doing, but call in each morning to let us know that you're still in the area. Now get out of here." Wow! Six months to study the Bible with Navy pay! That was incredible!

Since then, my wife Deborah and I have been able to minister in all fifty states and more than forty countries around the world. One of the most gratifying places God directed me was a return to Vietnam. While doing missionary work in the Philippines in the mid '80s, I was compelled to visit the Bataan refugee camp. There I found thousands of Vietnamese, Cambodians and Laotians who had risked their lives to escape governments that had become oppressive, or worse. I was taken aback by an overwhelming burden that fell upon me for them. God didn't let up until I investigated further. So in the early 1990s my wife and I made a trip into Vietnam with a fellow missionary. We started in Hanoi and worked our way down to HCMC (Ho Chi Minh

City).

While in Hanoi I spoke with people on the streets. They discovered I was an American and that I had fought in the war. A man approached me from the shadows and grabbed me. His embrace lasted much longer than was comfortable and I wondered if he was going to try and settle an old score. But then it registered. I couldn't speak Vietnamese and he couldn't speak English, and in his own way he was conveying to me that the war was over. I felt he was saying, "I've moved on. What about you?" I was the one who hadn't moved on.

That was the turning point. All my pentup emotions from years earlier had come to a head. The memories of losing eight friends, spending time in hospitals recovering from my leg wound, plus a thousand other feelings erupted all at once. Then I heard God say, "John, these are my people. I love them just like I love you. I want you to come back to this nation to share my Gospel with them. This time you won't be carrying an M-16, but the Holy Bible."

I spent several fabulous years in the '90s working among these precious people. I still make frequent trips to lend a hand in any way I can. Vietnam is predominately Buddhist. Less than one percent of the population of 87 million is fundamentally Christian. But the hunger is there.

When I travel throughout America and share my personal story, Vietnam veterans often seek me out. Some still have that faraway look in their eyes. Others are curious to know how I coped when I returned from the war. And others are surprised that I would be going back and forth to Vietnam as a missionary. There are still some lingering wounds that many of us carry at home and abroad, but through the help of the Lord, both sides have been able to move on with their lives.

The approval I longed for from my earthly father and never received came from a source that I hadn't expected. I'm not sure if my dad even had a clue as to what I so desperately longed for. He seemed incapable of providing me with the one thing I needed the most—love and affirmation.

My faith in God irritated him. It gave him fuel to criticize me. He loved to write but didn't have many pen pals, so I became his main source of correspondence. I scanned through each of his letters looking for something civil, and avoided the rest. I knew he was a terribly tormented and lonely soul, so I tolerated his barbs for years. One day I had enough. I wrote him a long letter expressing how I felt. I was tired of his constant insults and being put down. I asked him not to write me if he didn't have anything nice to say.

His letter writing slowed after that, but his tone was much softer when he did. Maybe he finally saw himself. I hope so. I even got one or two letters expressing in his own awkward way that he was proud of me. I soaked it up like a sponge. I was surprised by how much a little praise meant to me. I had been waiting my whole life for a few kind words from him.

I craved a relationship with my earthly father but it never came about. I don't think my dad knew how to have one. It was as if he was tied up inside. What he didn't know, and what I so desperately tried to help him discover, was that all that he needed in order to be set free was Jesus. He could have been a caring and loving parent, but he chose to run from the very One who could have made a difference.

The last time I saw him was just a few months before he passed away. He was in a veteran's home in Wisconsin. I flew from Georgia to Wisconsin, and my brother Gary and I drove three hours to see him. Dad was withdrawn. He looked old, just a shell of the man he had once been. Slumped in his wheelchair he seemed so frail and scared. I wanted to reach out to him, but he had built a thick wall around himself. I gave him an awkward hug and left.

On the long drive home I thought hard about the life my father had lived. He was able to conquer his drinking problem by seeking the help of *Alcoholics Anonymous* in the late '70s. We were all so very proud of him. But I still couldn't stop thinking about how his life could have been so much different. He passed away just one month short of his ninetieth birthday.

I wasn't there when he died, and only God knows how he spent those last few months. I heard he might have allowed someone to wheel him down to a church service or two. I don't know. Dad had left an envelope to be opened after he died. Inside was this letter:

To all my children,

No one will know what his life will be until he lives it. We all start out with good intentions, hopes and dreams, but somewhere along the way circumstances change things. I certainly am not proud of my own life and often tried to change it.

We all have our own cross to carry and I surely will not get the Nobel Prize as the father of the century. I often hoped to compensate for the past but years roll by and old age creeps up and all the opportunities are gone.

But by the same token if things were reversed, I know in my heart that I could understand the weakness of others. Perhaps if I had a better education I would have been a different man. Perhaps I'll do better the next time around. So just being sorry is not enough I know, but sorry I am and sorry I did not do better. So I hope you all will understand and not think too badly of me. I hope that my weakness and failures will spur you all on to do better and remember that you will never know what your own life will be until you live it.

Love,

Dad

My mother's passing was much different. It was comforting knowing I was the one who had baptized her. She was Spirit-filled and maintained a vital relationship with Jesus right to the end.

Her later years were not physically healthy ones. She had numerous ailments that made her life intolerable. Her fatal stroke was a blessing in disguise. She was in a coma when I arrived. I don't know if she knew we were around her bed or not, but when I held her hand, sang to her and read from the Bible, her spirit calmed down. I could feel the presence of the Lord all around her. I whispered to her to just let go and be with Jesus. "We'll be all right," I said. "Just go on and enjoy heaven. I'll meet you there."

She had lived a hard life. Raising six of us in tough times wasn't easy, but Mom managed. She was my hero. Her end was much better than her beginning. She had found her Savior. She is living in eternal peace.

Mom gave me birth. She nurtured me, loved and cared for me with all of her heart. In return I was able to help lead her to a close relationship with Jesus. She gave me a mother's love. I helped her find the source of that love.

Her passing was a promotion. I miss her dearly, yet I'm happy for her. Death for a Christian is reassuring. The Bible says that to be absent from the body is to be present with the Lord (2 Corinthians 5:8). There is no sting in death because Christ took our place that we might have eternal life (1 Corinthians 15: 55-57).

Looking back it's easy to see how the Lord was working in my life. It wasn't so obvious then. My childhood struggles worked together for good. God's Word says he has placed eternity in our hearts (Ecclesiastes 3:11). That means each of us has a longing for something greater than what this world has to offer. My world crumbling at an early age gave me an advantage. Working through problems I faced as a kid helped me focus on reasons for living. That quest led me to a loving God who sustained me, protected me, and reached for me. My early morning jaunts delivering papers and walking to school by myself gave me time to reflect. This also helped me to develop a listening ear so God could speak to me.

Seeing the world also helped. Visiting other countries, looking at different cultures and participating in a vulgar war gave me insight. The puzzle was complex, but my hunger helped me put the pieces together.

I have often wondered why some people become acutely aware of their need for God and hunger to know him, while others can't seemingly connect the dots enough to even acknowledge that he exists. I count myself fortunate.

The Holy Spirit guided me to a place where I could meet him. It took a few years for me to understand that it was God working behind the scenes, sometimes gently, other times less subtly, doing his best to make me aware of him. Life for me was like one of those mazes you see in comic books. You know the ones—where there are myriad of paths to take with many roadblocks and only one way out. Usually you are given the starting position then you have to work your way out of the maze, through many wrong choices and dead ends. Eventually, if you keep trying, you will find the one route that sets you free.

I spent most of my younger years around water. I took life saving classes, served as a lifeguard, swim coach and rescue swimmer with Underwater Demolition Team eleven. I had the honor of being the first man in the water to help rescue Neil Armstrong, Buzz Aldrin and Michael Collins when they returned from the moon. Little did I know then that while I was rescuing others, God was trying to rescue me.

Although my walk came in baby steps and stages, when He knocked I opened the door and invited Him in. I discovered he was the very reason for my existence and that there was no real meaning to my life without my Friend. He was always there when I needed Him, and when my life slowly deteriorated, the closer He seemed to be. At times He seemed like a bloodhound hot on my trail, searching for me from pillar to post, determined to take hold of me. Other times God was like a gentle wind, gently nudging me along, whispering to me.

On November 3, 1971, I walked out of the quarterdeck at UDT-11 in Coronado, California with my discharge papers. I was a civilian once again. Four years earlier I left my hometown on a hope and a thin promise. I had no assurance that I would actually become a Navy frogman. I put my best foot forward and achieved a teenage dream. Vietnam hadn't sunk in yet, and rescuing astronauts who had been to the moon was the farthest thing from my mind.

Someone said that a journey of a thousand miles begins with one small step. If I hadn't taken that first step, my dreams may have never been realized. I knew that beyond the city limits of where I was raised adventure awaited me. But never in my wildest dreams could I have imagined that the greatest discovery of all had been close to me all along.

"We are not limited to the air. We are not limited by the gravity of the Earth. We can overcome those limitations and move out any place we really want to go."

~ James E. Webb, former NASA administrator

Underwater Demolition Training Class— BUD/S Number 44

LTJG Gary R. Gray	Sherman, Texas
ENS John L. Hollow	Helena, Montana
ENS Ernest L. Jahncke	Greenwich, Connecticut
LTJG Christopher C. Lomas	Pound Ridge, New York
LTJG Paul D. Plumb	Coronado, California
LTJG Timothy G. Wettack	Coffeyville, Kansas
SA Donald F. Armstrong	Smyrna, Tennessee
SA James A. Berta	Ottowa, Illinois
AA Tommy W. Bracken	Fresno, California
SA Robert E. Brown	Cleburne, Texas
BTFN Raymond C. Clair	Hamburg, New York
FA Craig R. Danielson	Seattle, Washington
MM3 Roger F. Cochlin	Austin, Minnesota
FA Craig R. Danielson	Seattle, Washington
AA Rickard E. Doyle	Tacoma, Washington
FA John S. Durlin	Erie, Pennsylvania
AOAN Lance G. Farmer	Passlo, Washington
GMGSN Charles Free	Coronado, California
SA James R. Gore	Cut Bank, Montana
AA Forest B. Harness	Portland, Oregon
Qm3 Wayne W. Jacobs	Staten Island, New York
SA Fred J. Lang	North Platt, Nebraska
SN Patrick M. O'Meara	Owosso, Michigan
FA Richard J. Solano	Mountain View, California
SA Frank Sparks	Van Nuys, California
AN Michael J. Walsh	Dorchester, Massachusetts
AN Roger G. Werner	Chicago, Illinois
BUL2 Frank L. Willis	Oakland, California
FA Steven P. Wolf	Ann Arbor, Michigan
SA John M. Wolfram	Fort Atkinson, Wisconsin

Ollie's Famous Fire Brand Chili

2 pounds ground beef (course ground)
1 pound ground pork
¼ cup suet
3 large cans dark kidney beans
2 large onions chopped
3 cloves garlic minced
2 large cans crushed tomatoes
1 large can tomato paste
2 heaping tblsp. crushed chili pods
Grind fresh chili pods separate with one large can
   of crushed tomato in blender.
4 heaping tblsp. chili powder
2 tblsp. dried basil
3 crushed bay leaves
1 tsp. celery salt
½ tsp. caraway seed
⅛ tsp. sage
1 quart water
2 8oz cans heavy beef gravy
2 tblsp. soy sauce
salt to taste

    Fry meat and suet until browned. Boil all other ingredients in pot thirty minutes. Add to meat. Simmer one hour. Add beans last. Add vinegar to taste (about two shot glasses).

Musical Credits

Chapter Three
"I-Feel-Like-I'm-Fixin'-to-Die Rag" performed by Country Joe and the Fish.
Words and music by Joe McDonald.
© 1965, renewed 1993. Alkatraz Corner Music Co BMI

Chapter Sixteen
"Spirit in the Sky"
Written by Norman Greenbaum.
Copyright 1970. Great Honesty Music

Chapter Eighteen
"He Rescued Me"
From album *His Name is Holy*
by Genelle Tennant
© 1978 by Genelle Tennant

Note from the Author

For additional copies: <u>www.johnwolfram.com</u>

If you would like John Wolfram to minister at your church or speak at a civic function contact him at:

johnwolfram@me.com

Photo by Michelle Tacott, Expressions Photography